MW01092713

THE SKIN-EGO

THE SKIN-EGO

Didier Anzieu

Translated by Naomi Segal

Routledge
Taylor & Francis Group

LONDON AND NEW YORK

Originally published as *Le Moi-peau*, © Dunod, Paris, 1995.

First published 2016 by
Karnac Books Ltd.

Published 2018 by Routledge
2 Park Square, Milton Park, Abingdon, Oxon OX14 4RN
711 Third Avenue, New York, NY 10017, USA

Routledge is an imprint of the Taylor & Francis Group, an informa business

Copyright © 2016 to Naomi Segal for this English edition.

The rights of the contributors to be identified as the authors of this work have been asserted in accordance with §§ 77 and 78 of the Copyright Design and Patents Act 1988.

All rights reserved. No part of this book may be reprinted or reproduced or utilised in any form or by any electronic, mechanical, or other means, now known or hereafter invented, including photocopying and recording, or in any information storage or retrieval system, without permission in writing from the publishers.

Notice:
Product or corporate names may be trademarks or registered trademarks, and are used only for identification and explanation without intent to infringe.

British Library Cataloguing in Publication Data

A C.I.P. for this book is available from the British Library

ISBN-13: 9781782201007 (pbk)

Typeset by V Publishing Solutions Pvt Ltd., Chennai, India

CONTENTS

ABOUT THE AUTHOR AND TRANSLATOR

Didier Anzieu (1923–1999) was a French psychoanalyst and theorist whose work brings the body back to the centre of psychoanalytic enquiry. He was the author of numerous books and articles, on areas ranging from the psychology of groups and psychodrama to theories of creativity and thought; he also published short stories, literary criticism, a drama, a book of cartoons and a study of May '68 written from the heart of Nanterre. His research was always conducted alongside his academic and clinical practice, both characterised by inclusivity, curiosity, a broad mind and a gentle manner.

Naomi Segal is a professor of modern languages, specialising in comparative literary and cultural studies, gender, psychoanalysis and the body. In 2004 she created and then directed the Institute of Germanic & Romance Studies, University of London. She has published 15 books, of which the most recent monographs are *Consensuality: Didier Anzieu, gender and the sense of touch*, *André Gide: Pederasty and Pedagogy* and *The Adulteress's Child: authorship and desire in the nineteenth-century novel*. Naomi Segal is an Academic Associate of the British Psychoanalytical Society, a Chevalier dans l'Ordre des Palmes académiques and Member of the Academia Europaea.

SERIES EDITOR'S FOREWORD

In the spring of 1923, literally days after he discovered the cancerous lesions inside his mouth, Sigmund Freud received a welcome parcel in the post—a copy of one of the volumes of the *Obras Completas del Professor S. Freud*—a Spanish translation of his collected works—which had recently begun to appear in print. No doubt Freud derived considerable satisfaction that his works had finally penetrated Catholic Spain—a country long resistant to the overtly sexual and secular themes of psychoanalysis—and he wrote a letter, in Spanish, to the translator, Señor Luis López-Ballesteros y de Torres, congratulating him on his "very correct interpretation of my thoughts and of the elegance of your style" (Freud, 1923, p. 289).

Freud had, of course, studied Spanish rigorously as an adolescent; and consequently, he knew that López-Ballesteros y de Torres had acquitted himself splendidly. Whereas many of Freud's translators in other countries had studied with him directly and had already begun to practice clinical psychoanalysis, López-Ballesteros y de Torres—a *littérateur* and professional translator—had not. Knowing of López-Ballesteros y de Torres's non-clinical background, Freud (1923, p. 289) paid him high praise, noting, "I am above all astonished that one who, like you, is neither a doctor nor a psychiatrist by profession should have been able to obtain so absolute and precise a mastery over material which is intricate and at times obscure."

Had the eminent French psychoanalyst Didier Anzieu lived long enough to read Naomi Segal's magisterial translation of his classic *Le Moi-peau*, one suspects that he might have written a similar Freudian encomium. Though neither a "doctor nor a psychiatrist", Naomi Segal has enjoyed a long and distinguished career as professor of French and comparative literature and as a scholar of psychoanalysis; and happily, has generously offered us the benefits of her dual strengths by providing us with a completely new, refreshed, and deeply thoughtful translation of Anzieu's important theoretico-clinical work which has long proved to be of great value to clinical practitioners.

Professor Segal's careful study of the theory of psychoanalysis and its value to literary scholars began many decades ago. Her many books on varying aspects of French literature bear testament to her deep steepage in psychoanalytical ideas. And in 1986, as a young "don" at the University of Cambridge, she and her colleague Edward Timms— both soon to become professors—organised a landmark conference at the Institute of Germanic Studies in the University of London, co-sponsored by both the Austrian Institute of London and, also, the newly-founded Freud Museum, to mark the half-century of Freud's enforced emigration to London. The speakers included many eminent scholars and practitioners such as John Bowlby, Ernst Federn, and Pearl King, amongothers, and provided us with a feast of ideas, resulting in the publication of a much valued book of essays *Freud in Exile: Psychoanalysis and its Vicissitudes* (Timms & Segal, 1988). Thus, Segal could not be better qualified to have undertaken the nuanced and challenging task of rendering Anzieu's compelling and often complex clinical French prose into engaging and edifying English.

Both Professor Peter Rudnytsky—my fellow series co-editor—and I know how much care and attention Naomi Segal has devoted to this translation: a labour of scholarship and a labour of love, combined. Over the last year or more, she had kept us closely informed of her careful thinking about the best ways of translating certain seminal Anzieu concepts—not least that of "psychic envelopes", now rendered as "psychical wrappings"—as well as many other technical terms, at each step on the journey. We can testify that Segal has set a very high bar indeed for all future academics who endeavour to translate classic texts from their native language into English.

Naomi Segal has prepared her translation of Didier Anzieu's *The Skin-Ego* with the same care and attention that the clinical psychoanalytical practitioner devotes to his or her patients. No detail remains too small to merit close scrutiny; no phrase does not brim with rich meaning, waiting to be deciphered. We thank Anzieu for his lifetime of wisdom in the realms of clinical psychoanalysis and developmental psychology; and we thank Segal for her recognition of the value of this text—still not fully appreciated by English-speaking audiences—and for sharing her considerable literary capacities and psychoanalytical knowledge with us so that those not blessed with a fluency in Anzieu's native tongue can profit, nonetheless, from the rich feast contained herein.

Professor Brett Kahr
Series Co-Editor
February 2016

References

Freud, Sigmund (1923). Letter to Señor Luis Lopez-Ballesteros y de Torres. 7th May. James Strachey (Transl.). In Sigmund Freud (1961). *The Standard Edition of the Complete Psychological Works of Sigmund Freud: Volume XIX. (1923–1925). The Ego and the Id and Other Works.* James Strachey, Anna Freud, Alix Strachey, and Alan Tyson (Eds. and Transls.), p. 289. London: Hogarth Press and the Institute of Psycho-Analysis.

Timms, Edward, and Segal, Naomi (Eds.). (1988). *Freud in Exile: Psychoanalysis and its Vicissitudes.* New Haven, Connecticut: Yale University Press.

TRANSLATOR'S FOREWORD

This new translation of *Le Moi-peau* is based on the second and last (1995) edition, which is essentially similar to the 1985 edition, apart from the closing chapter, Chapter Eighteen. Because of the interest of the earlier Chapter Eighteen, I have translated it as an appendix following the main text. Three other regular elements of the translation may need explanation. First, I have translated *psychique* throughout as "psychical", in conformity with common psychoanalytic practice. Second, and perhaps more radically, I have chosen to translate *enveloppe* as "wrapping", rather than the word that appears in a number of earlier translations, "envelope". After much consideration, I concluded that "envelope" is misleading since its main and intuitive meaning in English is the object into which we put a letter: French is rare in using the same word for both this object and a more general wrapping or enclosure (neither German nor Italian nor Spanish do so); thus, even though Strachey renders Freud's *Hülle* as "envelope"—in German one puts a letter into an *Umschlag*—I considered it inappropriate for Anzieu's usage, which is much closer in meaning to "wrapping". Finally, to avoid sexist language, I have translated the French "gender-neutral" *il* by various English usages—"he or she", "they" with plural meaning or "they" with singular meaning.

I have adopted with gratitude a usage found in the 1989 translation by Chris Turner: he renders *contenant* as "container" and *conteneur* as "containor". I have followed Anzieu by capitalising *Moi* as "Ego" and *Soi* as "Self" (and used lower case where he occasionally does) and kept the opening capital for such compound versions as "Skin-ego", "Agent-ego", "Core-ego" etc. In the reference section I have substituted non-French original texts for some of Anzieu's items, when these are the texts I have quoted from, and in the text (but not in the References) I have translated titles cited, where I felt this may be useful to the reader. I have added the first names of authors referred to where I could ascertain them. Where, occasionally, a quotation lacked a page-reference I have added one if I could find it. Most errors in the original have been corrected silently, including misspellings of Fisher and Sheckley, though it should be noted that Anzieu incorrectly used the feminine pronoun for Barrie Biven and Isi Beller. Finally, some references mentioned by Anzieu in his text but not his bibliography have proved impossible to find; these therefore do not appear in the References of this translation, but the names have been left in the text: in order of appearance, these are Wallon, Ajuriaguerra, Ombredane, Martinet, Caffey and Moffitt, Butterfield, Wolff and Hall.

I am indebted to Peter Rudnytsky and Brett Kahr for giving me the opportunity to translate this wonderful book and bring Didier Anzieu's work to a new Anglophone readership. Thanks go also to Anne-Marie Smith-Di Biasio and Marc Lafrance for help with various sources, and to many other friends and colleagues for their thoughts on assorted translation knots. This translation is dedicated to Scarlet.

INTRODUCTION

On 10 December 1890, a fatal accident befell a five-year-old child called Marguerite Pantaine, the daughter of a farming family in Chalvignac, in the *département* of Cantal in the Massif central. Here are two versions of the event:

> The family talk a lot about a violent emotion the mother suffered while she was pregnant with my patient. The eldest daughter died as the result of a tragic accident: she fell, before her mother's very eyes, into the wide-open door of a lighted stove and died very rapidly of severe burns. (Lacan, 1975, pp. 174–175)

> [My mother] was the third child in the family, the third or fourth… That's the problem. Before her, in fact, three daughters were born. The family lived in a large stone house close to the stable and the fields. The main room was heated by a large fireplace filled with big burning logs […], and there were benches in it that you could sit on. This happened before my mother was born. It was a feast-day. Marguerite, the youngest of the three daughters, had an organdie dress on, ready to go to church. She'd been left for a moment in the charge of the eldest girl, the one who was to become

my godmother. The child was lightly dressed, it was cold, she went up to the fire to warm herself… and was burnt alive. It was a dreadful shock for her parents and her two sisters. So my mother was conceived as a replacement for the dead child. And since she was another girl, they gave her the same name, Marguerite. The living dead, in a way… It's no coincidence that my mother spent her life finding ways to escape from the flames of hell… It was a way of accepting her fate, a tragic fate. My mother only spoke openly of this once. But I knew it as a family legend. I think her depression goes back to this untenable position. (Anzieu, 1991, pp. 19–20)

The variation between these two versions shows how a "family legend" (which will also become a "fate" carried through several generations) twists and turns to serve the vagaries of later causalities. Was the dead girl the eldest or the youngest? Was it a gaping stove or an ingle-nook fireplace? Was it a sister or the mother who witnessed the terrible event and should have been taking better care? Was the mother pregnant when it happened or did she become so to replace her lost daughter, whether firstborn or lastborn? What they agree on is the shock to the whole family, and the long-lasting effects not just on the parents and living sisters but on the siblings that followed. In fact the child who died was the eldest, not the youngest, of the three sisters and the mother Jeanne was not pregnant with the second Marguerite when the first was killed, but (possibly) with a baby who was declared stillborn the following August (see Allouch, 1994; also Lessana, 2000, pp. 293–342). The second Marguerite was born in July 1892 (see Allouch, 1994, pp. 99–104, 156 and 248–260; also Roudinesco, 1997, p. 35).

The first version cited above is that of Jacques Lacan, who treated Marguerite Pantaine, by then Marguerite Anzieu, in April 1931, when she was arrested and then sent to Sainte-Anne for attacking a famous stage actress with a knife. In 1932 Lacan published his doctoral thesis on her under the pseudonym of "Aimée", using her case-history as a prototype of the role of personality in psychopathic development.

At eighteen, Marguerite started work in the administrative section of the Post Office. She was transferred to a village some way from her home and from there in 1913 to Melun, near Paris, where she met René Anzieu, also a Post Office employee, and they married in 1917. Her sister Élise, who could not have children after a total hysterectomy in 1914 and whose husband Guillaume (an uncle) had died as a result of war-wounds, came to live with the couple eight months after their wedding. Two children were born to Marguerite: a daughter who died at birth and, in 1923, a son, who was healthy but whose life seemed to his mother under constant threat—he was, of course, the replacement child of a replacement child. When Marguerite went off the rails and was sectioned, Elise took over the care of the child and later also took the wife's place with René, though the family put up energetic opposition when he wished to get divorced and marry her after Marguerite's final discharge from hospital in 1943—when, by yet another of the bizarre doublings that attend Anzieu's life, she became housekeeper to Lacan's father (and died the same year as Lacan, 1981).

The second version cited above is that of Didier Anzieu in a set of interviews conducted in 1983 when he was sixty. He goes on:

> I might put it this way—it sounds banal, but in my case it seems true: I became a psychoanalyst to care for my mother. Not so much to care for her in reality, even though I did succeed in helping her, in the last quarter of her life, to find a relatively happy, balanced life. What I mean is, to care for my mother in myself and other people. To care, in other people, for this threatening and threatened mother... (Anzieu, 1991, p. 20)

Looking back to his childhood, Didier Anzieu described himself in a draft autobiography rather dramatically as "unloved, the son of unloved people" (Anzieu, 1991, p. 36). But on another occasion he characterizes himself as over-loved:

> I couldn't go out of doors without being bundled up several times over: jumper, coat, beret, muffler. The layers of my parents' care, worries and warmth never left me, even when I lived far away from home. I carried it like a weight on my shoulders. My vitality was hidden at the core [au cœur] of an onion, under several skins. (Anzieu, 1991, pp. 14–15)

Yet Anzieu describes the influence of his father with warmth. Differently, almost contrary to Marguerite's longing for travel, frustrated by years of incarceration and the craziness of her projects, René's is internalized as mental geography, the pursuit of education and where it can take you. After some teenage conflicts and successful studies in Paris at the Lycée Henri IV and the Ecole Normale Supérieure, Didier Anzieu finally reached the goal of psychoanalysis via these two pathways, then: the wish to "care for my mother in myself and other people" and, reading Freud, the discovery of "a new geography which took the place of the one my father had taught me. I had got a map to guide me through the internal continent" (Anzieu, 1991, p. 26).

He entered the Ecole Normale Supérieure at the age of twenty-one, as part of the postwar cohort of 1944; he began as a student of philosophy but soon transferred to psychology and, after graduating, took a job running projective tests and psychodrama groups at the Centre Psychopédagogique Claude Bernard, a treatment centre for disturbed children. At the same time, "I did a practical psychology course at Prof Graciansky's dermatology unit, where I gave Rorschach tests to eczema sufferers [...]; that gave me a vague early intuition of the Skin-ego" (Anzieu, 1991, p. 30).

Anzieu's two doctoral theses were on Freud's self-analysis and psychodrama. In 1947 he married a schoolfriend, Annie Péghaire, who remained his colleague, published alongside him and is still practising; and their two children were born in 1950 and 1953. From 1949 to 1953 he was analysed by Lacan—who did not tell him he had already treated his mother. When, in 1961, Anzieu reported to the IPA commission, his main criticisms of Lacan's technique were three: "an almost total lack of interpretations, an inability to bear the negative transference, and a failure to understand the specificity of the early relationship with the maternal imago" (Roudinesco, 1994, pp. 335–336).

Among what she calls the "third generation" of French psychoanalysts, born in the 1920s, Elisabeth Roudinesco groups Anzieu as one of the "academics" (Roudinesco, 1994, p. 290), and this is where he made his career, as a lifelong educator as well as clinician. But in 1992 he himself describes a familiar ambivalence towards that world: "I have loved the academic institution like a foster-mother. Like my real mother, it was often disappointing—and doubtless often disappointed by me" (Parot & Richelle, 1992, p. 259). Less active than many in the series of dramatic schisms that rent the French scene from the 1950s onwards, and determined never to form a set of followers unable to emancipate themselves from his influence, Anzieu holds a central place in the "hundred years of psychoanalysis" (Roudinesco, 1994, p. 683 *et passim*) less because of his problematic relationship with Lacan—this he shares with all the major names of his generation—than because of his unswerving independence of thought.

In 1954 he succeeded Juliette Favez-Boutonier as professor of clinical psychology at the University of Strasbourg, bringing "with him his encyclopaedic knowledge" (Jean Muller, cited in Kaës, 2000, p. 63) and developing particularly innovative courses on social psychology, group psychology and psychodrama. Active in the local community, he lectured at hospitals, prisons and businesses; in 1956 he took part in an international seminar on group dynamics run, under the Marshall Plan, by disciples of its founder Kurt Lewin (see Hubert Touzard cited in Kaës, 2000, pp. 67–70 & Chabert, 1996, pp. 17–18). His combined interest in groups and drama led to the founding, in 1962, of CEFFRAP (the Cercle d'études françaises pour la formation et la recherche active en psychologie), and in the same year he ran the first regional seminar on psycho-sociology in Murbach, Alsace.

Anzieu was appointed to chair the newly founded Department of Psychology at the University of Paris X (Nanterre) in 1964.

> Committed to the principles of Lagache [his erstwhile doctoral supervisor], whom he admired unreservedly, on the epistemic unity of psychology, he was inspired by the wish to realize this unity at the level of both teaching and research. Curriculum development, the kind of posts he wanted to create, the staff appointed to these posts, all these depended on a long-term project of creating a balance between the various currents, methodologies and approaches in the field of psychology. Experimental psychology, clinical psychology, training psychology and psychoanalysis: all were *equally* recognized. (Jean-Claude Filloux, cited in Kaës, 2000, pp. 72–73)

By 1967–1968, the Nanterre department had over five hundred students, and Anzieu organized his staff with a stress on consultation and collegiality that was "pretty atypical at that time" (Filloux in Kaës, 2000, p. 75). He wrote a short account of the events of May 1968 under the pseudonym "Epistémon"; it was published the same year and much read at the time and after. Dedicated to the aim of "understanding the students" (Anzieu, 1968: n. p. and Anzieu, 1991, pp. 121–140), it takes as its premise the belief that the academics and their pupils, for all the old entrenched hierarchies, were on the same side, "the side of non-knowledge" (Anzieu, 1968, p. 20), and that the issue was both a "generational conflict" (Anzieu, 1968, p. 35) and a question of epistemology.

On 2 May, after two hundred demonstrators disrupted a French studies lecture, terrorising in particular staff who had lived through the Occupation not so long before, the Dean announced the closure of the Faculty of Nanterre. The students moved on to the Latin Quarter. "[On 10 May], I walked around there most of the night, crossing the smaller barricades with difficulty, blocked by others. An extraordinary atmosphere of collective enthusiasm inspired these young people [... among whom] I recognized many of my own students" (Anzieu, 1968, p. 73).

> From the morning of Tuesday 14 March, an explosion of talk, all the talk that had been repressed before, began to spread, by chain reaction, through schools and universities, among intellectuals and artists and the liberal professions. Joint committees of staff and students started meeting in the university buildings which were occupied now without interruption by their natural users. I attended almost every day up to Pentecost weekend (1–3 June), which I spent drawing up a detailed plan for this book. After that the tension had reached such a level that I began to suffer from fatigue and my attendance dropped off. Various learned societies that I belong to had their own revolutions and I was part of that. I cut into meal-times and night-times to write, but at other times I stayed with the students as much as possible. I took part in several meetings of colleagues where we were trying to take stock collectively and think through our attitudes by confronting them directly. Those who had understood more quickly gave patient explanations to the slower ones. (Anzieu, 1968, p. 75)

Anzieu insists, here and elsewhere, that, though fundamentally liberal and materialist, he was never politically minded: "regimes may come and go but the unconscious remains" (Anzieu, 1991, p. 95; see also 54 and 92; and Kaës, 2000, p. 50). But his pseudonym was quickly seen through and, far from causing him difficulties, it rather raised his profile. Edgar Faure, the newly appointed minister of education, asked him to devise a professional status for psychologists, and he worked on this during the following year; the issue was so vexed, with particular resistance from the psychologists themselves, that it was not finally resolved until twenty years later.

In the early 1970s, Anzieu continued to publish books and articles, including in the recently founded *Nouvelle revue de psychanalyse*, and in 1972 he set up two series with the publisher Dunod, "Psychismes" and "Inconscient et culture". He spent two sabbatical years concentrating on research in 1973–1975, and 1974 saw the publication of his first article on the Skin-ego. A year later he published an article called "La psychanalyse encore" ["Still psychoanalysis"], in which he argues that

> Psychoanalysis has become sick with its own success [...]. The problem is not to repeat what Freud discovered in relation to the crisis of the Victorian era. It is to find a psychoanalytic answer to the discontents of modern man in our present civilisation [...] We need to do work of a psychoanalytic kind wherever the unconscious emerges: standing, sitting or lying down; individually, in groups or families, during a session, on the doorstep, at the foot of a hospital bed, etc., wherever a subject is able to let his or her anxieties and phantasies speak to someone presumed capable of hearing them and giving back an account of them. (repr. in Anzieu, 2000, pp. 257–268; see also the extract cited by Kaës in Anzieu, 1992, p. 33)

In 1978, he met a painter, Charles Breuil, who, without any knowledge of Anzieu's work, had painted the image of a man wearing a woman's skin. On the back of the painting he had sketched various titles: "Ta peau" [Your skin], "Ma peau" [My skin], "Peau-Moi" [Ego-Skin], "PO" and "Moi-peau" [Skin-ego], deciding finally on the title "L'Enveloppe" [The Wrapping]. Delighted by this "coincidence between an artist's intuition and a psychoanalyst's idea" (Anzieu, 1991, p. 109), Anzieu bought the painting after the two met in 1985, and hung it next to his analytic armchair.

Anzieu retired from Nanterre in 1983 at the age of sixty. He went on researching, with *Le Moi-peau* appearing in book form first in 1985 and then in a second edition in 1995; translations of it into Italian, Spanish, Portuguese, English and German came out in the later 1980s and early 1990s. His creative writings—a book of short stories, a tiny volume of cartoons and a play—chimed in with continuing work on the creativity of others, from Freud to Bacon via Borges, Henry James and, in his last years, Beckett. First published in 1998, *Beckett* is shaped by thoughts of death: "if I stop moving, I die" (Anzieu, 1999a, p. 237). The main text ends at the Montparnasse cemetery, where Anzieu visits both his parents' grave and that of the Becketts. There follow seven "postscripts", the penultimate one ending "This time, it's finished. Indefinitely"

(Anzieu, 1999a, 287), and the very last page giving a "finale" which includes the lines:

> To marry the masculine and the feminine in the mind, immobility and movement in the body. To tolerate anxiety and joy, hatred and laughter. To sustain love in the gap between abandonment to the other and abandonment of the other. To foil the seductions, perversions and ruses of the death drive. To turn the negative against itself. To deny, cut, tear and transgress in order to progress. To enwrap, unfold, unfurl, unroll, curl up, interleave, in order to exist and coexist. To give, indefinitely, to our human finitude, a form that is never definitive. (Anzieu, 1999a, p. 289)

But I want to "wrap up" this biographical introduction by returning to a description Anzieu gave, with characteristic wit, at a celebration of his seventieth birthday in 1993, of his family origin and where it placed him psychologically:

> Ten years later, Marguerite was freed. Her husband asked for a divorce. Another drama—I was going to say, psychodrama—Marguerite's family rose up against René and scuppered his plan of legalising his union with his sister-in-law. A fresh scandal. But also, for the adolescent son, what an experience to find himself confronting the private psychosis of a mother and the neurosis of the family group! And what luck to have been sustained by the competitive three-way love of his father and two women! What an introduction to the twinned knowledge of Oedipus and Narcissus! Yes, the history of this child is the epitome of banality! (Kaës, 2000, p. 50)

In 1993, Didier Anzieu considered his career, marked by its intellectual richness and variety, and noted: "Looking back on my life and work, I think I can grasp a guiding idea: unity in diversity, the convergence of parts in a whole" (Kaës, 2000, p. 50). In this section, I want to give a brief presentation of the main lines of his theory, keeping in mind always that they are converging lines, whose fundamental point of connection is the image in that closing phrase: a movement-into, a co-presence inside. What does it mean to contain or be contained? How do these processes work and what do they mean psychically? How does containment function dynamically?

Taking Anzieu's published works roughly chronologically, beginning with the two theses he first published in the 1950s, and echoing his own three-way presentation in the introduction to *Créer/Détruire* (1996), I am going to start with Anzieu's work on psychodrama and groups; then look at his theories of self-analysis and creation; and finally I will come to his major work, that of the Skin-ego, and its development into a theory of thought.

Le psychodrame analytique chez l'enfant et l'adolescent [*Analytic psychodrama used with children and adolescents*] was published in 1956, and was the shorter of Anzieu's two doctoral theses. In the preface to the 1994 edition, he declares: "Like the Rorschach test as a clinical technique for individuals, the use of psychodrama in group therapy is still one of the key methods for psychologists, especially when both methods are fortified by psychoanalytic thought" (Anzieu, 1994a, p. 1; on the Rorschach and other projective tests, see Anzieu & Chabert [1961] 2003). Psychodrama is a "composite matrix of energies" (Anzieu, 1994a, p. 7) which allows subjects "to *be* [...], to *feel* [...] and ultimately to *know* the meaning and range of what they feel" (Anzieu, 1994a, p. 98). If it is developed psychoanalytically, Anzieu suggests that it can incorporate the key rules of the analytic setting, non-omission and abstinence. Psychodrama "stands exactly midway between bodily expression and verbal communication" (Anzieu, 1994a, p. 83; see also 105). Thus, "as in individual psychoanalysis, the balance of permissiveness and frustration produces changes in the subject" (Anzieu, 1994a, p. 141), bringing out resistances and defence mechanisms in all participants. Everyone experiences the effects of the transference and the counter-transference; the key difference, and this applies to all group analysis, is that it necessarily incorporates work on "common transferential material" (Anzieu, 1994a, p. 155). Its effect is a *"symbolic effectiveness"* (Anzieu, 1994a, p. 163) that both revives and repairs the participants' unconscious concerns, leading them to "emotional catharsis" (Anzieu, 1994a, p. 171).

Group theory appears in two main contexts. The first is *La Dynamique des groupes restreints* [*The Dynamics of Small Groups*], coauthored with Jacques-Yves Martin, first published in 1968. Introducing the seventh edition in 1982, Anzieu comments:

> To human beings the small group represents a place invested simul-
> taneously or alternately with hopes and threats. Situated between
> intimacy (the life of the couple or private solitude) and social

life (governed by collective representations and institutions), the small group can provide an intermediary space which sometimes reinvigorates a sense of contact and sometimes helps to reconstruct the essential gaps between the individual and society. (Anzieu, 1997, p. 11)

In two significant metaphors Anzieu suggests that the group provides an environment which imitates in key ways the child's fantasmatic relationship with its mother. The first is the image of a mutual mirroring: "a group of equals or peers is, after the mother, the second mirror in which each one can seek an identity through reciprocal recognition" (Anzieu, 1997, p. 308). In these circumstances, the group serves as a safe haven, even if it is a gang of egocentric individuals, and consensus may well reign (for other instances of such consensus, see Anzieu, 1997, pp. 179–181, 310 and 319). In the second, he cites the theory of his colleague René Kaës that "the space of a large group is experienced like an image of the inside of the mother's body" (Anzieu, 1997, p. 41); by this he is referring to the way that members seek safety and enclosure as well as a sense of cohesion.

In his monograph *Le Groupe et l'inconscient* [*The Group and the Unconscious*] (1975) Anzieu picks up on Kaës's theory of the "group psychical apparatus" (Anzieu, 1999b, p. 13). He opens the 1999 edition:

A group is a wrapping that holds individuals together [...]. A living wrapping, like the skin that regenerates itself around the body, like the ego which is meant to enclose the psyche, is a double-faced membrane [...]. Its inner face allows the group to establish a transindividual psyche which I propose to call the group Self [...]. This Self is the container inside which a traffic of fantasies and identifications circulates among the participants. (Anzieu, 1999b, pp. 1–2)

At the time of the break with Lacan, Anzieu had begun a self-analysis, and he continued this throughout his life; indeed, he describes his retroactive recognition of his mother's importance in these terms: "it was through a long work of self-analysis that I was able to reconstruct in my mind the problems of my mother's contact with me in the first months of my life" (Anzieu, 1991, p. 17). From one viewpoint, of course, self-analysis makes no more sense than parthenogenesis: the lineage of psychoanalysis insists on the production of each new analyst out of the teacher-pupil bond of at least one training analysis. From another, it is clear that, like parthenogenesis, self-analysis is a powerful fantasy: to reproduce oneself single-handed, through a mode of communication with oneself, not another. Perverse, absurd or megalomaniac, this is, for Anzieu, the base fantasy of all creativity.

The longer of Anzieu's doctoral theses, *L'Auto-analyse de Freud et la découverte de la psychanalyse* [*Freud's self-analysis and the discovery of psychoanalysis*] (1959), argues that Freud discovered—or, more accurately, created—psychoanalysis as a result of the work of self-analysis that followed a number of mid-life crises: the unplanned sixth pregnancy of his wife, a period of psychological and physical illness, a loosening of the intense tie to Fliess, and finally the death of his father on 23 October 1896. From July 1895, Freud analysed a number of his own dreams, setting this work alongside the dreams of his patients (for Anzieu always assumes at least one Winnicottian, Beckettian virtual other overseeing the act of "being alone") and what emerged was the formation of dreams as wish-fulfilments, the discovery of castration anxiety and ultimately *The Interpretation of Dreams* (1900) and the whole theory of psychoanalysis. Anzieu in his turn analyses Freud's dream analyses, insists on the relevance of the life to the work, and derives from all this a theory of creation.

Freud is the first example explored in the fullest presentation of Anzieu's theory of creation, *Le Corps de l'œuvre* [*The Body of the Creative Work*] (1981), his favourite and, he believed, least appreciated book (see Anzieu, 1992, p. 8). This is a study not of creativity, more often a potential than a realization, but of the act of creation, where it originates and how it is carried through into the production of a work. Familiarly, Anzieu links this to the life-cycle. His theory is derived, he announces, from three sources: himself, his patients and "contact with 'great works'" (Anzieu, 1981, p. 9); and it stands in contrast to other uses of psychoanalysis in relation to creativity, which either claim to analyse "the unconscious of the text" or to give a psychoanalytic reading of the semiotics of language. His premise is that

> it is the unconscious of the author, a living and individual reality, that gives a text its life and singularity. The unconscious of the reader [...] brings to it a new life, another originality. This is the same as what occurs, in the cure, between analyst and analysand. Cut off from these two unconsciouses, the text is simply an

inanimate, anonymous body, a corpus of dead letters. (Anzieu, 1981, p. 12)

This is, as the first section title of the book—"Entering into creation" (Anzieu, 1981, pp. 15–23)—suggests, a highly gendered representation of the psychology of the creative act, a fact I have critiqued elsewhere (see Segal, 2009, pp. 67–72). Though in his theory elements of creativity belong to the five spheres of the maternal, the paternal, femininity, masculinity and indeterminate, they typically take place in a male body, for

> the greater frequency of male creators is due largely to the fact that the paternal mental function is generally more developed in boys than girls, because it is the resumption, in terms of thought, of the biological function of the father, endowing the Ego with a new function, the ability to conceive codes. (Anzieu, 1981, p. 83)

Thus, as aware as Anzieu is that the traditional metaphor of creativity is female reproduction—again a reason why it is traditionally ascribed to men, on the grounds that women cannot properly do both things—he sets out in this book to present an account of how male creativity is a consolidation, not a contradiction, of masculinity.

Locally, the opening moment of a creative act is a version of "take-off" or "lift-off" [*décollage*]. This metaphor is borrowed from Proust, in love with an amateur pilot, his secretary-chauffeur Alfred Agostinelli, who died in a accident while flying under the pseudonym of Marcel Swann; Anzieu uses it to describe the ability of the creator to "fly above" [*survoler*] other people (Anzieu, 1981, p. 17; and see Segal, 2009, pp. 171–179). From the longer viewpoint, the occasion is likely to be a life-cycle crisis, that of old age between sixty and eighty, middle age around forty, or youth around twenty. All these crises carry intimations of mortality, but they present themselves differently and produce different kinds of artwork: the old man seeks "'a piece' of immortality" (50), the middle-aged man a substitute for his declining potency and the solution to his mid-life depression in the form of a repaired "loved, lost and destroyed object" (Anzieu, 1981, p. 53), the young man creates explosively and violently as his "work of art is an attempt to re-establish the continuity, totality, perfection and brilliance of the narcissistic wrapping" (Anzieu, 1981, p. 55).

The actual work of creation goes typically (but not universally) by five phases:

> experiencing a state of sudden shock [*saisissement*]; becoming aware of an unconscious piece of representative psychical material; raising it into a code to organize the work of art and choosing a material that can give a body to that code; composing the work in detail; producing it in the outside world. (Anzieu, 1981, p. 93)

It is, as Anzieu himself pointed out, in his work on creation that he began to develop the concept of the Skin-ego (see Kaës, 2000, p. 34). A work of art is like a body fleshed forth, a poem is "a skin that holds together sensuality, motivity [*motricité*] and affectivity, a wrapping that unifies momentarily the past, the present and the expectation of a future, a membrane that harmonizes the vibrations of the body with the internal rhythm of the code" (Anzieu, 1981, p. 158). Like the Skin-ego, it has an inward- and an outward-looking face; but it also establishes an "empty space" (Anzieu, 1981, p. 208) between the kernel and the shell of the creator's psyche, filling that space as best it might.

As we have seen already, Anzieu's last book, *Beckett* (1998), returns to the concept of self-analysis. It does this in two ways. First it argues, as he had done earlier in a section of *Créer/Détruire*, that Beckett's writing is an extended response to the failure of his analysis with the young Bion, a soliloquy that is more exactly a free association directed to the virtual interlocutor of the invisible analyst. Half the self speaks, the other half listens, and what is spoken is "a universal message about psychical pain" (Anzieu, 1996, p. 124). The book implicitly brings together two people suffering from Parkinson's disease: the mother whom it was Beckett's unconscious purpose to "*vomit*" (Anzieu, 1996, p. 116) as he vomited his works and Anzieu himself, whose relation to Beckett's literature of immobilization is, as we have seen, at once deadly and life-preserving. Vividly written and enacting repeatedly the fear of ending, this book intersperses invented dialogues between "Beckett" and "Bion" with anecdotes, readings and diary-entries from the three months 18 October 1990 to 15 January 1991. It is offered as "a piece of jewellery mounted on a Moebius strip that is not spatial but temporal" (Anzieu, 1999a, p. 13), an "immense enterprise in the service of an act of negative thought" (Anzieu, 1999a, p. 32). For Anzieu, who waited a lifetime to undertake it, it represents, like Beckett's *œuvre*, "a long, hard and meticulous work of composition" (Anzieu, 1999a, p. 114) expressing the quintessentially creative, self-analytic "project of not dying" (Anzieu, 1999a, p. 219).

As noted earlier, Anzieu's concept of the Skin-ego first appeared in print in spring 1974, in an article published in a number of the *Nouvelle revue de psychanalyse* entitled "Le dehors et le dedans" [Outside and Inside]. *Le Moi-peau* was first published as a monograph in 1985 and reprinted, in the expanded form which is translated in this volume, in 1995. But, by a coincidence of cultural history, the actual term had first seen the light forty years earlier, in a note by Robert Musil to *Der Mann ohne Eigenschaften* [*The Man Without Qualities*] (1930–1943), in which he refers to the visibility of emotions on the skin under the rubric "das Hautich" [the skin-ego] (Musil, 1978, p. 1974; see also Benthien, 2002, p. 208).

It is of course the best known of Anzieu's theories and its influence has already been considerable, including in the English-speaking world—though Judith Butler notes that "unfortunately, [it] does not consider the implications of its account for the sexed body" (Butler, 1990, p. 163 n43).[1] The theory is premised on the central importance of the body to psychical life. Whereas in Freud's time "what was repressed […] was sex" (Anzieu, 1995, p. 43; this volume, p. 23), in the 1980s the ignored and repressed issue was the body. Since Lacan, the stress on language had meant that the body was not being psychoanalytically theorized; yet "every psychical activity leans anaclitically on a biological function" (Anzieu, 1995, p. 61; this volume, p. 44). Anzieu's aim was to fill this gap. "Psychical space and physical space constitute each other in reciprocal metaphors", he wrote in 1990: "the Skin-ego is one of these metaphors" (Anzieu, 1990, p. 58; see also Anzieu, 1995, p. 28; this volume, p. 6).

The reader will, of course, discover the richness of the argument, its sources, vagaries and illustrations, in the pages that follow. Among

---

NB Where not otherwise specified, all translations are my own and page-references are to the original text (except in the case of this translation of *Le Moi-peau*); italics within quotations are the author's.

[1] For other discussions of *Le Moi-peau* in English, see (alphabetically): Ahmed & Stacey 2001, Benthien [1991] 2002, Connor 2004, Deleuze & Guattari 1972, Grosz 1994, Lafrance 2007, Lafrance 2009, Moorjani 2000, Prosser 1998, Segal 1998, Segal 2009, Silverman 1988, Syrotinski & Maclachlan 2001 and Ulnik 2007. More recently, he is cited in eds. Birksted-Breen, Flanders & Gibeault 2010, Cavanagh, Failler and Hurst 2013, Diamond 2013, Howells 2011, ed. Lafrance forthcoming 2016 and Lemma 2010.

its key insights are the principle that—as cited above—"the problem is not to repeat what Freud discovered in relation to the crisis of the Victorian era. It is to find a psychoanalytic answer to the discontents of modern man in our present civilisation". In the late twentieth century, with a world running out of control, in what Zygmunt Bauman was later to call "liquid modernity" (Bauman, 2000), Anzieu saw a need "to set limits" (Anzieu, 1995, p. 28; this volume, p. 7): the typical patient is no longer a neurotic suffering from hysteria or obsessions but a borderline case whose problem is a lack of boundaries. If maths, biology, and neuro-physiology had all become sciences of interfaces, membranes and borders, and embryology had shown that the ectoderm forms both the brain and the skin, this meant that "the centre is [...] to be found at the periphery" (Anzieu, 1995, p. 31; this volume, p. 78), and it is this complex structure of surfaces, rather than the old image of thought penetrating through into a truth-core, that could help us understand our physical, psychical and intellectual worlds in a different way.

The theory takes up and develops the work of figures as mainstream as Freud, Winnicott and Bion, on the one hand, and on the other scientists whose specialisms are somewhat or even very different, like (alphabetically) Abraham and Török, Esther Bick, John Bowlby, T. Berry Brazelton, Paul Federn, André Green, Harry Harlow, René Kaës, Jean Laplanche, Donald Meltzer, Ashley Montagu, Michel de M'Uzan, Mahmoud Sami-Ali, Paul Schilder, René Spitz, René Thom and Frances Tustin. It invokes research in autism, dermatology, embryology, ethology, mathematics and paediatrics, as well as theories of consciousness, development and linguistics. Above all, Anzieu exploits his presiding metaphor wherever it can be found: in the discourse of everyday life, in the actions of groups, in myth, folktale and science fiction (Adolfo Bioy Casares, Gérard Klein, Robert Sheckley, John Varley) and, supremely, in his own case studies. He considers love in many contexts, experienced in material and phantasmatic form. If the baby develops the illusion of a "an interface, represented as a skin common to the mother and the child, with the mother on one side and the child on the other" (Anzieu, 1995, p. 85; this volume, p. 67), that phantasy of reciprocal inclusion "is revived later in life in the experience of being in love, in which each of the lovers encloses the other in their arms while at the same time being enclosed by them" (Anzieu, 1995, p. 85; this volume, p. 68). But for every function of the Skin-ego imagined as positive, holding or receptive, there are pathologies to be ranged and detailed, toxicities like the bitter gift of the last fairy at Sleeping Beauty's christening.

Ultimately, growing out of this first configuration, "the Skin-ego is the basis for the very possibility of thought" (Anzieu, 1995, p. 62; this volume, p. 44). From the eight functions of the Skin-ego, after the individual has passed through the double taboo on touching, eight corresponding functions of the thought-ego will develop.

It is not for nothing that Anzieu named his set of interviews with Gilbert Tarrab *Une Peau pour les pensées* [*A skin for thought*]. Just as he began his research life with the study of Pascal and his *Pensées* (1660), so he ends it, in *Le Penser* [*Thinking*] (1994) with a theory that complements the psychical skin with a skin that contains—enables, controls and holds—the way we think. In psychoanalytic terms, the capacity for thought is the third term: first there is the body, then the primary process (impulses, drives, unconscious feelings) and finally there is the secondary process (consciousness, organisation, thought); it is what confronts the pleasure principle with the reality principle, deferral of gratification, acceptance of what is impossible or out of reach. We reason away our frustration, as far as we can. We mourn what is lost and transform it into knowledge. "*The reality principle* is a function that the ego imposes on the id" (Anzieu, 1994b, p. 60). The capacity to think "aspires to the ideal of a unique [utopian, universal] logic" (Anzieu, 1994b, p. 7)—though of course it is always disrupted by psychical impulses and failures—and "it is a moving moment for a psychoanalyst when a patient achieves the ability to think about him- or herself and about other people" (Anzieu, 1994b, p. 166).

Anzieu distinguishes between "thoughts" [*pensées*] and the capacity for thought, the act of thinking [*penser*].

> Thoughts precede thinking. They need to be thought in order to be recognized as thoughts. They invoke the creation of an apparatus for thinking (the function creates the organ). Thinking is the part of the ego where it intersects with the mind seeking to know the object. The first object is the body; then, by analogy (in the fullest sense) with one's own body, the next is ideas.
>
> In sum, all thoughts are thoughts of the body: one's own body, other bodies; thinking seeks to bring thoughts together in a body of thoughts. (Anzieu, 1994b, p. 21)

Developmentally, we first think through the thoughts of others. Bion, Bick and Winnicott see the work of infancy as letting the child internalize maternal care as a wrapping that forms the kernel of thought—a curious play with inside outsides typical of Anzieu's insights. The next stage is a doubly negative one. The taboo on touching, imposed on the child, means that "putting desires and needs into action becomes dependent on putting them into words. Putting them into words becomes dependent on putting them into thought" (Anzieu, 1994b, p. 33). But the child itself also has a capacity to negate. In conflict with its mother over feeding, the baby of about six months may spit, keep its mouth shut or move its head away from the nipple, teat or spoon; by fifteen months, it uses a consistent shake of the head or the word "no". Equal and opposite to the nod or smile, this gesture "marks the earliest acquisition of a system of communication" (Anzieu, 1994c, p. 4, citing the work of René Spitz). Once "no" is established as a word, "it is an act of *thought*" (Anzieu, 1994b, p. 48).

The theory of thinking in Anzieu is triadic:

> the skin envelops the body; by analogy with the skin, the ego envelops the psyche; by analogy with the ego, thought [*la pensée*] envelops thoughts [*les pensées*]. Analogy is not a vague resemblance, but a term-by-term correspondence of the elements of each of these wholes. (Anzieu, 1993, p. 31)

In the "Preamble" to *Le Penser*, Anzieu writes: "the person to whom I owe my capacity to think is essentially my father: unconditionally supporting my studies and my intellectual ambitions, he gave me two complementary experiences: the taboo and unconditional love" (Anzieu, 1994b, p. 1).

But, as we saw in the last section, describing his mother in *Une Peau pour les pensées* as having "intellectual tastes and gifts that I have certainly inherited" (Anzieu, 1991, p. 16), he also succeeded in "bringing my disunited parents back together" (Anzieu, 1991, p. 23). Referring, in 1992, to his writing in general, he concludes: "I have formed with my superego a couple united in the way a horseman is with his mount—and I don't know exactly which of us was the man and which the steed" (Parot & Richelle, 1992, p. 257).

To conclude this introduction, let us return to the comments of Anzieu's colleagues, who knew him best. Jean-Michel Petot, Anzieu's successor in 2000 in the chair of clinical psychology at Nanterre, describes him in 1973 or 1974, during a doctoral seminar, guessing from the evidence of Rorschach and other projective tests alone not only the appropriate diagnosis but also "the family situation, the profession, the favourite leisure activity and the form of treatment (a sleep cure) undergone by a patient" (cited in Kaës, 2000, pp. 102–103). "Above all", he goes on, "after amazing us by this, he took care to explain the processes of interpretation, so that divination became a transmissible technique" (Kaës, 2000, p. 103). Another colleague, René Kaës, drawing an implicit contrast with Lacan, points out that "everyone who knows Anzieu is grateful to him for the fact that he never formed a 'school' [...]; instead of a school, he formed a 'university', assisting those who chose to enter into dialogue with him to find for themselves, within the open network of his approaches, the thread that would guide them" (Kaës, 2000, p. 6).

To those readers who have the pleasure of discovering Anzieu through the pages of this book, the dialogue begins here; to those who are returning to him in this new translation, may the dialogue with this remarkable thinker long continue and evolve.

References

Ahmed, Sara & Jackie Stacey (eds) (2001). *Thinking Through the Skin*. London and New York: Routledge.

Allouch, Jean (1994 [1990]). *Marguerite, ou l'Aimée de Lacan*. Paris: EPEL.

Anzieu, Didier and Jacques-Yves Martin. (1997 [1968]). *La Dynamique des groupes restreints* Paris: PUF.

Anzieu, Didier *et al.* (1992). *Portrait d'Anzieu avec groupe* Paris: Hommes et Perspectives.

Anzieu, Didier *et al.* (1993). *Les Contenants de pensée*. Paris: Dunod.

Anzieu, Didier *et al.* (1994c). *L'Activité de la pensée* [republished in 2000 as *Émergences et troubles de la pensée*]. Paris: Dunod.

Anzieu, Didier (1968). *Ces Idées qui ont ébranlé la France*. Paris: Fayard.

Anzieu, Didier (1974). "Le Moi-peau". *Nouvelle revue de psychanalyse, Le dehors et le dedans*, 9, 195–208.

Anzieu, Didier (1981). *Le Corps de l'œuvre*. Paris: Gallimard.

Anzieu, Didier (1990). *L'Epiderme nomade et la peau psychique*. Paris: Les Editions du Collège de psychanalyse groupale et familiale.

Anzieu, Didier (1991). *Une Peau pour les pensées*. Paris: Apsygée.

Anzieu, Didier (1994a [1956]). *Le Psychodrame analytique*. Paris: PUF.

Anzieu, Didier (1994b). *Le Penser* . Paris: Dunod.

Anzieu, Didier (1995 [1985]). *Le Moi-peau*. Paris: Dunod.

Anzieu, Didier (1996). *Créer/Détruire*. Paris: Dunod.

Anzieu, Didier (1998 [1959]). *L'Auto-analyse de Freud et la découverte de la psychanalyse*. Paris: PUF.

Anzieu, Didier (1999a [1998]). *Beckett*. Paris: Gallimard.

Anzieu, Didier (1999b [1975]). *Le Groupe et l'inconscient* Paris: Dunod.

Anzieu, Didier (2000). *Psychanalyser*. Paris: Dunod.

Bauman, Zygmunt. (2000). *Liquid Modernity* Cambridge: Polity

Benthien, Claudia. (2002 [1999]). *Skin*, tr. by Thomas Dunlap. New York and Chichester: Columbia UP.

Birksted-Breen, Dana, Sara Flanders & Alain Gibeault. (2010). (eds) *Reading French Psychoanalysis*. Hove & New York: Routledge.

Butler, Judith (1990). *Gender Trouble*. New York and London: Routledge.

Cavanagh, Sheila L., Angela Failler & Rachel Alpha Johnston Hurst (2013). *Skin, Culture and Psychoanalysis*. Houndmills: Palgrave Macmillan.

Chabert, Catherine (1996). *Didier Anzieu*. Paris: PUF.

Connor, Steven (2004). *The Book of Skin*. London: Reaktion.

Deleuze, Gilles and Félix Guattari (1972). *L'Anti-Œdipe*. Paris: Minuit.

Diamond, Nicola (2013). *Between Skins*. Chichester: Wiley Blackwell.

Grosz, Elizabeth (1994). *Volatile Bodies*. Bloomington and Indianapolis: Indiana University Press.

Howells, Christina. (2011). *Mortal Subjects*. Cambridge: Polity.

Kaës, René *et al.* (2000). *Les Voies de la psychè: hommage à Didier Anzieu*. Paris: Dunod.

Lacan, Jacques (1975 [1932]). *De la psychose paranoïaque dans ses rapports avec la personnalité*. Paris: Seuil.

Lafrance, Marc. (2007). "Embodying the Subject: Feminist Theory and Contemporary Clinical Psychoanalysis." *Feminist Theory*, 8 (3), 263–279.

Lafrance, Marc. (2009). "Skin and the Self: Cultural Theory and Anglo-American Psychoanalysis." *Body and Society*, 15 (3), 3–24.

Lafrance, Marc. (2016). (ed.) *Skin Matters: Thinking the Body's Surface across the Disciplines' Body and Society*. Forthcoming.

Lemma, Alessandra. (2010). *Under the Skin*. Hove and New York: Routledge.

Lessana, Marie-Magdeleine (2000). *Entre mère et fille: un ravage*. Paris: Fayard.

Moorjani, Angela (2000). *Beyond Fetishism and Other Excursions in Psychopragmatics*. Basingstoke and London: Palgrave.

Musil, Robert (1978 [1930–43]). *Gesammelte Werke I: Der Mann ohne Eigenschafter*. Ed. By Adolf Frisé. Reinbeck bei Hamburg: Rowohlt.

Parot, Françoise & Marc Richelle (eds) (1992). *Psychologues de langue française*. Paris: PUF.

Prosser, Jay (1998). *Second Skins*. New York: Columbia University Press.

Roudinesco, Élisabeth (1994 [1986]). *Histoire de la psychanalyse en France*, 2 vols. Paris: Fayard.

Roudinesco, Élisabeth (1997 [1994]). *Jacques Lacan*, tr Barbara Bray. Cambridge: Polity.

Segal, Naomi (1998). *André Gide: Pederasty and Pedagogy*. Oxford: Oxford University Press.

Segal, Naomi (2009). *Consensuality: Didier Anzieu, Gender and the Sense of Touch*. Amsterdam and New York: Rodopi.

Silverman, Kaja. (1988). *The Acoustic Mirror*. Bloomington & Indianapolis: Indiana University Press.

Syrotinski, Michael & Ian Maclachlan (eds) (2001). *Sensual Reading*. Lewisburg and London: Bucknell University Press & Associated University Presses.

Ulnik, Jorge (2007). *Skin in Psychoanalysis*. London: Karnac.

PART I

DISCOVERY

CHAPTER ONE

Epistemological preliminaries

Some general principles

1. The dependence of thought and the will on the cortex and the dependence of the emotions on the thalamus are well known and scientifically proven. Contemporary psycho-pharmacological research is extending and even transforming our understanding of these areas. At the same time, such advances have narrowed both the field of observation and the theoretical field: psycho-physiologists tend to reduce the living body to the nervous system and behaviour to the brain activities that programme it by collecting, analysing, and synthesising information. However fruitful this model has proved for biologists, it has also increasingly been imposed by state-funded research institutions on psychology, which is fast becoming the poor relation of brain neurophysiology. Indeed, it is often imposed with authoritarianism by the very "scientists" who insist on freedom of research, especially basic research, in their own disciplines. By focusing on the skin, a primary datum which has elements of both the organic and the imaginary, which is at once a system for protecting our individuality and a primary instrument and site of exchange with others, my aim is to propose a different model, solidly based in

3

biology, that is the foundation of our interaction with those around us and respects the specificity of psychical phenomena as they relate to both organic and social realities—in sum, a model which I believe is capable of enriching the practice as well as the theory of psychology and psychoanalysis.

2. The functioning of the psyche, both conscious and unconscious, has its own laws. One of these laws is that part of it strives for independence, whereas in fact, from the beginning, it is doubly dependent— on the living organism that supports it and on the stimuli, beliefs, norms, cathexes, and representations emanating from the social groups the subject belongs to—first the family, later the cultural environment. Any theory of the psyche must hold these two threads together, without falling back on a combination of simplistic determinisms. Thus, following René Kaës (1979b, 1984), I shall postulate that the psyche has two anaclitic relationships: on the one hand a double anaclisis on the biological body and the social body and on the other a mutual anaclisis since, among humans at least, organic life and social life have just as much need for the virtually constant support of the individual psyche—as we can tell from both psychosomatic approaches to physical illness and the study of how myths or social innovations come to be—as the latter has for the reciprocal support of a living body and a living social group.

Nonetheless, the viewpoint of psychoanalysis is fundamentally different from that of psycho-physiology or psycho-sociology, for psychoanalysis is always aware of the existence and importance of individual phantasy—conscious, preconscious, and unconscious— and its role as a bridge and screen mediating between the psyche and the body, the world and other psyches. The Skin-ego is a phantasmatic reality: it appears in phantasies, dreams, everyday speech, body language, and thought disorders; and it provides the imaginary space in which phantasies, dreams, thought, and all psychopathological formations are set up.

There is an internal conflict in psychoanalytic thought between an empiricist, pragmatic, psychogenetic tendency, most common among the British and Americans, which holds that the organisation of the psyche is the result of unconscious experiences in childhood (especially those with object relations) and a structuralist tendency, predominant in France in the last few decades, which denies that structure may emerge out of experience, arguing on the contrary that any experience must itself have been organised by a pre-existing structure. I refuse to take sides in this conflict. The two attitudes are complementary and the antagonism between them should be preserved only so long as it enriches psychoanalytic research. The Skin-ego is an intermediate structure of the psychical apparatus: it mediates chronologically between the mother and the infant and structurally between the mutual inclusion of psyches in the state of original fusion and the differentiation of psychical agencies that corresponds to Freud's second topography. If the appropriate experiences do not occur at the right moment, this structure will not be acquired or, more commonly, will be distorted. But the many different configurations of the Skin-ego, which I shall describe in Part III, are variants on a basic topographical structure, whose universal character may suggest that it is already inscribed in virtual form (pre-programmed) in the psyche at birth, and the aim of achieving it is always implicitly felt by the psyche (in this respect, my thinking is close to the theory known as epigenetics or "interactive spiral theory").

Freud proposed, but did not formalise, a "model" of the psychical apparatus as a system of sub-systems, each governed by its own functioning principle—the reality principle, the pleasure-unpleasure principle, the compulsion to repeat, the principle of constancy and the Nirvana principle. With the Skin-ego we must add two more: a principle of internal differentiation and a principle of containment, both of which were hinted at by Freud in his "Project for a scientific psychology" (1950a) of 1895. The most serious pathologies of the Skin-ego—the autistic wrapping, for example—might even offer the possibility of importing into psychoanalysis the principle of self-regulation of open systems in response to "noise" which has been popularised by systems theorists such as Henri Atlan (1979). However, this principle, which helps living organisms to evolve, seems to be reversed when we move from biology to psychology, in which it appears chiefly to create psychopathological structures.

3. The sciences progress by means of an oscillation between two epistemological attitudes, which vary according to the personalities of the scientists and the requirements or the dead ends of a particular science at a particular moment. In the first case, the science possesses a valid theory which the ingenuity of laboratory workers is devoted to confirming, applying or developing; it remains useful as long as

it goes on producing valuable insights or until its major arguments are refuted. In the second, the science is renewed by the inspiration of one researcher—sometimes from another discipline—who casts doubt on accepted ideas; this individual's intuitions arise more from the creative imagination than from reasoning or calculations; moved by a kind of personal myth, which they cleanse of its phantasmatic baggage (though the latter may be projected into religious beliefs, philosophical speculation or related literary or artistic activities), they use it to draw out ideas that can be formulated in simple terms, verified under certain conditions and perhaps translated and transported into other fields. In the study of individual psychical functioning, Freud embodies this second attitude—it is no coincidence that as a young man I was interested in how he deployed his creative imagination through self-analysis, in his own youth, to discover psychoanalysis (see Anzieu, 1975a). Within this new discipline defined by Freud, the two opposing epistemological tendencies have continued to confront each other. Klein, Winnicott, Bion or Kohut, for example, invented new concepts (the paranoid-schizoid and depressive positions; transitional phenomena; attacks on linking; transferences of mirroring or the grandiose self) specific to new domains of study—the child, the psychotic, borderline states, and the narcissistic personality—which have expanded the scope of psychoanalytic theory and practice. Yet the majority of psychoanalysts cleave more and more to the first attitude: the return to Freud, with endless, almost Talmudic commentaries on his texts, mechanistic applications or adaptations of his ideas, not in the light of new practices but following "advances" in philosophy, the social sciences or the humanities, especially in the field of language (typified in France by Lacan). Now, in the last decades of the twentieth century, it seems to me that psychoanalysis has a greater need of people who think in images than of scholars, scholiasts, abstract or formalistic thinkers. My idea of the Skin-ego is not yet a concept; it is instead, intentionally, a vast metaphor—or, to be more exact, I believe it partakes of that fluctuation between metaphor and metonymy so well described by Guy Rosolato (1978). It is my hope that this idea will inspire psychoanalysts to think more freely and will enrich their spectrum of responses to their patients. Can this metaphor lead to a coherent set of operating concepts that may be factually verified or properly refuted? The task of this book is to convince the reader that it can.

4. Every piece of research takes place within a personal and social context; I shall now try to describe the context of this one. At the end of the eighteenth century, the *idéologues* introduced to France and, beyond it, to Europe the notion of unlimited progress in thought, science, and civilisation. This idea was dominant for a long time but at last the bubble had to burst. If I were to sum up the situation of the west—perhaps of all humanity—at the end of the twentieth century, I would emphasise the need to set limits: limits to demographic expansion, to the arms race, to nuclear explosions, to the speeding-up of history, to economic growth, to insatiable consumption, to the widening gap between the rich nations and the third world, the huge scale of scientific projects or economic enterprises, the invasion of the private sphere by the media of mass communication, the incessant pressure to break records, at the cost of over-training and doping, the compulsion to go faster, farther, more expensively, at the price of congestion, nervous tension, cardiovascular diseases and general discontent. We need to set limits on the violence against nature as well as against human beings—air pollution, ground pollution, water pollution, the squandering of energy resources in the name of producing everything we are technically capable of, down to mechanical, architectural or biological monstrosities; limits on the breaking of moral laws or social rules, on the assertion of individual desire, on the threat of technological advances to the integrity of our bodies and the freedom of our minds, to natural human reproduction and the survival of the species.

To speak only of a field in which I am involved—not just as an ordinary citizen but through my near-daily professional experience: in the thirty years since I began therapeutic work I have noticed a significant change in the nature of the suffering of patients who come for psychoanalytic treatment, and this change is confirmed by my colleagues. In Freud's day and in the first two generations of his followers, psychoanalysts found themselves dealing with clear-cut neuroses—hysteria, obsession, phobias or a mixture. Nowadays over half of a psychoanalyst's practice typically consists of what is known as borderline cases and/or narcissistic personalities (assuming, with Kohut, that these are two separate categories). Etymologically, "borderline" refers to states at the border between neurosis and psychosis, which combine traits from those two traditional categories. In actual fact, these patients suffer from a lack of limits—they cannot perceive the frontiers between the psychical and bodily Egos, between the reality Ego and the ideal Ego, between what depends on the Self and what depends on other people; or these frontiers shift without warning and the patient has a depressive breakdown, can no longer differentiate between erogenous zones, gets confused between pleasant experiences and painful ones, and cannot distinguish between the drives, so that a drive, when it arises, is experienced as violence rather than desire (what François Gantheret calls the "Uncertainties of Eros", *Incertitudes d'Éros*, 1984). These patients also suffer from narcissistic wounds, owing to weaknesses or flaws in their psychical wrapping: they have a diffuse feeling of malaise, of not living their own lives, of observing their mind or body from the outside, of being the spectator of something that both is and is not their own existence. The psychoanalytic treatment of borderline states and narcissistic personalities demands both technical adjustments and a new set of concepts, which would allow better clinical understanding; such adaptations are well described by René Kaës's term "transitional psychoanalysis" (Kaës, 1979a; Anzieu, 1979).

Small wonder that a civilisation which fosters outsize ambitions, panders to the demand of the couple, the family and social institutions to take charge of the individual, passively encourages the collapse of all boundaries in the artificial ecstasy of chemical or other drugs, exposes the child, who is more and more often an only child, to the traumatic focus of the unconsciouses of both parents in a household that is more and more restricted in size and solidity; small wonder, then, that such a culture favours immaturity and provokes a proliferation of borderline psychical disturbances. To this one might add the dispiriting impression that, in no longer setting itself any limits, humanity is heading straight for a catastrophe which contemporary artists and thinkers are outbidding each other to represent as equally appalling and inescapable.

Thus, in my view, we face a task of the greatest psychological and social urgency: to rebuild limits, restore frontiers and create for ourselves recognisable and habitable territories. These limits and frontiers must both institute differences and enable exchanges between the newly defined regions—regions of the psyche, of knowledge, of society and humanity. Without being explicitly aware of this overall goal, scientists in a variety of fields have begun to take on the task, each within their own sphere of activity. In the abstract, the mathematician René Thom (1972) has studied the interfaces separating various regions of space, and it is no accident that he uses the term "theory of catastrophes" to denote the description and classification of sudden changes in their form. My own work is much in his debt. The eyes and ears of today's astronomers, with the help of ever more refined instruments, are reaching towards the edge of the universe; and this universe has both spatial limits, constantly expanding, in which the matter in quasars, moving at almost the speed of light, is transformed into energy, and temporal limits, starting from the big bang whose echo still survives in the background noise of the universe and whose original deflagration created the primitive nebula. Biologists have transferred their interest from the cell nucleus to its outer membrane, discovering in the latter a kind of active brain which programmes the exchange of ions between the protoplasm and what lies outside; and errors in the genetic code may explain the increasing propensity for such serious illnesses as high blood pressure, diabetes, perhaps even certain cancers. The concept of the Skin-ego, which I am proposing in psychoanalysis, points in the same direction. How are the psychical wrappings formed, what are their structures, interleaved series and pathologies? And how, by means of "transitional" psychoanalytic treatment of the individual and perhaps even of groups and institutions, can they be re-established? These are the questions I ask myself and which I hope this book will begin to answer.

5. Ever since the Renaissance, western thought has been obsessed with one epistemological notion: the idea that we acquire knowledge by breaking through an outer shell to reach an inner nucleus or kernel. This notion is now exhausted, after having achieved some successes and also created many serious dangers—after all, it was *nuclear* physics that led scientists and the military to the point of atomic explosions. As early as the nineteenth century, neurophysiology called a halt to this, though it was not much noticed at the time. The brain is in fact the upper and frontal section of the encephalon; the cortex—the word means bark or shell in Latin and entered the vocabulary of anatomy in 1907—denotes the outer layer of grey matter that caps the white matter. We are faced with a paradox: the centre is situated at the periphery. In his article and later his

book of the same name, the late Nicolas Abraham (1978) set out the dialectic between "the shell and the kernel". His arguments confirmed my own findings and added weight to my hypothesis: what if thought were as much a matter of the skin as of the brain? And what if the Ego, now defined as the Skin-ego, had the structure of a wrapping?

Embryology can help us break away from certain habits of so-called logical thought. At the gastrula stage, the embryo takes on the form of a sac through the "invagination" of one of its sides, forming two layers, the ectoderm and the endoderm. This is, in fact, a more or less universal phenomenon in biology: with rare exceptions, the peel of all plants and the membranes of all animals consist of two layers, one internal and the other external. To go back to the embryo—its ectoderm forms both the skin (including the sense organs) and the brain. The brain, a sensitive surface protected by the cranium, is in constant contact with this skin and its organs; and the skin is a sensitive epidermis protected by the thickening and hardening of the parts nearest to the surface. Both the brain and the skin are surface entities, the cortex or internal surface—internal, that is, in relation to the body as a whole—being in contact with the outside world through the mediation of an outer surface or skin; and each of these two casings consists of at least two layers: a protective layer on the outside and, underneath it or in its orifices, another layer which collects information and filters exchanges. If we follow this model of the organisation of the nervous system, thought no longer appears as the segregation, juxtaposition, and association of kernels, but as a matter of relations between surfaces, themselves arranged, as Abraham astutely observed, in a series of interleaved levels in which each in turn takes the position of shell and then the position of kernel in relation to another.

"Invagination", the term used by anatomy and physiology, wisely reminds us that the vagina is not an organ with a specific structure but a fold of the skin, like the lips, anus, nose or eyelids, without a hardened layer or protective cornea to act as a shield against stimuli and whose mucous membrane is exposed, so that its sensitivity and erogeneity are on the surface, reaching a climax on contact with the equally sensitive surface of the tip of the erect penis. And everyone knows perfectly well, unless they find it amusing to reduce love to the contact of two epidermises,[1] which does not always result in the full expected pleasure, that love has the paradoxical quality of bringing us, at the same time and with the same person, the deepest psychical contact and the finest epidermal contact. Thus, the three bedrocks of human thought—the skin, the cortex, and sexual union—correspond to three configurations of the surface: the wrapping, the cap, and the pouch.

Every cell is surrounded by a cytoplasmic membrane. In addition, plant cells possess a cellulose membrane which has pores enabling exchanges; this membrane covers the cytoplasmic one and gives the cell—and consequently the plant itself—a degree of rigidity; for example a nut has a hard outer shell and also a fine skin surrounding the kernel. An animal cell is supple and gives way easily when it meets an obstacle, which ensures mobility. The physico-chemical exchanges required for sustaining life take place through the cytoplasmic membrane.

Recent research has revealed the double-layered structure of this membrane—which corresponds to Freud's intuitive grasp, in his "Note upon the 'mystic writing-pad'" (1925a), of the two layers of the Ego, one a shield against stimuli, the other a surface for registering impressions. Using electron microscopy, the two layers can be seen as separate, sometimes with an intervening space. Two kinds of fungus have been distinguished, one with a skin that is difficult to peel apart, the other whose skin consists of two distinct layers. In another observable structure, membranes are superimposed like the layers of an onion—this motif has been discussed by Annie Anzieu (1974).

6. Psychoanalysis presents itself—or is generally presented—as a theory of unconscious and preconscious psychical contents. The concept of psychoanalytic technique that follows from this aims to make those contents, respectively, preconscious and conscious. But there cannot be a content without it being related to a container. A psychoanalytic theory of the psyche as container does exist, but

---

[1] *Translator's note:* Anzieu is referring here to a well-known aphorism by Sébastien-Roch Nicolas, known as Chamfort (1741–1794). The 359th of his *Maximes et pensées* (1796) reads: *"L'amour, tel qu'il existe dans la société, n'est que l'échange de deux fantaisies et le contact de deux épidermes"* [*Love, as it exists in society, is nothing more than the exchange of two fantasies and the contact of two epidermises*].

it is far more fragmentary, approximate, and scattered. And yet the pathologies which the practising psychoanalyst encounters nowadays more and more often derive mainly from disturbances of the container-content relationship; and post-Freudian thinking has led analysts to pay increasing attention to the relation between the analytic setting and the analytic process, thinking about when and how the variables of the setting might be adjusted by the psychoanalyst or when and how the patient makes those variables into a substitute for process or a non-process (cf. José Bleger, 1967). The technical consequences of this epistemological reversal are significant: psychoanalysts now not only have to use the transference to interpret the flaws and defensive hypercathexes of the container, to "construct" the early encroachments, cumulative traumas, and prosthetic idealisations that created these flaws and defences, but also to offer their patients an inner disposition and a way of communicating which provide the possibility of a containing function that may be fully interiorised. My own focus for this theoretical reworking is the idea of the Skin-ego and the consequent readjustment of clinical practice is the above-mentioned technique of "transitional analysis".

Psychoanalytic theory thus both needs complementing and expanding. Here are five areas, among others, in which such developments strike me as desirable:

- to complete Freud's "topical" [*topische*] perspective on the psychical apparatus by a more strictly topographical one, which would relate to the spatial organisation of the bodily Ego and the psychical Ego;
- to complete the study of phantasies of psychical contents with a study of phantasies of psychical containers;
- to complete the understanding of the oral phase as being based on the activity of sucking by adding to it the importance of body-to-body contact between the baby and its mother or primary carer, i.e., by extending the breast-mouth relation to a breast-skin relation;
- to complete the double Oedipal prohibition by adding a double prohibition on touching, which is its precursor;

- to complete the typical psychoanalytic "setting",[2] not only by making some adjustments—for instance through the use of transitional psychoanalysis—but also by considering the positioning of the patient's body and their representation of analytic space within the analytic set-up.

A sixth issue is that of the drive. As we know, Freud's conceptions of the drive varied over time. First he contrasted the drive for self-preservation to the sexual drive, then the object libido to Ego libido and lastly the life drives to the death drives. He was undecided how to articulate the drive with the principle of constancy and later with the principle of inertia or Nirvana. Without ever abandoning the four parameters of the drive—source, pressure, aim, and object—he always insisted that the list of drives was not complete and more could be discovered. I therefore feel justified in considering a drive for attachment (to use Bowlby's term) or clinging (to use Hermann's), not as a proven case but as a useful working hypothesis. If I had to position it in relation to Freud's classifications, I would probably align it with the drives for self-preservation. Freud also describes a drive for mastery, which stands in an ambiguous, intermediate position in relation to the contrasting pairs outlined above. Insofar as it leans anaclitically on the muscles and especially on the activity of the hands, the drive for mastery must be said to complete the attachment drive, which aims to constitute the image of the skin as a containing, passively sensitive surface. One can see why these theoretical problems—and I have pointed out only some of them—should have caused analysts to question more and more the value of retaining the concept of the drive.[3]

The tactile and cutaneous universe

Even before they are born, the young of the human species are introduced by cutaneous sensations into a rich and highly complex universe,

---

[2] *Translator's note*: Anzieu uses the English term here.
[3] See the Acts of the conference *La Pulsion, pour quoi faire?* [*What is the use of the drive?*] (1984), published by the Association Psychanalytique de France, especially the article by Daniel Widlöcher, "Quel usage faisons-nous du concept de pulsion?" [What use do we make of the concept of the drive?]. See also Paul Denis (1992) and Roger Dorey (1992) on the drive for mastery.

which remains diffuse but awakens the perception-consciousness system, lays down a global, episodic sense of existence and creates the possibility of an initial psychical space. The skin is an almost inexhaustible subject of research, care, and discussion. Let us begin with a summary of what is known about it.

1. Both scientific and everyday language is full of expressions about the skin. To start with the lexical field: every living thing, every organ and cell, has a skin or a shell, tunica, wrapping, carapace, membrane, meninx, armour, pellicle, septum or pleura. As for the synonyms of "membrane", these are manifold: amnion, aponeurosis, blastoderm, cap, corium, diaphragm, endocardium, endocarp, ependyma, fascia, filter, fraenum, hymen, mantle, mesentery, operculum, pericardium, perichondrium, periosteum, peritoneum... A key example is the "pia mater", which is the direct covering of the nerve centres: this innermost layer of the meninges contains the blood vessels that lead to the medulla and the encephalon; etymologically the term means "the skin-mother", which conveys nicely the preconscious notion that the primordial skin is the mother's. In the French Grand Robert dictionary, the entries for *peau* [skin], *main* [hand], *toucher* [to touch] and *prendre* [to take] are among the fullest, not much less extensive than the entries for *faire* [to do, make], *tête* [head] and *être* [to be]. The entry for "touch" is the longest in the Oxford English Dictionary.

    Let us turn now to the semantic field. Numerous expressions in everyday speech refer to the many joint functions of the skin and the Ego. Here is a small selection.

    • The function of tactile pleasure: French: *Caresser quelqu'un dans le sens du poil* [to cosy up to someone], *avoir la main heureuse* [to have a lucky hand]; English: to feel good in one's skin.
    • The function of elimination: French: *Tu me fais suer* [you make me sweat, i.e. make me mad]; English: you rub me up the wrong way.
    • The aggressive-defensive function: French: *C'est une peau de vache* [he's a real bastard]; French: *se faire crever la peau* [to get a bullet in your hide]; English: it's no skin off my nose.
    • The function of identification: French: *Entrer dans la peau d'un personnage* [to get inside the skin of a character]; *faire peau neuve* [to have a makeover]; English: I've got you under my skin; sisters under the skin.

- The function of reality-testing: French: *Toucher la réalité du doigt*; English: put your finger on it.
- The function of communication: French: *entrer en contact* [to get in touch]; *mon petit doigt me l'a dit* [something tells me]; English: by the pricking of my thumbs.

And here are two words with multiple, vague meanings that signify the resonant subjective effects that objects have inside us; both refer originally to skin contact—*sentir* [to feel] and *impression* [impression].

I shall not embark on a study of the representation of the skin in the plastic arts or in societies other than our own. Michel Thévoz's richly illustrated book *Le Corps peint* (1984) [*The painted body*] is a first step in that research.

2. In both its structure and its functions, the skin is not a single organ, it is a collection of different organs. Its anatomical, physiological, and cultural complexity prefigures on the organic plane the complexity of the Ego on the psychical plane. Of all the sense organs, it is the most vital: one can live without sight, hearing, taste or smell, but if most of one's skin is not intact, one cannot survive. The skin is heavier (twenty per cent of the total body weight of a new-born baby, eighteen per cent of that of an adult) and covers a greater surface-area (2,500 cm^2 in the new-born, 18,000 cm^2 in the adult) than any other sense-organ. It appears in the embryo before any other sensory system (towards the end of the second month of gestation, preceding the two other proximal systems, the olfactory and gustatory, the vestibular system and the two distal systems, auditory and visual), following the biological law that the earlier a system develops the more fundamental it is. It has a great density of receptors—fifty per 100 cm^2.

   Itself a system comprising several sense-organs (touch, pressure, pain, warmth) the skin is also closely connected to the other external sensory organs (hearing, sight, smell, and taste) and to the awareness of body movement and balance. In young babies the complex sensitivity of the epidermis—to touch, heat or pain—remains diffuse and undifferentiated for a long time. When it develops it transforms the organism into a sensitive system capable of experiencing other kinds of sensation (the function of initiative), either connecting them to sensations of the skin (the associative function) or differentiating and localising them as figures emerging against the backcloth of an overall body surface (the screen function). A fourth function appears later: the skin provides the prototype and basis for it but it extends to the exchange of signals with other people in the close environment, in the form of the "double feedback loop", which I shall examine presently.

The skin can estimate time (less well than the ear) and space (less well than the eye), but it alone combines the dimensions of space and time. The skin can perceive distance on its surface more accurately than the ear can judge the position of distant sounds.

The skin responds to a variety of stimuli: the alphabet has been encoded into electric impulses on the skin which can be taught to blind people. The skin is almost constantly able to receive signs or learn codes, without these interfering with other cognate systems. The skin cannot refuse any vibro-tactile or electro-tactile signal; it cannot shut its eyes or its mouth or stop up its ears or nose. The skin is also not overburdened with excessive verbiage, as speech or writing may be.

But the skin is more than just an organ (or organs) of sense. It fulfils the related roles of several other biological functions: it breathes and perspires, secretes and expels, it maintains muscle-tone, stimulates respiration, circulation, digestion, excretion, and of course reproduction; it plays its part in the metabolic function.

Alongside its specific sensory roles and its role as all-purpose auxiliary to various organic systems, the skin carries out a series of other tasks that are essential to the living body, considered now as a whole individual, continuous in space and time: it maintains the body around its skeleton and keeps it upright, it protects it against external attack—by means of the surface corneal layer, the veneer of keratin and the layer of subcutaneous fat—and it registers and transmits stimuli and useful information.

3. In many mammals, particularly the insectivores, physiologists have identified the existence of two distinct, complementary organs in a single structure:

   • fur, which covers almost the whole body and fulfils the function of what, following Freud, can be called the shield against stimuli [*Reizschutz*]; it plays the same role as the plumage in birds or scales in fish, but in addition it has qualities of touch, warmth and smell that make it one of the anatomical bases of the clinging or attachment drive which is so important in mammals; and this also makes the parts of the body where hair remains one of the favoured erogenous zones in humans;

- hair follicles or vibrissae (a long bristle or a tuft of such hairs growing out of a fleshy mound, such as a cat's whiskers) in direct communication with a nerve ending that gives them high tactile sensitivity. Their distribution on the body varies by species, individuals and stages of development. Among primates the vibrissae are in decline; they have disappeared altogether in humans, at least in adults, but they can be found in the foetus or the neonate; in these species, the epidermis fulfils the double function of shielding against stimuli and allowing tactile sensitivity, by dint of an *anastomosis* with the horny or corneal layer which protects the nerve endings. To cite François Vincent: "The study of the skin structure, particularly among the order Primates, enables us to attribute a definite phylogenetic value to several characteristics: the implantation of the hairs, the thickness of the epidermis, the extent of development of skin wrinkles and the greater or lesser complexity of sub-epidermal capillaries" (1972).

To an outside observer, the skin of a human being displays variable characteristics according to the individual's age, sex, ethnicity, personal history, etc., which, like the clothing that forms a second layer over it, make it easy (or difficult) to identify the person. These characteristics include pigmentation, folds, ridges or wrinkles, the pattern of the pores, body hair, head hair, nails, scars, pimples, "beauty spots", not to mention the texture of the skin, its odour (reinforced or modified by perfume), its smoothness or roughness (accentuated by creams, lotions and lifestyle)…

4. A histological analysis of the skin reveals an even greater complexity—an enmeshing of tissues with different structures whose tight system of interweaving ensures the overall maintenance of the body, its shield against stimuli and its rich sensitivity.

    a. The surface epidermis or corneal layer is made up of a dense amalgamation (like that of rubble stones in a wall) of four layers of cells, in which the keratin produced by some of them forms a layer around the others, leaving them as empty shells, though all the more solid for that.

b. The subjacent epidermis, or mucous body, is a stratification of six to eight layers of large polyhedral cells of dense protoplasm, connected to each other by many filaments in a mesh network, the last layer structured like a palisade.

c. The upper dermis contains numerous papillae, rich in blood vessels, which actively absorb certain substances found in the liver and adrenals; they are articulated with the mucous body (described above) by a gear structure. In combination, b. and c. (the mucous and capillary bodies) serve the regenerative function of healing wounds and resistance against ageing—by emptying themselves of their protoplasm, they constantly push the worn-out subjacent layers up to the surface.

d. The dermis, or corium, is a highly structured retaining tissue; it has a felt-like texture, both resistant and elastic, an "amorphous cement" made up of interlocking clusters of fibrillae.

e. The hypodermis is an insulator; it has a sponge-like structure, allowing blood vessels and nerves to pass through to the dermis and—though without a clear dividing line—separating the integuments from the underlying tissues.

The skin also contains various glands, which secrete odours, sweat, and lubricating sebum, respectively: sensory nerves with free endings, sensing pain or contact, or ending in specialised corpuscles, sensing heat, cold or pressure; motor nerves, which control gestural expressions; and vasomotor nerves, which control the functioning of the glands.

5. If we turn now from the anatomy of the skin to its psychophysiology, we find so many paradoxical instances that one wonders whether psychological paradox is not partly based anaclitically on the skin. The skin preserves the balance of our inner environment from exogenous disturbances but in its form, texture, colouring, and scars it retains the marks of those disturbances. In turn, however much the skin is said to keep that inner state safe, it is revealed on the surface of the skin for all to see; it tells other people whether we are well or ill and acts as the mirror of the soul. In their turn, the non-verbal messages spontaneously emitted by the skin are deliberately

inflected or inverted by cosmetics, tanning, make-up, bathing or even cosmetic surgery. Few organs attract the interest or attention of quite so many specialists: hairdressers, perfumers, beauticians, kinesiologists, physiotherapists, not to mention advertisers, hygienists, palmists, healers, dermatologists, allergy specialists, prostitutes, ascetics, hermits, forensic police officers (using fingerprints), the poet seeking a skin of words to weave on a blank page or the novelist unveiling the psychology of characters through descriptions of their faces or bodies, and—if we include animal skins—tanners, furriers, and parchment-makers.

These are not the only paradoxes. The skin is permeable and impermeable. It is superficial and profound. It is truthful and deceptive. It regenerates, yet is always drying out. It is elastic, yet a piece of skin cut out of the whole will shrink substantially. It provokes libidinal investments that are as often narcissistic as sexual. It is the seat of well-being and seduction. It provides us with pains as well as pleasures. It communicates messages from the outside world to the brain, including "intangible" ones which its job is, precisely, to "feel" without the Ego being aware of them. The skin is both strong and fragile. It is the servant of the brain, yet it is capable of regeneration while the nerve cells are not. In its nakedness, it shows us denuded and bare but also reveals our sexual excitement. In its thinness and vulnerability, it represents our native helplessness, greater than that of any other species, but at the same time highlights our evolutionary adaptiveness. It separates and unites the various sense-faculties. In all these dimensions—and my list is far from exhaustive—it has the status of an intermediary, an in-between, a transitional thing.

6. In his richly documented work, *Touching: The Human Significance of the Skin* (1971), Ashley Montagu makes three main general points:

a. The early and prolonged effect of tactile stimulation on the functioning and development of the organism: in the evolution of mammals we find the following stages of the mother's tactile contact with her young, which serves both organic stimulation and social communication—she uses her tongue to lick it, her teeth to comb its fur and her fingers to delouse it or, in humans, to touch and stroke it. These stimulations help to trigger essential new activities immediately after birth: the baby's breathing, excretion, immune defences, and awareness; and later, its sociability, confidence, and sense of security.

   b. The effect of tactile exchanges on sexual development: seeking the partner, openness to sexual excitation, forepleasure, the achievement of orgasm or the let-down of breast-milk.

   c. The great range of cultural attitudes towards touch and the skin: an Inuit baby is carried naked against the middle of its mother's back, its belly against her warmth, inside her fur garment, held in place with a scarf knotted around their two bodies. The mother and child speak to each other through their skin. When the baby is hungry, it scratches its mother's back and nuzzles her skin; she brings it round to the front and gives it her breast. The baby's need to move is satisfied by the mother's activity. It eliminates urine or faeces without leaving the mother's back; she unties the baby and cleans it up, more for its comfort than her own. She anticipates all its needs, intuiting them by touch. The baby rarely cries. If its face or hands need cleaning she licks them, for frozen water is expensive to melt. This explains the calm attitude to adversity of the Inuit in later life—the fundamental confidence which helps them live and survive in a physically hostile environment, their altruistic behaviour, and their exceptional spatial and mechanical skills.

   In many countries, taboos on touching are set up to prevent sexual excitation, depriving people of the tender skin contact of the whole body, while at the same time favouring harsh contacts of hands or muscles, rough-and-tumble play, corporal punishment applied to the skin. Some societies systematically inflict painful practices on their children's skin—Montagu provides an impressive list of these—either in the form of initiatory rites or else to promote growth and/or beautify the body; in all cases, these practices raises the child's social status.

7. Psychoanalysts have shown relatively little interest in the skin. In a thoroughly documented article, "The role of the skin in normal and abnormal development, with a note on the poet Sylvia Plath" (1982, [2005]), American analyst Barrie M. Biven has made a useful survey of psychoanalytic publications on this subject. He does not offer any single organising principle but presents a large range of data, interpretations, and comments; in the next few pages I will summarise his main points.

- The skin provides a phantasmatic core to patients who have suffered early deprivations. For example, they may turn to suicide in the hope of restoring a common skin with the love object.
- A baby's mouth serves not only to absorb food but also to touch things and thus contributes to its sense of identity and ability to distinguish between animate and inanimate objects. Incorporating an object through the skin may occur earlier than absorbing it through the mouth. The desire to be incorporated in this way is found as frequently as the desire to be incorporated through the mouth.
- The Self does not necessarily coincide with the psychical apparatus: many patients experience parts of their body and/or their psyche as alien.
- The skin which the new-born gets to know best is that of its mother's hands and breasts.
- It is common for very young children to project the skin onto the object. This is also found in painting, in which the canvas (often thickly painted or cross-hatched) becomes a symbolic skin (often a fragile one) that functions for the painter as a protection against depression. An auto-erotic investment in their own skin is found more prematurely in infants who have been separated too soon from their mothers.
- In the Bible we find the running sores of Job, which express his depression, and the deceit of Rebecca covering the hands and neck of her beardless son Jacob with kidskin so that their blind father Isaac will mistake him for his hairy brother Esau.
- Helen Keller and Laura Bridgman, both deaf-blind and thus cut off from the world, were able to learn to communicate through the skin.
- The theme of skin is dominant in the work of the American poet and novelist Sylvia Plath, who committed suicide in 1963 at the age of thirty-one. This is her childhood memory, as she presents it, of her mother arriving home with a baby:

I hated babies. I who for two and a half years had been the centre of a tender universe felt the axis wrench and a polar chill immobilise my bones [...] Hugging my grudge, ugly, and prickly, a sad sea-urchin I trudged off on my own, in the opposite direction toward the forbidding prison. As from a star I saw, coldly and soberly, the *separateness* of everything. I felt the wall of my skin: I am I. That stone is a stone. My beautiful fusion with the things of this world was over. (Ocean, 1212–W)

And again: "Skin […] peels away easy as paper".

- As far as skin problems are concerned, scratching is one of the earliest modes of turning aggression back onto the body (rather than onto the Ego, which presumes a more highly developed Superego). The resulting shame derives from the feeling that once one begins to scratch one will not be able to stop, that one is led by a hidden and uncontrollable force, that one is opening up a breach in the surface of the skin. Shame,[4] in its turn, tends to be erased by the return of erotic excitation through the act of scratching, in an increasingly pathological circular reaction.
- Skin mutilations—sometimes real, but most often imaginary—are drastic attempts to maintain the boundaries of the body and the Ego, to restore a feeling of being intact and cohesive. The Viennese artist Rudolf Schwarzhogler, who used his own body in his art, amputated his own skin, piece by piece, until he died. He was photographed throughout this process and the photo series was exhibited in the German town of Kassel.
- Phantasies of skin mutilation are often found in Western art, from the fifteenth century on, in the guise of anatomical art. A character in the work of Jean Valverde is holding his skin at arm's length; Joachim Remmelini (1619) shows a man with his skin wrapped around his belly like a loincloth; Félix Vicq-d'Azyr (1786) has one with his scalp hanging down over his face. A man represented by van den Spiegel (1927) strips skin off his femurs to make gaiters; Berrettini's man is blinded by shreds of his own skin; and the wrists of a woman painted by Bidloo (1685) are tied with shreds of skin taken from her back.

To conclude my summary of Biven's article, I would add that, long before writers and scientists recognised and represented the specific relation between perverse masochism and the skin, painters were already doing so.[5]

---

[4] See Serge Tisseron, *La Honte, psychanalyse d'un lien social* [*Shame: The Psychoanalysis of a Social Bond*] (1992).
[5] See Didier Anzieu and Michèle Montjauze, *Francis Bacon* (1993).

CHAPTER TWO

Four sets of data

In Freud's day, what was repressed, both in the speech of individuals and in collective representations, was sex; this was the external reason (the internal one was his self-analysis) which led the inventor of psychoanalysis to emphasise questions of sexuality. For almost the whole third quarter of the twentieth century, the thing that has been misunderstood, denied or entirely absent—in education, in everyday life, in the rise of structuralism, in the psychologism of many therapists and sometimes even in child-rearing practices—was, and to a great extent still is, the body: as a vital element of human reality, as a general, irreducible, pre-sexual given, as the thing that all psychical functions lean on anaclitically. It is no accident that the notion of the body image, invented by the Viennese psychoanalyst Paul Schilder (1950), is missing from Laplanche and Pontalis's *Vocabulary of Psychoanalysis* (1967), which is otherwise a very well documented account, nor that contemporary western civilisation is coloured by a wholesale destruction of natural balances, the degradation of the environment and an ignorance of the laws of life. It is also no accident that the avant-garde theatre of the 1960s saw itself as a theatre of gesture rather than language, nor that the success of group methods, in the USA since that time and in Europe a little later, no longer relies on verbal exchanges inspired by the psychoanalytic process of free association but on bodily contact and the pre-verbal communications it creates. Throughout this period, what progress has psychoanalytic knowledge achieved in its search for the origins of psychical functioning?

Psychoanalytic research into the psychical effects of maternal deprivation has been carried out by scholars who, before they became psychoanalysts or at the same time, were, became or remained child psychiatrists or paediatricians. This applies to Bowlby from 1940, Winnicott from 1945, and Spitz from 1946, to cite only the dates of their first publications on the subject—not to mention the research conducted earlier by the two first child analysts, who were not medically qualified: Melanie Klein and Anna Freud. From those dates, it was clear to the three analysts that the way a child develops depends to a great extent on the whole pattern of care it is given during childhood, not simply on the relationship of breastfeeding; that if a baby's psyche has suffered attacks, its libido will not follow the series of developmental stages described by Freud; and that a major disruption of the early relationship between mother and child will seriously impair the latter's economic equilibrium and topographic organisation. In their view, Freudian metapsychology was no longer adequate to treat children who had suffered deprivation. In the USA, Spitz used the somewhat unfortunate term "hospitalism" to describe the serious and rapidly irreversible decline seen in children who have been deprived of their mother by an early hospital stay; this occurs if the staff provide routine or indeed scrupulous care but that care lacks the emotional warmth and free communications of smell, sound and touch that are available as a matter of course in what Winnicott calls "primary maternal preoccupation".

Recording facts in a scientific domain can only bring about real progress if those findings are placed within an observational grid that allows essential points (often hitherto unrecognised) to be picked up and if, on the one hand, the ideas drawn from that research coincide with existing knowledge from elsewhere and, on the other, they can be applied or fruitfully transposed to new domains. Four sets of data have, thus, directed, interrogated and fed into psychoanalytic research on the early genesis and problems of the psychical apparatus.

Ethological data

Around 1950, two major ethological works were published in English— Lorenz (1949) and Tinbergen (1951). The British psychoanalyst Bowlby

(1961) took from them the phenomenon of "imprinting", according to which the young of most birds and some mammals are predisposed to keep close to a particular individual who is singled out in the first hours or days after birth and preferred to all others. Generally this is the mother, but experiments show that it could be a mother of a different species, a foam ball, a cardboard box or Lorenz himself. What is interesting to psychoanalysts in this experiment is that the child does not only stay near its mother or follow her around but looks for her when she is not there and calls out to her in the greatest distress. This distress in the little bird or mammal is analogous to the anxiety displayed by a human infant when it is separated from its mother, and it ends as soon as contact is restored. Bowlby was struck by the primary character of this manifestation and by the fact that it is not connected to the "oral" phenomena in the narrow sense (breastfeeding, weaning, loss followed by hallucination of the breast), which had been considered by Freud and other psychoanalysts researching on infants as the only important point of reference. He believed that Spitz, Melanie Klein, and Anna Freud, trapped in the Freudian theoretical apparatus, had been unable or unwilling to take this finding on board, and he turned to the work of the Hungarian school of filial instinct and the clinging drive (Imre Hermann 1930, taken up in France by Nicolas Abraham, 1978) and on primary love (Alice and Michael Balint, 1952) to base his theory of the attachment drive. To summarise Hermann's argument: young mammals find both physical and psychical security in clinging to their mother's hair. The near-complete disappearance of fur from the surface of the human body facilitates significant early tactile exchanges between mother and baby and prepares the way to acquire language and other semiotic codes, but it means that for the young human the chance of satisfying the clinging drive is more random. It seems that by gripping on to the mother's breast or hands or her whole body or clothing, the child triggers behaviour in her that had hitherto been attributed to a utopian maternal instinct. The disaster that haunts the nascent psyche of the human baby is the loss of that clinging grip; if that happens, the baby is plunged—to borrow a term later coined by Bion—into "a nameless dread".

In recent decades, clinical psychoanalysis has found itself having to introduce new nosological categories, among which that of borderline states is the most sound and commonly applied. Patients in this category, we might say, are individuals who had difficulty in breaking away from the clinging relationship or, more precisely, who experienced the contradiction of premature and repeated alternations between excessive clinging and sudden and unpredictable detachments, which did violence to their bodily and/or psychical Ego. Certain characteristics of their psychical functioning result from this: unsure of what they feel themselves, they are much more preoccupied by what they believe other people desire and feel; they live in the here and now and communicate in the narrative mode; they do not have the right mindset to—borrowing another expression from Bion (1962)—"learn from experience" which belongs to them, represent that experience to themselves, draw a fresh perspective from it. Indeed, the idea of doing this remains a source of anxiety: they find it hard to stop clinging intellectually to a nebulous mixture of their own and others' life-experiences, to let go of contact through touch and restructure their relationship to the world in terms of sight, to access a conceptual "vision" of things and psychical reality and acquire the capacity for abstract reasoning; they remain fused to other people in their social lives, fused to sensations and emotions in their mental lives; and they dread penetration, whether in the form of the other's gaze or in genital coitus.

To return to Bowlby: in an article of 1958, "The nature of the child's tie to his mother", he offers the hypothesis of an attachment drive as a primary non-sexual instinct independent of the oral drive. He distinguishes five fundamental variables in the mother–child relation: sucking, clinging, crying, smiling, and following. This stimulated the research of the ethologists, who were themselves moving towards a similar hypothesis, which had recently been demonstrated in the famous, elegant experiment of Harlow in the USA (also published in 1958) in an article titled "The nature of love". Harlow compared the reactions of baby macaque monkeys to an artificial mother made of a block of wood covered in soft terry cloth, whether or not it gave milk (i.e., with or without a feeding bottle attached), to their reactions to artificial mothers, again feeding or not, that were made out of wire, and noted that if the variable of feeding is removed the baby always prefers the cloth mother to the wire-mesh mother as an object of attachment and that even when the variable of feeding is taken into account the difference is not statistically significant.

From this point on and continuing into the 1960s, the experiments of Harlow and his team focused on measuring the relative weight of the various factors in the infant's attachment to its mother. The comfort provided by contact with the softness of skin or fur proved to be the most significant. In the other three factors—feeding, the physical warmth experienced through contact and the rocking effect of the mother's movement when she carries the baby or it holds on to her—comfort was only a secondary effect. If the comfort of contact is maintained, baby monkeys prefer an artificial mother that provides milk to one that does not, and this lasts for 100 days; and they also prefer a surrogate that swings back and forth to a stable one, for 150 days. The only thing that proved stronger, in some cases, than the desire for contact was the desire for warmth: a baby rhesus monkey placed in contact with an artificial mother covered in soft cloth but unheated embraced her just once and then ran to the other side of the cage, where it stayed for the whole month of the experiment; another preferred an electrically heated wire mother to a cloth-covered mother at room temperature (see also I. C. Kaufman, 1961).

Clinical observation of normal human infants had long demonstrated similar phenomena, so Bowlby (1961) set out to revise psychoanalytic theory to take these findings into account. He took as his model the theory of control systems, which had originated in mechanics and then been developed in electronics and later in neurophysiology. Behaviour was no longer defined in terms of tension and reduction of tension but in terms of fixed goals, processes leading to the achievement of these goals and signals that activate or inhibit those processes. In this perspective he viewed attachment as a form of homeostasis. The child's aim is to keep its mother at a distance where she remains accessible. The processes are those that help it preserve or increase proximity (moving towards her, crying, clinging) or which encourage the mother to do so (smiling and other friendly overtures). The function is to protect the infant, particularly against predators. A proof of this is that the attachment behaviour can be observed not only towards the mother but also towards the male monkey whose role is to defend the group against predators and the little monkeys against the bigger ones. The mother's attachment to her offspring changes as it grows up, but its reaction of distress on losing her remains unaltered. The infant can tolerate longer and longer absences on the mother's part, but it becomes upset in the same overwhelming way if she does not return at the time it expects her to. Adolescents maintain this reaction, but internalise it, tending to hide it from other people and even themselves.

Bowlby devoted three volumes, under the general title *Attachment and Loss*, to developing his thesis. I have just summarised the first volume, *Attachment* (1969). The second, *Separation* (1973), explains overdependence, anxiety, and phobia. The third, *Loss, Sadness and Depression* (1980), is devoted to unconscious processes and the defence mechanisms that keep them unconscious.

Winnicott (1951) did not compare human children to animal young, nor did he offer such a systematic theory, but his descriptions of transitional phenomena and of the transitional space that the mother creates for the child between herself and the world could well be understood as effects of attachment. Monique Piñol-Douriez's observation of the child Hélène (1974) is a good example: falling asleep, Hélène would blink or wrinkle her nose with an air of total contentment, while exploring her eyelashes with her finger; later she extended this to exploring her mother's eyelashes, then her doll's, while rubbing her nose with her teddy-bear's ear; and finally she would touch or call out to her mother when she came back after an absence, or crawl towards other babies or a cat or a pair of wool-lined shoes or fleecy pyjamas. The author describes all this, correctly, as a transitional phenomenon. For my part, I would add that the common denominator in all these actions of Hélène's is the desire to touch parts of the body or objects covered in hair that is particularly soft to the touch or made of material producing a similar sensation. This contact sent her into a state of ecstasy which it would be difficult to describe as erogenous: the pleasure obtained through the attachment drive seems to be of a different quality from that obtained through the oral sexual drive; and in Hélène's case it clearly helped her, first, to fall asleep with confidence, then to trust in her mother's return and finally to arrive at a classification of people and objects that she could trust.

Winnicott chose to work in an aetiological perspective: he set out in more detail than his predecessors the connection between serious mental damage and early maternal deprivation. He summarises the issue in "Providing for the child in health and crisis" (1962b, pp. 22–23): if the deprivation occurs before the baby has become a person, it causes childhood schizophrenia, non-organic mental defects and a predisposition to clinical mental disorders at a later date; if the deprivation causes a trauma in an individual who is developed enough to be traumatised, it produces a tendency to affective and antisocial disorders; if it occurs when the child is trying to assert its independence, it provokes pathological dependence, pathological defiance, and outbreaks of violence.

Winnicott (1962a) also specifies the diversity of needs of the infant, which indeed survive in all human beings. As well as bodily needs, the baby has psychical needs which are satisfied by a "good enough" mother; insufficient responses from its environment to these needs will cause it to have difficulty in distinguishing between "me" and "not-me", while excessive responses make for a defensive over-development of its intellectual and phantasmatic capacities. Alongside the need to communicate, the young child has a need not to communicate and occasionally to experience a state of well-being that derives from the "unintegration" (1962a, p. 61) of its psyche and its soma.

After this historical summary, let us pause to reflect. Here is a list of the facts that have been established. To begin with ethological research:

1. The search for bodily contact between mother and child is an essential factor in the latter's affective, cognitive, and social development.
2. This factor is independent of feeding; a young monkey given free access to a feeding-bottle attached to a metal support will not approach it and appears scared; if the researchers arrange soft cloths or fur on the support (not necessarily monkey fur), it snuggles up to it and its behaviour becomes calm and reassured.
3. Being deprived of the mother or her surrogate causes disturbances that may become irreversible. Thus a young chimpanzee deprived of physical contact with its peers is incapable of mating later on. Monkeys of all kinds will fail to take up the correct postures in response to the social stimuli of their fellows, which triggers all manner of brutal behaviour from those others and violent outbursts from the affected individual.
4. Behavioural problems in a young monkey deprived of its mother can be prevented to a great extent if it is in contact with others that are similarly deprived; a group of companions is a substitute for the mother. Ethnological research on black African societies had already come to the same conclusion: the peer-group can replace the mother and take over her function. In young monkeys, the most favourable form of development is seen in those who benefit first from contact with the mother and then from contact with their group.
5. At the appropriate age, the baby monkey—in the wild as well as in the laboratory—leaves its mother and explores the world around it. She guides and supports it in doing this. At the slightest sign of danger, whether real or imaginary, it rushes into her arms or grips

on to her fur. The pleasure of touching or clinging to the mother's body is thus at the root of both attachment and separation. If the external stimuli are only slightly hostile, the baby familiarises itself with them and has less and less need of the mother's comfort; if they are terrifying—in one of his experiments, Harlow used a mechanical dog or a toy bear banging a drum—the baby monkey still goes on seeking the safety of its mother even after it has managed to touch and explore these monsters. Once the infant has gained and established trust in the world around it, real separation from the mother is achieved, either through its actions or through hers.

6. In monkeys, access to sexual maturity is achieved in three stages. The first stage is a satisfying childhood experience of non-sexual attachment to the mother. Next comes the possibility of practising playful manipulations of the body of a partner from the same age-group, these manipulations becoming increasingly sexualised (the discovery of childhood sexuality). This attachment followed by these games prepare and, in some species, condition the achievement of adult sexuality. In monkeys, as in many mammals and birds, the mother is *never* the object of sexual behaviour on the part of her sons. Ethologists explain this incest taboo by the fact that the mother is—and remains—the dominant animal for the young male. A macaque that becomes the leader of his mother's troop has the right of sexual access to all the females, so he generally chooses to leave the troop rather than mate with his mother. Entry into adult sexuality is marked by the end of the very permissive education provided by the troop in the form of childhood play and the introduction of savage constraints on the part of the dominant males who arrogate to themselves and then distribute rights of access to all the troop's females.[1]

---

[1] The two earliest studies published in French on this subject are François Duyckaerts, "l'Objet d'attachement: médiateur entre l'enfant et le milieu" [The object of attachment as mediator between the child and its environment], in *Milieu et développement* [*Environment and development*] (1972) and René Zazzo, "L'Attachement. Une nouvelle théorie sur les origines de l'affectivité" [Attachment: A new theory of the origins of affectivity] (1972). Two collected volumes combine essays by French and non-French authors on various issues relating to attachment: *Modèles animaux du comportement humain* [*Animal models for human behaviour*], a CNRS Colloquium, edited by Rémy Chauvin (1970) and *L'Attachement*, edited by René Zazzo (1974).

Data from the theory of groups

A second set of findings is provided by the observation of human groups formed for the purposes of either training or psychotherapy, once this study was extended from looking only at smaller groups to looking at large groups of thirty to sixty people, and to thinking about how a group inhabits its location and what imaginary space the group members project onto that location. With small groups it had already been observed that the participants tend to fill up empty space—if the room is very big they bunch together in one part of it; if the chairs are set out in a circle they put tables in the middle—or stop up gaps: they do not like to have empty seats between people; they pile up spare chairs in a corner; the empty place of an absentee makes them uncomfortable; they keep doors and windows closed, even if this makes the atmosphere physically suffocating. In a large group, in which anonymity is more marked, fears of fragmentation are reawakened and members experience the threat of losing ego identity, individuals feel lost and try to stay safe by withdrawing inside themselves or into silence. The three main defence mechanisms of the paranoid-schizoid position—splitting of the object, projection of aggression, and the search for a bond—all reappear. Splitting: the bad object is projected onto the large group as a whole or onto the monitors or one member who is treated as a scapegoat; the good object is projected onto small groups in which it helps create the group illusion. Projection of aggression: I perceive other people as devouring me when someone speaks and I cannot tell who it is or if they are looking at me without me being able to see them do so. Seeking a bond: if there is no seating-plan and participants are free to choose where they sit, the majority will tend to huddle together. Later on, or out of defensiveness, they adopt a seating pattern in one or more concentric ovals—like a closed egg, providing the reconstituted safety of a collective narcissistic wrapping. Turquet (1974) notes that a group participant will try to emerge as a subject out of that initial state of anonymity and isolation by making visual, gestural or verbal contact with the one or two people closest to them. This establishes what Turquet calls "the relational boundary of the I with my neighbour's skin":

> In a large group, the threat of breaking the boundary with "my neighbour's skin" is ever-present, and this is not only due to the

above-mentioned centrifugal forces which cause the I to withdraw, making it more and more isolated, idiosyncratic, and alienated in its relations with others. The continuity with one's neighbour's skin is also endangered because a large group raises numerous problems such as where, who, and of what type the I's neighbours are, especially when their personal space changes position, which happens all the time as another person may be near, then far, in front, then behind, first on the left, now the right, etc. These repeated changes of place give rise to questions: Why this change? What is it based on? Where has my neighbour gone? Towards what? Where shall I go now? etc. A typical characteristic of the large group is its instability; instead of stability it offers a kaleidoscopic experience. As a result, the I experiences a distended skin which attaches itself to the neighbour who spoke last but is now far away. Such distension may reach the point where the skin is about to burst open; to avoid that, the I breaks away and abandons the group, becoming a "singleton" and thus a deserter. (1974)

Although Turquet does not state this directly, his description lends support to Bowlby's theory, for it shows how the attachment drive operates in humans through the search for a contact—in both senses: bodily and social—which can provide a double form of protection, against external dangers and internal psychical distress, and which allows the reciprocal exchange of communicative signs, with each partner feeling recognised by the other. In groups, the development of techniques of bodily contact, physical expression, mutual massage, etc., points in the same direction. As we saw in the use of variables in Harlow's monkey experiments, the desire for warmth and a rocking movement also has a role to play. Trainees complain of the "coldness", both physical and moral, of a large group. In psychodrama or physical exercises, there is always one collective mime in which several participants cling tightly to one another, their bodies swaying together. This fusion sometimes ends with the simulation of a volcanic explosion, representing a common discharge of the tonic tension that has built up in each individual, like the baby Wallon liked to describe who, on being stroked rhythmically, discharged its excessive muscular tonus by laughing more and more loudly until, when a certain threshold was overstepped, the laughter turned to sobs.

Turquet points out that when, in the course of reconstituting itself, the psychical Ego creates a boundary-skin with its neighbour, the main result is the possibility of delegation: a person who is re-emerging as a subject "wants another member of the large group to speak for them, in order to hear something said that seems similar to what they are thinking or feeling and to be able to observe or find out, by putting this other in their place, how the group may respond to what that person has said on my behalf". The same process applies to the gaze. A group member reports that he was sitting opposite someone with "a kind face" and that made him feel better about himself. This might be kindness in the face or look, or a gentle voice: "the quality of the monitors' voices has more effect than what they are trying to say—for a gentle, calm, soothing tone is introjected by the listeners while the words themselves may be ignored". Here we can see the typical tone of voice that the attachment drive aims for—softness, sweetness, furriness, hairiness—a quality that started out as tactile and is then extended metaphorically to the other sense-organs.

Let us not forget that in Winnicott's theory (1962a, pp. 12–13) the integration of the Ego in both time and space depends on the mother's way of "holding" the baby, the personalisation of the Ego depends on her way of "handling" it and the Ego's establishment of the object relation depends on the mother presenting objects (such as the breast, the bottle, milk) that allow the infant to satisfy its needs. It is the second of these processes that interests us here: "the ego is based on a body ego, but it is only when all goes well that the person of the baby starts to be linked with the body and the body-functions, with the skin as the limiting membrane" (1962a, p. 59). Winnicott offers proof of the contrary: "a loss of firm union between ego and body, including id-drives and id satisfactions".

Data from projective testing

My third set of data is taken from work on projective tests. In the course of their research on body image and personality, two American scientists, Seymour Fisher and Sidney Earl Cleveland (1958), isolated two new variables among the responses to Rorschach inkblot tests, which have continued to prove very useful: they called these the "Barrier" and "Penetration" scores. The Barrier score is given to any response that implies a protective surface such as a membrane, shell or skin which can be linked symbolically to the perception of the borders of the body image—clothing or animal skins, in which the grainy or downy, spotted or striped texture of the surface is emphasised; a hollow in the ground or a protuberant belly; protective or overhanging surfaces; an armour-plated object or one having the form of a container; creatures or objects covered by or hidden behind something. The Penetration variable is the opposite: it relates to all responses that may express symbolically a sense that the body is a weak protective covering that can easily be penetrated. Fisher and Cleveland specify three versions of the representation of penetration:

a. the piercing, bursting or stripping back of a body surface (wound, fracture, abrasion, crushing, bleeding);
b. routes or modes of penetrating into something or expelling something from inside (an open mouth, an orifice of the body or doorway of a house, a hole in the ground from which liquids gush out, X-rays or cross-sections of organs that allow a direct view of the inside);
c. representations of the surface of an object that show it as permeable and fragile (things that are flabby or insubstantial, without clear boundaries, transparent or with a withered, faded, diseased or damaged surface).

Administering the Rorschach test to people suffering from psychosomatic illnesses, Fisher and Cleveland found that those whose symptoms were located on the outside imagined a body surrounded by a strong defensive wall, while those with symptoms in their internal organs had a conception of their body as easily penetrated, lacking a protective barrier. They consider it a proven fact that these imaginary representations pre-exist the appearance of symptoms and thus have aetiological value. They also believe that treatments which mobilise the body, such as massage or relaxation, can help patients to release these imaginary representations.

Defined by these two variables, the notion of body image is no substitute for that of the Ego but, as far as a person's knowledge of their own body is concerned, it does have the advantage of focusing on the perception of the body's borders. A sense of the boundaries of the body image (or of the image of the body's boundaries) is acquired by a baby as it becomes detached from the fusion with its mother: these boundaries are to some degree analogous to the borders of the Ego which are shown by Paul Federn (1952) to be decathected in the process of depersonalisation. If we take the body image not as an agency or function of the psyche but simply as a representation developed early on by the Ego itself as it takes shape, we may conclude, with René Angelergues (1975), that what is involved here is

> […] the symbolic process of representing a boundary that functions as a "stabilising image" and protective wrapping. This action posits the body as an object of cathexis and its image as the product of that cathexis. This cathexis captures an object that is not interchangeable, except in states of delusion, and must at all costs be kept intact. The function of borders is connected to the imperative of maintaining integrity. The body image belongs to the order of phantasy and secondary elaboration; it is a representation that acts upon the body.

Dermatological data

A fourth set of data is derived from dermatology. Apart from those caused by accidental injuries, skin ailments are related closely to everyday stress, emotional upheavals and—most relevant to my argument here—narcissistic flaws and problems in the structuring of the Ego. Though they first appear spontaneously, these ailments are often maintained or aggravated by compulsive scratching, which transforms them into symptoms the subject can no longer do without. If the symptoms are localised in the organs corresponding to the various stages of libidinal development, they obviously combine erotic pleasure with the physical pain and moral shame required to satisfy the punitive demands of the Superego. But, in such pathomimetic disorders, one sometimes finds cases in which the skin lesion is deliberately irritated and exacerbated, for example by rubbing it each day with broken glass (on this issue, see the work of Jacques Corraze, 1976). In this case, the secondary benefit to the supposedly incurable patient was receiving a disability pension; the primary benefit was not sexual but consisted in the tyranny they were able to wield over those around them, as well as the prolonged satisfaction of triumphing over medical know-how and power; thus, the drive to mastery is at play but it is not the only factor. There is a sneaky undercurrent of aggression in this behaviour, an aggression which is the reaction against a nagging inner need for dependency that these malingerers find intolerable. They attempt to recover this need by making other people dependent on them, people who replicate the earliest objects of their attachment drive, who frustrated them in the past and who seem ever since to have been inviting revenge. This intense need for dependency correlates with the fragility and immaturity of the pithiatic's psyche, its poorly differentiated topographic structure, inadequate cohesion of the Self and weak development of the Ego in relation to the other psychical agencies. These patients too manifest a pathological attachment drive. Because their Skin-ego is so fragile, malingerers veer between a terror of abandonment if the object of their attachment is not within reach and a terror of persecution if he or she is too close.

The psychosomatic approach to skin disorders has broadened out these findings. Pruritus is not only linked to guilty sexual desires, in a circulatory play between auto-eroticism and self-punishment; it is also, more than anything, a way of drawing attention to oneself, especially to one's skin if, in earliest childhood, the mothering and family environment did not provide contacts that were (as outlined above) gentle, warm, firm, reassuring, and above all meaningful. The itch is the itch to be understood by one's love-object. Through the effect of the repetition compulsion, the physical symptom revives old frustrations in the primal form of the "language" of the skin, with the suffering visible on the surface and the underlying anger suppressed; and, since these patients are fixated on a stage before soma and psyche were properly differentiated, skin irritation is confused with mental irritation and the eroticisation of the damaged part of the body emerges belatedly to make pain and hatred tolerable and to try to turn unpleasure into pleasure. The condition known as "pudendal" erythema does not cause anxiety only because the skin, acting as "the mirror of the soul" rather than as a boundary, allows an interlocutor to read directly the sexual and aggressive desires the patient is ashamed of but also because the skin is revealed to the other person as a fragile wrapping that invites physical penetrations and psychical intrusions.

Generalised eczema may represent the regression to a childhood state of complete dependence, the somatic conversion of a terror of psychical collapse and a mute, desperate appeal to an auxiliary Ego offering total support. In children under two years, eczema can mark the lack of a tender, enveloping physical touch on the part of the mother. Spitz (1965) hesitates between two interpretations:

> We have been wondering whether these skin problems are an adaptive strategy or a defensive reaction. When a child reacts in the form of eczema this may be a demand to its mother to touch

it more often; or on the other hand, it may be a form of narcissistic withdrawal, since through eczema it can obtain the somatic stimuli she has refused to provide. We cannot know.

I myself remain equally hesitant, ever since I first worked, as a young trainee psychologist in the 1950s, in Professor de Graciansky's dermatological unit at the Hôpital Saint-Louis in Paris. Are some skin disorders typical of patients who, as children, both benefited and suffered from the mother's over-stimulation of their skin in the course of everyday care, while the conditions of other patients repeat the results or after-effects of a dearth of childhood contact with the mother's body and skin? In fact, the unconscious problematic in both cases would seem to centre on the primary taboo on touching, which I shall describe later—if the mother failed to caress or embrace the baby enough, its growing psyche will have experienced this unconsciously as the excessive, premature, violent application of the prohibition on clinging tightly to another person's body; overstimulation by the mother would also be unpleasant because it overwhelms the child's protective shield, which is as yet insecure, and dangerous because it transgresses and switches off the taboo on touching, which the psyche knows it needs in order to create a psychical wrapping that is truly its own.

For the moment, in the light of all these clinical observations, the simplest and safest hypothesis is the following: "the depth of the damage to the skin is in proportion to the depth of psychical harm done".[2]

I prefer to reformulate this hypothesis by bringing in my concept of the Skin-ego, which I am about to present: the seriousness of the damage to the skin (which can be measured by the increasing resistance of the patient to chemical or psychotherapeutic treatments) is related to the quantitative and qualitative extent of flaws in the Skin-ego.

---

[2] See articles by Danièle Pomey-Rey, a dermatologist, psychiatrist, psychoanalyst, and consultant fellow in psychodermatology at the Hôpital Saint-Louis; esp. "Pour mourir guérie" [She died cured], *Cutis* 3 (Feb 1979), which discusses the tragic case of Mlle P. See also her book, *Bien dans sa peau, bien dans sa tête* [*Feeling good in one's skin, feeling right in the head*], Centurion, 1989.

CHAPTER THREE

The notion of a Skin-ego

The four sets of data I have outlined above—from ethology, group theory, projective testing, and dermatology—have led me to the hypothesis of the Skin-ego, first formulated in an article of 1974 in the *Nouvelle Revue de Psychanalyse*. Before returning to this hypothesis and expanding on it, it will be helpful to revisit the notion of the oral stage.

Mouth-breast and skin-breast

Freud did not limit the stage he termed "oral" to the activity of the bucco-pharyngeal zone and the pleasure of sucking; he also focused on the subsequent pleasure of the feeling of repletion. The mouth provides the first, vivid, brief experience of a differentiating contact, a site of passage and incorporation, but repletion gives the baby the more diffuse, long-lasting experience of a central mass, a fullness, a centre of gravity. It is no surprise that contemporary psychopathology has come to attach more and more importance to what some patients describe as a sense of inner emptiness, nor that a relaxation therapy such as Schultz's autogenic training begins by suggesting to participants that they feel simultaneously in their bodies a sensation of warmth (the flow of milk) and heaviness (repletion).

While it is being breastfed and during daily care, the baby has a third, concomitant experience: that of being held in its mother's arms, pressed to her body, sensing its warmth, smell, and movements, and being carried, rocked, rubbed, washed, and caressed, while at the same time being bathed in her murmuring and humming. These experiences taken together characterise the attachment drive described by Bowlby and Harlow and evoke the idea of what Spitz and Balint call the primal cavity. Bit by bit these activities lead the baby to differentiate a surface with an inner and outer face, an interface that allows the distinction between inside and outside, and a volume within whose atmosphere it feels itself bathed; both the surface and the volume give it the experience of a container.

The "breast" is the term commonly used by psychoanalysts for the total reality experienced by an infant at this time: it combines four characteristics that the analyst, like the baby, tends to confuse—the breast is on the one hand a source of nourishment and on the other an object that fills; its skin is warm and soft to the touch and it is also an active, stimulating receptacle. The mother's breast, as a generalised, syncretic thing, is the earliest mental object, and it is doubly to the credit of Melanie Klein to have shown how it is able to feature in the first metonymic substitutions (mouth-breast, cavity-breast, faeces-breast, urine-breast, penis-breast, rival-baby-breast) and how it attracts the competing cathexes of the two basic drives. The intense pleasure that it brings to the life drives—the pleasure of sharing in its creativity—evokes gratitude; but, by contrast, destructive envy is directed against the breast because of this very creativity when, to the baby's frustration, that pleasure is given to someone else. Yet in focusing only on phantasy, Klein neglects the qualities of more specifically bodily experiences (by emphasising the "holding" and "handling" actions of the real mother, Winnicott, 1962a, was reacting against this) and in insisting on the relations between certain parts of the body and their products (milk, sperm, excrement) within a creative-destructive dynamic, she neglected the one thing that links them all into a unifying whole—the skin. The surface of the body is missing from Klein's theory, and this gap is particularly surprising given that an essential element of that theory, the opposition of introjection (modelled on feeding) and projection (modelled on excretion) is premised on the formation of a boundary between inside and outside. This helps us to understand certain objections raised against Kleinian techniques: bombarding the patient with interpretations may remove not only the Ego's defences but also its protective wrapping. It is true that in referring to the "inner world" or to "internal objects", Klein must be presupposing the notion of internal space (see Didier Houzel, 1985a).

Many of her followers, sensitive to this deficiency and trying to mitigate it, developed new concepts (among which the Skin-ego finds its natural place): the infant's introjection of the mother-baby relation as a container-contained relation and the resulting formation of an "emotional space" and a "space for thought"—the earliest thought, that of the absence of the breast, makes the frustration of that absence bearable—leading to an apparatus for thinking thoughts (Bion, 1962); alternative representations of a soft, flaccid amoeba-Ego and a hard crustacean-Ego in the two forms of childhood autism, abnormal primary and encapsulated secondary (Tustin, 1972); the second, muscular skin as a defensive-offensive armour in schizophrenics (Bick, 1968); the formation of three psychical borders, one with the internal space of external objects, one with the internal space of internal objects, and one with the outside world, but which leave a "black hole" (analogous to that of astrophysics) that swallows up any psychical element that comes near—madness, autistic whirlwind (Meltzer, 1975).

I must also mention here without further ado four French psychoanalysts—the first two born in Hungary, the other two in Italy and Egypt—whose clinical intuitions and theoretical thinking, along similar lines to my own, have enlightened, stimulated, and encouraged me. All unconscious psychical conflicts unfold not only in relation to oedipal issues but also to narcissistic ones (Grunberger, 1971). All the sub-systems of the psychical system as well as the psychical system as a whole conform to a dialectical interaction between shell and kernel (Abraham, 1978). The psychical apparatus has an original pictogrammatic mode of functioning which is more archaic than the primary and secondary modes (Castoriadis-Aulagnier, 1975). An imaginary space develops on the basis of the mutual inclusion of the bodies of the mother and the child, through a dual process of sensory and phantasmatic projection (Sami-Ali, 1974).

Every figure presupposes a ground against which it appears: this elementary truth is easily ignored because our attention is normally drawn to the emerging figure, not the background from which it stands out. The baby's experience of its orifices as allowing things to pass either inwards (incorporation) or outwards (expulsion) is important, of course, but no orifice can be perceived without relating to a sensation of surface and volume, however vague. The *infans* begins to perceive its skin as a surface when it experiences contact between its body and that of its mother, in the framework of a secure relationship of attachment to her. Through these experiences it comes to develop not only the notion of a boundary between the inside and the outside but also the confidence it will need to control its orifices, for it can only feel confident of their functions if it also has a fundamental certainty of the integrity of its bodily wrapping. In this, clinical practice confirms Bion's (1962) theoretical notion of the psychical "container":[1] the dangers of depersonalisation are linked to the image of a perforable wrapping and the terror—primary, according to Bion—of vital substance flowing out through its holes, which is a fear not of fragmentation but of being drained; many patients describe this when they talk of themselves as an egg with a pierced shell through which either the white or the yolk leaks away. Moreover, the skin is the seat of proprioceptive sensations, whose important role in the development of character and thought has been emphasised by Henri Wallon: it is one of the organs that regulate muscle tone. If we think in economic terms—accumulation, displacement, and discharge of tension—we are presupposing a Skin-ego.

In a baby, the whole surface of its body and that of its mother is the object of experiences that are as important, for their emotional quality, stimulation of confidence, pleasure and thought, as experiences connected to sucking and excretion (Freud) or to the phantasmatic presence of internal objects representing the products of the functioning orifices (Klein). As she bathes, washes, rubs, carries or embraces her baby, the mother is unknowingly stimulating its skin. Indeed, mothers are well aware of the existence of skin pleasure in their baby—and themselves—because they provoke them knowingly through caresses and play. The little one accepts these gestures, first as a form of excitation and later as communication. Massage becomes message. This kind of early pre-verbal communication is a necessary preliminary to learning to

---

[1] I am indebted to René Kaës for distinguishing between two French terms for "container"—*contenant* and *conteneur*—though I use them in the opposite way to him: in my usage, the *conteneur* is passive, and the *contenant* active.

speak. The novel (1938) and film (1971) *Johnny Got his Gun* illustrate this well. A seriously injured soldier has lost his sight, hearing, and mobility, but by tracing letters on his chest and abdomen, a nurse succeeds in establishing contact with him—and later, responding to his wordless plea with a kindly masturbation, she gives him the pleasure and relief of sexual discharge. This restores the wounded man's will to live by making him feel, in turn, recognised and satisfied in his need to communicate and his masculine desire. It is undeniable that, as a child develops, its skin becomes eroticised: skin pleasures are part of the preliminaries to adult sexual activity and retain a major role in female homosexuality. Nevertheless it remains true that genital, even auto-erotic, sexuality is only achieved by people who have acquired a minimal basic sense of security in their own skins. Moreover, as Federn (1952) has suggested, when the borders of the body and the Ego are eroticised, the earlier psychical stages of the Self are consigned to repression and amnesia.

The idea of a Skin-ego

The Skin-ego arises in response to the need for a narcissistic wrapping and provides the psychical apparatus with a secure and consistent state of basic well-being. As a corollary, the psychical apparatus may test out sadistic and libidinous object cathexes: the psychical Ego is strengthened by identification with these objects and the bodily Ego can enjoy pregenital and later genital pleasures.

By "Skin-ego" I am referring to a mental image used by the child's Ego during its early stages of development to represent itself as an Ego containing psychical contents, based on its experience of the surface of the body. This corresponds to the moment when the psychical Ego differentiates itself from the bodily Ego in operative terms but remains mixed up with it in figurative terms. Viktor Tausk (1919) shows particularly well that the syndrome of the "influencing machine" could only be properly understood through the distinction between these two Egos: the psychical Ego continues to be recognised by the subject as his or her own (it is this Ego that implements defence mechanisms against the dangerous sexual drives and interprets logically any perceptible data that reach it) whilst the bodily Ego is not recognised as belonging to the self and the cutaneous or sexual sensations that emanate from it are attributed to the "influencing machine" controlled by the machinations of a seducer-persecutor.

Every psychical activity leans anaclitically on a biological function. The Skin-ego is supported by the various functions of the skin. Later I shall examine these more systematically; for the moment I shall limit myself to three—the three I detailed in my original article of 1974. The first function of the skin is to be the sac that contains and retains inside itself all the good, full material that has accumulated through breast-feeding, everyday care, and the experience of being bathed in words. Its second function is to be the interface that marks the border with the external world, which it keeps on the outside, the barrier that protects one against being penetrated by the aggression and greed of others, whether people or objects. The third function of the skin, which it shares with the mouth and carries out at least as much as the mouth does, is to be a site and primary mode of communication with other people, to establish meaningful relations; in addition, it is a surface for registering the traces left by those others.

From this epidermal, proprioceptive origin, the Ego inherits the double faculty of setting up barriers (which become psychical defence mechanisms) and filtering exchanges (with the Id, the superego and the outside world). If the attachment drive is well satisfied early on, it is my opinion that it provides the infant with the basis on which to establish what Luquet (1962) calls the integrative impulse of the Self. And there is a later consequence: the Skin-ego is the basis for the very possibility of thought.

The phantasy of a common skin and its narcissistic and masochistic variants

There are arguments here that may support and clarify the disputed notion of primary masochism and make it clearer. Before it is eroticised at a secondary stage and develops into sexual or moral masochism, masochistic suffering can initially be explained in terms of drastic alter-nations, which occur before the child can walk or talk or has passed the mirror phase, between overstimulation and lack of contact with the mother or her substitutes, and thus between satisfaction and frustration of the need for attachment.

The constitution of the Skin-ego is one of the conditions of the dual passage from primary to secondary narcissism and from primary to secondary masochism.

In psychoanalytic treatment of patients presenting either masochistic sexual behaviour or a partial fixation to a perverse masochistic position, I have often encountered the following: they spoke of experiencing an actual physical injury to their skin in early childhood and this episode had furnished crucial material for the organisation of their phantasies. This may have been a superficial surgical intervention, by which I mean one basically affecting the surface of the body; or an episode of dermatitis or alopecia; or an accidental fall or knock in which a substantial piece of skin was torn away. Or it may have been the early symptoms of conversion hysteria.

The unconscious phantasy which these diverse observations helped me bring to light is not that of a "dismembered body", as certain psychoanalysts have proposed—this seems to me more typical of psychotic organisations. Instead, I believe that the underlying phantasy of the perverse masochist is that of the "flayed body".

Referring to the "Rat Man", Freud writes of his "horror at pleasure of his own of which he himself was unaware" (1909d, p. 167). The masochist's pleasure reaches its apogee of horror when the corporal punishment applied to the skin surface (spanking, flagellation or piercing) is taken to the point at which pieces of skin are actually torn, gouged or ripped away. Masochistic ecstasy, as is well known, requires the subject to imagine that the blows have left marks on the surface of their skin. Among the pregenital pleasures that normally accompany genital sexual orgasm, one often finds that of leaving traces behind on the partner's skin, by biting or scratching them; this represents an incidental fantasy which, in the case of the masochist, moves to centre-stage.

As we shall see in the next chapter, which is focused on the Greek myth of Marsyas, the originating phantasy of masochism is made up of two representations: (i) that a single skin is shared by the child and its mother, figurative of their symbiotic union; and (ii) that the process of detachment by which the child attains its autonomy involves the breaking off or tearing of that common skin. This phantasy of being skinned is borne out by seeing domestic animals slaughtered and prepared for the table or of oneself being spanked or having cuts or scabs looked after.

Most of the patients I have treated who have displayed a marked masochistic fixation presented more or less conscious phantasies of skin fusion with the mother. What seems to me particularly revealing is the closeness of the unconscious phantasy of the flayed body to the preconscious phantasy of fusion. In the language of archaic thought, the symbiotic union with the mother appears in the form of a tactile (and probably olfactory) image of the two bodies of mother and child sharing a common interface. Separation from the mother is represented by the tearing of this common skin. Certain real-life experiences lend credence to this phantasmatic representation: after an illness, an operation or an accident involving a wound, when the dressing sticks to the skin, the mother or her substitute tears off—or is imagined to be able to tear off—pieces of epidermis along with the dressing. Thus the woman who provides the care is also the one who flays; yet the woman who has torn the common wrapping is also the one who could repair it.

In masochistic phantasy, such as Sacher-Masoch's *Venus in Furs* (1870), the fur carries over the figurative representation of a recovered skin-to-skin contact, velvety, voluptuous, and scented (nothing is so strong as the scent of a new fur garment), to the conjoining of bodies that is one of the pleasures associated with genital orgasm. The fact that Sacher-Masoch's flagellating Venus—in life as in the novel—may be naked under her furs confirms the primary value of the fur-skin as an object of attachment before it acquires the value of denoting the sexual object. Need we remind ourselves that a fur is actually the hide of an animal and its presence refers back to a flayed, skinned animal? The child Severin, fascinated by Venus or Wanda dressed in furs, imagines his mother covered in a skin that simultaneously signifies fusion and stripping-away. The fur represents the physical softness and sensual tenderness of a mother lovingly caring for her child. But Venus in furs also stands for the mother whom the child tried to see naked or whom he tried to seduce by displaying his penis to her, in reality or imagination: the mother who beat him in reality, imagined as having flayed him until he was skinned alive, now triumphing, draped in the skin of her vanquished enemy, just as the hunter-heroes of ancient mythology or of so-called primitive societies dress in the skins of the wild animals or humans they have killed.

It is time to introduce a fundamental distinction between two types of contact that the mother and other carers have with the baby's body and skin. Some contacts communicate excitation—for example, in the course of taking care of its body, the mother may give her baby a strongly libidinised stimulation which has an erotic effect so premature and excessive in relation to its state of psychical development that it is experienced as a traumatic seduction. Other contacts communicate information—these may be related to the baby's basic needs, the feelings of both partners, the dangers of the outside world, various ways of dealing with objects depending on whether they are animate or inanimate. The baby cannot at first differentiate between these two types of contact, and this will continue unchanged as long as the mother and other carers go on inverting, mixing or confusing them. In a hysteric, they tend to remain permanently confused: he or she will direct towards the partner information, under the guise of stimuli, which is so veiled that the partner is most likely to try to respond to the stimulation, not the information, and this leads to disappointment, resentment and complaints from the hysteric. In certain forms of depression one finds the opposite dynamic: the baby has received the necessary and adequate bodily care, with the usual set of accompanying instinctual excitations, but the mother, preoccupied with the death of a close relative, the distress of a failed marriage or a post-partum depression, is incapable of the focus required to pick up the baby's signals or send out signals in her turn. When such children grow into an adults they become depressed every time they receive material or spiritual nourishment that is not accompanied by meaningful exchanges, and absorbing that nourishment simply makes them feel their inner emptiness more intensely.

These two types of contact—excitation and significance—lead to effects related, respectively, to masochism and narcissism.

The paradox of excitatory contacts lies in the fact that the bodily care provided by the mother, who serves as the baby's primary shield against the attacks of the outside world, brings with it such intensely libidinal stimuli that it causes the child an instinctual over-excitement of internal origin which sooner or later becomes excessive and unpleasant. This sets up permanently a psychical wrapping of excitation and suffering that blocks the establishment of the Skin-ego, which would have been both a shield against stimuli and a wrapping of well-being. It lays the economic and topographical groundwork for the development of masochism, with its compulsion to repeat the experiences that reactivate both the wrapping of excitation and that of suffering.

The paradox of signifying contacts lies in the fact that a mother who is attentive not only to her baby's bodily needs but also to its psychical ones does more than simply satisfy these needs: by the sensory echoes she sends back, as much as by the concrete actions she performs, she shows that she has correctly interpreted them. The baby's needs are satisfied and at the same time so is its need to have those needs understood. This creates both a wrapping of well-being, which it cathects narcissistically, and the illusion, essential for the formation of the Skin-ego, that the person on the other side of that wrapping will respond immediately, and in exact complementarity, to its signals; this is the reassuring illusion of an omniscient narcissistic double always at its beck and call.

What underlies both these cases—that of secondary narcissism and that of secondary masochism—is the phantasy of a skin surface common to the mother and the child, dominated in the one case by a direct exchange of excitations and in the other by a direct exchange of meanings.

When the Skin-ego develops markedly in the direction of narcissism, the primary phantasy of the common skin changes into the phantasy of a reinforced, invulnerable skin (typically having the double-wall structure described on pp. 141–143). When the Skin-ego develops more in the direction of masochism, the common skin is felt in phantasy to be torn off and damaged. If we list the various skin phantasies found in mythology (see Anzieu, 1984) they fall into two types—the skin as shield (the aegis of Zeus) or as ornamental costume (celestial robes or the animal garment of "Peau d'âne" [Donkey Skin]) for the first type; the bruised, flayed, deadly skin for the second.

Sylvie Consoli has presented the case of a masochistic patient who gets pleasure from imagining himself humiliated by a woman under the following circumstances: she is standing dressed in the skin of a sheep or cow while he, on all fours at her feet, identifies as that sheep or cow.[2] This scenario represents a skin common to the man (in the form of the animal) and to the woman who is dominating him, wearing the skin of the same animal, and this complementarity of roles strengthens the illusion of a narcissistic continuity. Body to body, each of them is not so much an "extension" of the other, as Consoli argues, but rather one of the two sides of the common cutaneous interface I have just described. It is worth adding that in many perverse scenarios, as well as in ordinary erotic fantasies, fur often plays a fetishistic role based on its resemblance to the body hair that conceals the genital organs and thus the difference between the sexes.

---

[2] Paper delivered at a day conference on *Peau et Psychisme* [*Skin and the Psyche*], Hôpital Tarnier, Paris, 19th February 1983.

CHAPTER FOUR

The Greek myth of Marsyas

The socio-cultural framework

According to historians of religion, the myth of Marsyas—whose name, derived etymologically from the Greek verb *marnamai*, means "fighter"—echoes the battles fought by the Greeks to subdue Phrygia (a state in Asia Minor situated to the east of Troy) and its citadel Celaenae and to impose the worship of the Greek gods, here represented by Apollo, on the inhabitants in place of their local cults, especially those of Cybele and Marsyas. The victory of Apollo, with his lyre, over Marsyas, who plays a double-reed flute, is followed and sealed by his victory in Arcadia over Pan, the inventor of the single-reed flute, or syrinx.[1]

---

[1] It is said that Marsyas had a brother, Babys, who played the one-reed flute, but so badly that Apollo spared him; this recalls the theme of the foreign, crude, absurd mountain peasants whom the conquering Greeks, in their civilised way, allowed to keep their old beliefs as long as they worshipped the Greek gods at the same time. With his flute and pine-branch, Pan is a mythological double for Marsyas. He is a god of Arcadia, a mountainous region at the centre of the Peloponnese, and he represents its nimble, hairy shepherds, whose ways are as rough and brutish as those of their flocks, with animal-like appearance and a simple taste for afternoon naps in the shade, primitive music and polymorphous sexuality (the Greek word "pan" means "all" and the god Pan has the

Apollo's victories over Marsyas and Pan commemorate the Hellenic conquests of Phrygia and Arcadia, and the consequent supersession in those regions of wind instruments by stringed ones, except among the peasantry. Marsyas' punishment may refer to the ritual flaying of a sacred king—as Athene stripped Pallas of his magical aegis—or the removal of the entire bark from an alder-shoot to make a shepherd's pipe, the alder being personified as a god or demi-god. (Graves, 1960, p. 81)

The musical contest between Marsyas and Apollo condenses a whole series of oppositions: between the barbarians and the Greeks; between the mountain shepherds with their semi-bestial ways and the cultivated city-dwellers; between wind-instruments (the single- or double-reed flute) and string-instruments (the lyre has seven strings); between a cruel monarchic political succession, in which the king or high priest was periodically executed and flayed, and democratic succession; between Dionysiac and Apollonian cults; between the arrogance of youth and the outdated beliefs of old age, which must both give way to the power and laws of maturity. Marsyas is in fact represented sometimes as a silenus, an old satyr, and sometimes as the young companion of Cybele, the great mother-goddess of Phrygia, inconsolable after the death of her servant, who was also apparently her son and lover, Attis.[2] Marsyas calms her grief by playing the flute. The healing-seductive power that Marsyas has over the mother of the gods makes him ambitious and presumptuous, which provokes Apollo to challenge him to see which of the two makes the finer music with his instrument. Cybele gave her name to Mount Sipylus, from which the river Marsyas springs and on whose summit the Phrygian citadel of Celaenae was built.

As I argued some time ago (Anzieu, 1970), a myth follows a double process of encoding. It encodes external reality—botanical,

---

reputation of enjoying homosexual, heterosexual, and solitary pleasures equally; a late legend has it that before Ulysses returned Penelope slept with all her suitors one after the other and Pan was the offspring of that multiple adultery).
[2] It was James Frazer, in *The Golden Bough* (1929, p. 354), who had the idea of connecting Marsyas with Attis. The common theme is the tragic fate of a son whose mother loves him too much and wants to keep his love for herself.

cosmological, socio-political, toponymic, religious, etc.—and it encodes internal, psychical reality by placing it in a direct relation to the elements of external reality. It is my view that the myth of Marsyas encodes the psychical reality that I have named the Skin-ego.

Indeed, what interests me most in the myth of Marsyas and makes it unique among the Greek myths is the fact, first, that the sound wrapping (the element of music) changes into the tactile wrapping (in the form of the skin) and second, that an evil fate (inscribed on and through the flayed skin) is turned into a blessing (the skin is conserved whole and this ensures the resurrection of the God, the sustaining of life and the restoration of fertility throughout the country). In my analysis of this Greek myth, I shall focus only on the basic elements, the mythemes that refer directly to the skin (and which we can recognise from the common usage of everyday speech: when you triumph over your enemy you "have his hide'; you feel "good in your skin" when it is whole; and women are more likely to be impregnated by a man whom they have "got under their skin"). A comparison with other Greek myths in which the skin features only tangentially will allow me to verify and complete the list of fundamental skin mythemes and to glimpse how we may be able to classify them structurally according to whether any of these mythemes is found in them or not, what order they appear in and how they are combined.

The first part of the myth

I shall begin by recounting briefly the story of Marsyas before the skin comes into play: it is a familiar enough tale of open rivalry and covert incestuous desire; this seems to me to make clear how, in onto-psychogenesis, the original functions of the Skin-ego are obscured, hidden and distorted by the primary and later secondary processes linked to the pregenital and genital developments and the oedipalisation of psychical functioning.

> One day, Athene made a double-flute from stag's bones, and played on it at a banquet of the gods. She could not understand, at first, why Hera and Aphrodite were laughing silently behind their hands, although her music seemed to delight the other deities; she therefore went away by herself into a Phrygian wood, took up the

flute again beside a stream, and watched her image in the water, as she played. Realizing at once how ludicrous that bluish face and those swollen cheeks made her look,[3] she threw down the flute, and laid a curse on anyone who picked it up.

Marsyas was the innocent victim of this curse. He stumbled upon the flute, which he had no sooner put to his lips than it played of itself, inspired by the memory of Athene's music; and he went about Phrygia in Cybele's train, delighting the ignorant peasants. They cried out that Apollo himself could not have made better music, even on his lyre, and Marsyas was foolish enough not to contradict them. This, of course, provoked the anger of Apollo, who invited him to a contest, the winner of which should inflict whatever punishment he pleased on the loser. Marsyas consented, and Apollo impanelled the Muses as a jury.[4] The contest proved an equal one, the Muses being charmed by both instruments, until Apollo cried out to Marsyas: "I challenge you to do with your instrument as much as I can do with mine. Turn it upside down, and both play and sing at the same time."

This, with a flute, was manifestly impossible, and Marsyas failed to meet the challenge. But Apollo reversed his lyre, and sang such delightful hymns in honour of the Olympian gods that the Muses could not do less than give the verdict in his favour.

(Graves, 1960, p. 77)

Here begins the second part of the myth, which is specifically concerned with the skin. I am following the account given by Frazer (1929, pp. 396–400), picking up the underlying mythemes as I go.

---

[3] This episode illustrates what we might call—by contrast to penis envy—a woman's horror of the penis: Athene, the virgin warrior, is horrified by the sight of her face transformed into a pair of buttocks, with a penis hanging or rather standing up between them.
[4] In certain versions, the panel of judges is chaired by the god of Mount Tmolos, where the contest was held, and also included Midas, the king of Phrygia, who introduced the cult of Dionysus to the country. It is said that when Tmolos declared Apollo the winner, Midas disputed his decision. To punish him, Apollo made him grow the famous ass's ears (an appropriate punishment for someone with no ear for music!); he tried in vain to hide them under a Phrygian cap, but they ended up causing him mortal shame (see Graves, 1960, p. 283). In other versions, Midas judges the second contest, the one between Apollo and Pan.

The second part: the eight mythemes

First mytheme: Marsyas is hanged by Apollo from a pine tree. He is suspended not in the usual way, by the neck, causing strangulation, but by his arms from a branch, which allows the victim to be more easily cut up or bled. Frazer has collected an impressive list of examples of hanged gods—as well as priests or women who hang themselves by choice or ritual. These sacrifices, originally all human, were gradually replaced by animal sacrifices and later by sacrifices in effigy.

This mytheme seems to me to relate to the verticality of human posture, as opposed to the horizontality of animals. After leaving behind childhood and animality, a human being stands upright supported on the ground, just as a baby holds on to its mother's hand when it first stands up. This is the positive aspect of verticality, buttressed by the pine, that most vertical of trees. The punishment consists in inflicting a negative verticality on the victim: he remains vertical but hanging in the air (sometimes upside down), which is both painful and humiliating, exposing him to all manner of torments and reproducing the original distress of an infant that is poorly held or not held at all by its mother.

Second mytheme: the skin of the victim, who is suspended naked, is cut or pierced with a lance, to drain it of blood—either to fertilise the earth or to distract vampires from attacking family members, etc. This mytheme is absent from the myth of Marsyas but elsewhere is always found together with the above-mentioned one: the new-born Oedipus has his ankles pierced and is carried suspended from a pole; Oedipus the King puts out his eyes at the sight of the strangled Jocasta hanging from a rope; Christ is nailed to a cross; St. Sebastian is bound to a tree and pierced with arrows; some saint, hanging in the same position, has her breasts cut off; upside down, tied with their backs against a huge rock, prisoners of the Aztecs have their hearts torn out, etc.

This mytheme seems to me to relate to the skin's capacity to contain the body and the blood: the torture consists of destroying the continuity of the containing surface by riddling it with artificial orifices. In the case of Marsyas, the containing capacity is respected by the Greek god.

Third mytheme: while still alive, Marsyas is entirely flayed by Apollo and his empty skin is left hanging or nailed to the pine tree. Among the Aztecs, the skin of the prisoner sacrificed by the priests was worn for twenty days by his master. St. Bartholomew was flayed alive but his skin was not preserved. In *Le Jardin des supplices* [*The Torture Garden*]

(1899), Octave Mirbeau describes a man who has been flayed dragging his skin around behind him like a shadow, etc.

In my view, the skin torn away from the body, if it is kept whole, represents the protective wrapping, the shield against stimuli, which in phantasy one imagines taking from another person in order to have it for oneself or to duplicate and strengthen one's own—but this carries the risk of retaliation.

As a shield against stimuli, this skin is precious. One example is the Golden Fleece, guarded by a terrifying dragon, which Jason is commanded to capture—it is the golden hide of a sacred winged ram that Zeus once gave to two children whose stepmother was threatening to kill them. His lover, the sorceress Medea, protects him by giving him a balm to coat his whole body, which keeps him safe from burns and other injuries for twenty-four hours. Another is the skin of Achilles, whom his mother, a goddess, makes invulnerable by hanging him up by his heel (first mytheme) and dipping him in the infernal waters of the Styx (see Anzieu, 1984).

This is the mytheme that reverses the fate of Marsyas: keeping the skin whole turns his evil destiny into a blessing.

Fourth mytheme: the intact skin of Marsyas was preserved, well into the historical era, at the foot of the citadel of Celaenae: it hung in the cave where the river Marsyas, a tributary of the Meander, gushed forth. For the Phrygians it was a sign of the resurrection of their hanged and flayed god. This surely represents the intuition that a personal soul—a psychical Self—will exist as long as there is a bodily wrapping to guarantee its individuality.

The first, third, fourth, fifth, and sixth mythemes are combined in the story of Zeus's aegis. Saved by his mother's cunning from being devoured by his father, Zeus is suckled by a nanny-goat, Amaltheia, who keeps him hidden by hanging his cradle from a branch and, when she dies, leaves him her skin to make into armour. His daughter Athene, protected by this aegis, conquers the giant Pallas and takes his skin. The aegis not only makes a perfect shield in battle but also allows Zeus's strength to flourish, leading him to his unique destiny as the master of Olympus.

A *fifth mytheme*: common in the rituals and legends of many cultures, appears at first reading to be absent from the myth of Marsyas. It is, in a sense, the negative counterpart of the fourth mytheme. The victim's head is cut off from his body (which may be burned, consumed or buried) and those who preserved it kept it as a precious relic, either to frighten enemies or to attract the favour of the dead man's spirit by tending with great care to a particular organ of his head—the mouth, the nose, the eyes or ears...

The fifth mytheme seems to me to be based on the following antinomy: either the head is cut off from the body and preserved on its own or the whole skin is preserved, face and skull included. What is destroyed or recognised here is not only the link between the periphery (the skin) and the centre (the brain) but also the link between tactile sensitivity, which is scattered all over the body's surface, and the four other external senses, which are localised in or on the face. A person's individuality, expressed in the fourth mytheme which lays stress on resurrection (for example the regular recovery of consciousness on waking up), requires all the different sensory qualities to be brought together against the background of the fundamental continuum provided by the representation of the complete skin.

If the severed head remains captive while the rest of the body is discarded or destroyed, the dead person's spirit loses its independent will; it is taken over by whoever owns the head. To be oneself one must first have one's own skin and second use it as a space in which one's sensations can be felt.

Not only did Zeus's aegis keep him safe from his enemies but once the Medusa's head was fastened to it it petrified them. With the help of a burnished bronze shield held above his head by Athene, Perseus had overcome the hideous Gorgon and cut off her head; he gave it in gratitude to Athene, who used it to reinforce the power of the aegis.

Sixth mytheme: beneath the emblem of the immortal, suspended skin of the flautist god Marsyas, there gushes the noisy, impetuous river Marsyas, with its abundant waters, full of the promise of life for the region; its murmuring sound, echoing around the cave walls, creates a music that delights the Phrygian people.

The metaphor is clear. On the one hand, this river represents the life drives, with their power and charms. On the other, it seems that this instinctual energy is available only to those who have preserved the integrity of their Skin-ego, supported anaclitically on both the wrapping of sound and the cutaneous surface.

Seventh mytheme: the river Marsyas is also a source of fertility for the region: it ensures that plants will germinate, animals will breed and women will give birth. Here too the metaphor is explicit: to reach sexual maturity one needs to have a secure narcissistic base, a sense of feeling good in one's skin.

The myth of Marsyas tells us nothing of what qualities of the skin stimulate sexual desire. Other myths, folktales or fictional narratives may be taken as a guide: the boy desiring his mother's skin experiences it as the *Venus in Furs* (Sacher-Masoch); the skin of the father who has incestuous designs on his daughter is experienced by the girl as "Donkey Skin" (Perrault).

Excessive sexual desire is as threatening to fertility as the lack of it. Oedipus, who fathered no fewer than four children on his own mother, plunged Thebes into sterility.

Eighth mytheme: the skin of Marsyas, left hanging in the cave of Celaenae, was still sensitive to the music of the river and the songs of the faithful; it trembled at the sound of Phrygian melodies, but remained deaf and immobile when tunes were played in honour of Apollo. This mytheme illustrates the fact that the earliest communication between a baby and its carers and family is a mirror of both sound and touch. To communicate is, above all, to resonate or vibrate in harmony with the other.

Here the myth of Marsyas ends; but other myths lead me to propose an ultimate, negative mytheme.

Last, negative mytheme: the skin destroys itself or is destroyed by another skin. The first case is illustrated by the allegory of Balzac's *La Peau de chagrin* [*The wild ass's skin*]: the skin shrinks symbolically in proportion to the energy it allows the individual to expend on living and, paradoxically, the better it works the closer it gets and brings us to death, through a process of wearing out. The second case is that of the murderous skin, illustrated by two famous Greek myths: the dress and jewels which Medea deliberately poisons and sends to her rival set the latter on fire the moment she places them on her skin; along with her they burn her father, who has run to her aid, and the whole royal palace. The tunic which Deianeira unintentionally poisons by soaking it in the blood and sperm of the treacherous centaur Nessus (who has abused her physically and morally) adheres to the skin of her unfaithful husband Hercules, and as the poison heats up it penetrates his epidermis and gnaws at it. As he tries to rip away this corrosive second skin, Hercules tears off shreds of his own flesh; crazed with pain, he can think of no other way to get rid of the self-destructive wrapping than to immolate himself on a pyre which, out of pity, his friend Philoctetes lights for him.

What is the psychological correlative of this mytheme? To these phantasies of attacks against the contents of the body or mind (which may be accompanied by real acting out), we must add the notion of attacks on the container, or of turning attacks on the content into attacks on the container, or even of the container attacking itself; without these notions the problematic of masochism makes little sense. The first eight mythemes, in order, make up the specific myth of Marsyas: each of them is in its own way the site of a parallel struggle, an inner conflict illustrated figuratively by the contest between Apollo and Marsyas.

It seems to me that this destructive reversal has an analogous creative reversal; as Jean Guillaumin (1980) has shown, the latter consists of turning the skin inside out like a glove, making the content into a container, the space inside into a model for structuring the outside and what is felt inwardly into a reality that can be known.

Let us return to Sacher-Masoch's novel. The final episode of *Venus in Furs* offers a variant on the first mytheme of Marsyas. From a hiding-place, Severin has watched his mistress Wanda in a sexual encounter with her lover, the Greek: thus it is Severin's voyeuristic desire, like the exhibitionistic desire of Marsyas, that must be punished. Wanda hands him over, bound fast to a column, to be flogged by the Greek with a riding-crop, just as by her curse Athene delivered Marsyas to Apollo to be flayed. In fact, the Greek texts imply that she is present during his torture. The analogy between the two stories is reinforced by two further details. Sacher-Masoch evokes the beauty of the Greek by comparing him to the statue of a classical ephebe, which is an indirect way of saying that he is as handsome as Apollo. And the last sentences of the novel explain why Severin has abandoned his masochistic dream: to be whipped by a woman, even if she is disguised as a man, is fine; but "to be flayed by Apollo"—this is the penultimate line of the text—by a sturdy Greek with the ambiguous appearance of a female transvestite, is too much. Sensual pleasure has reached the point where it turns into intolerable horror.

The eight mythemes of the Greek myth of Marsyas bring indirect confirmation to the theory of the eight functions of the Skin-ego, which I shall develop in Chapter Seven.

as 1905, Freud demonstrated how the skin is an erogenous

In scopophilia and exhibitionism the eye corresponds to an erotogenic zone; while in the case of the elements of the sexual instinct
which involve pain and cruelty the same role is assumed by the
skin—the skin, which in particular parts of the body has become
differentiated into sense organs or modified into mucous membrane, and is thus the erotogenic zone *par excellence*. (1905d, p. 169)

CHAPTER FIVE

The psychogenesis of the Skin-ego

The double feedback in the mother–child dyadic system

Since the 1970s, there has been extensive scientific interest in new-born babies. In particular, the research of paediatrician Thomas Berry Brazelton (1981) in England and later in the USA, which was developed independently of my own work on the Skin-ego but ran parallel to it, adds interesting confirmation and complementary detail. In 1973, in order to study as systematically as possible the earliest stages of the dyad of the nursling with its mothering environment (I prefer "mothering" to "maternal", so as not to limit the caring environment to the biological mother), Brazelton developed the Neonatal Behavioral Assessment Scale, which has been widely applied in the USA. He drew the following conclusions:

1. At birth and in its first few days, the child manifests a rudimentary Ego, as a result of sense experiences it has had towards the end of its intra-uterine life and also no doubt as a result of the genetic code that has predetermined its development in this direction. If it is to survive, the new-born baby not only needs to receive repeated and adaptive care from its mothering environment, but also (i) to give

out signals to the mothering environment which will trigger and refine that care and (ii) to explore the physical environment in search of the necessary stimuli to exercise its potentialities and activate its sensorimotor development. This leads to the two wrappings of excitation and inscription.

2. In its dyadic situation, the baby is not a passive but an active partner (see Monique Piñol-Douriez, 1984): it is constantly interacting with the environment in general and the people who mother it in particular, when they are present—and the baby quickly develops techniques for bringing those people to it whenever it feels the need for them.

3. The baby calls upon the adults around it (primarily its mother) just as much as those adults call upon it. This double appeal—which corresponds to epigenetic determinisms that are themselves prefigured or prepared by the genetic code—follows a process that Brazelton compares to the physical phenomenon of feedback, i.e., in cybernetics, the self-regulation loop characteristic of assisted systems. The mutual appeal allows the baby to act upon its human environment (and through the latter on its physical environment), to learn the fundamental difference between what is animate and what is inanimate, to imitate the imitations of some of its gestures which the adults reflect back to it, and thus to prepare itself to acquire speech. This assumes—I shall come back to this later—that we can consider the mother–infant dyad as a single system made up of interdependent elements communicating information to each other, going in both directions, from mother to baby and from baby to mother.

4. If the mothering environment does not enter into this play of reciprocal appeals, building up the double feedback, or if a deficiency in the baby's nervous system makes it unable to take sensorimotor initiatives towards its carers and/or to respond to their signals, the baby will display reactions of withdrawal and/or anger. Such reactions will be temporary if the coldness, indifference or absence of the mothering environment is itself temporary—as Brazelton established by asking normally communicative mothers to keep their faces blank and hold back for several minutes from showing any expression towards their babies). The reactions tend to become lasting, intense, and pathological if the non-response of the mothering environment persists.

5. Parents who are sensitive to the baby's feedback will let it guide their own behaviour, occasionally even changing their attitudes as this helps them feel secure in their parental role. A baby who is passive and indifferent (as the result of an intra-uterine trauma or a flaw in the genetic code) throws its carers into confusion and disarray: it can even happen, as Michel Soulé (1978) has observed, that it drives its mother mad, though she may have had no such problems with her other children.

6. As a result of these interactions early models of psychomotor behaviour begin to form in the baby; if they are successfully repeated and learned, they will become its preferred behaviours and the precursors of later cognitive models. They ensure the development of the infant's own style and temperament, and these in their turn form a schedule that allows carers to anticipate the baby's reactions—its cycles of feeding, sleep or particular activities—and determines the level of awareness they need to maintain (see Julian de Ajuriaguerra: the child as "the creator of the mother"). At this point they start to think of it as a person, i.e., as having an individual Ego. They surround it by what Brazelton calls a "wrapping of mothering",[1] which consists of a set of responses adapted to its unique personality. Brazelton also refers to a "wrapping of control" which is the counterpart of the latter: the baby creates this wrapping for its carers, forcing them to take account of its reactions. Brazelton also refers to the double feedback system as a "wrapping" that surrounds the mother and infant together—which corresponds to what I call the Skin-ego.

7. The experimental study of new-born babies has helped to specify the nature of some of those feedback loops that are made possible at successive stages in the maturing of the nervous system and which the baby will experience if its carers give it the opportunity:

   • the baby's prolonged gaze "deep into the eyes" of its mother, somewhere between the age of six weeks and four months

---

[1] *Translator's note:* Brazelton uses the term "envelope", generally in scare-quotes, in *The Earliest Relationship: Parents, Infants and the Drama of Early Attachment* (1990), for instance "mother providing an envelope for interactive behaviours, father a base from which play can emerge" (p. 106). The text referred to here by Anzieu is translated into French by Aviva Luke, and indeed has *"enveloppe protectrice d'adultes maternants"* [protective wrapping provided by the mothering adults] and *"enveloppe de contrôle"* [wrapping of control] (both p. 15), but the exact phrase "enveloppe de maternage" does not appear.

(up to three or four months, the baby attracts an adult's attention by gazing; after that it uses bodily contact, and later vocalisation);

- the early identification by the baby (aged just a few days or weeks) of the characteristic melody of the mother's voice, with its ability to calm distress or stimulate certain activities;
- the same effects occur if the baby is offered a cloth carrying the mother's smell;
- the reflex distinction made by the baby, six hours after birth, between tastes that are nice (sweet), neutral (tasteless water) and nasty (in ascending order: salty, sour and bitter). In the course of the next few months, these distinctions are modulated gradually by the encouragement, prohibitions or exhortations of the mothering environment: the baby learns to read from its mother's signs what she considers good or bad for it, though this does not always correspond exactly—sometimes not at all—to its own original reflex model (see Matty Chiva, 1984);
- the perception of verbal sounds as distinct from other sounds, and the ability to differentiate them according to the same categories as adults use, as early as two months.

8. The baby's success in setting up the various successive feedback loops with its mothering environment adds to its ability to make sensory discriminations, achieve motor performance and send out signifying communications, a power which impels it to try out other feedback loops and attempt new skills. It acquires a power of endogenous mastery that develops from a sense of confidence into a euphoric feeling of unlimited omnipotence: as each new step is mastered, the energy is not dissipated by being discharged into action but, on the contrary, is increased by success (what psychoanalysis calls the "recharging of the libido") and invested in anticipation of the next stage. This feeling of having an inner power is essential for the baby to achieve the reorganisations of its sensorimotor and affective models that become necessary as its maturity and experiences develop.

The baby's success in dealing with its physical and human environment earns it not only the approval of the latter but other gratifying signs which it tries to elicit again for the pleasure they give it: now there is an addition to the powerful desire to embark on ever new experiences— the desire to fulfil or even anticipate the expectations of the grown-ups.

Differences between cognitive and psychoanalytic
points of view

Experimental psychology and psychoanalysis agree on the fact that the new-born child has a bodily pre-Ego which is endowed with the impulse to integrate various sense data, has a tendency to seek out objects and set in motion strategies to deal with them, to establish object relations (attachment being a special case) with the people caring for it and to use experience to regulate the bodily and psychical functions that its genetic code and life in the womb have made available to it. One of these is the ability to distinguish noises from verbal sounds and to recognise, within the latter group, relevant phonological distinctions in the language spoken around it. Similarly it has the capacity to direct signals to other people—at first mimicry and crying and perhaps giving off smells, later gazing and posture, still later gestures and vocalisations. This bodily pre-Ego is a precursor of the feeling of having a personal identity and a sense of reality that typifies the psychical Ego proper. It accounts for two facts that can be verified objectively as well as subjectively—first, the fact that pretty soon after birth the human person is an individual with their own distinctive style and probably the sense of being a unique Self; and second, the fact that their success in the experiments listed above fills their pre-Ego with a dynamism that drives it to attempt new experiments, accompanied by a plausible feeling of jubilation.

Nevertheless there are significant differences between a cognitivist theory and a psychoanalytic one. The former stresses the symmetry between the mothering environment and the infant and sees this couple as tending to constitute a homeostatic system. It does not surprise me that the study of babies generates delusions in scientists through the distorting lens behind which they make their observations. The deluded belief in a passive baby whose psyche is a *tabula rasa* or a piece of pliable wax is long gone. It has been replaced by the delusion a of competent, dynamic baby who is more or less an equal partner in the interactive process and forms with its mother—assuming she too is a competent, dynamic partner—a perfectly well-adjusted and happy couple, more like a pair of twins than the complementary but asymmetrical dyad they really are: one an adult, who is presumably fully developed, and the other a child whose development is, if not premature, at least far from complete. This delusion of twinning is similarly revived in an adult who falls in love: Isidoro Berenstein and Janine Puget (1984) have shown the fundamental role it plays in the relationship between lovers. Yet symmetry cannot exist without a central plane (or axis): in this case, I would argue, the plane is provided by the phantasy— ignored by experimental scientists—of a common skin between the mother and the child. This phantasy is structured as an interface of a particular kind, one that separates two areas of space sharing a single system and between which it thus creates a symmetry (if the systems are different, or if there are more than two of them, the structure of the interface is modified, for example by the addition of pouches or fracture points).

Psychoanalysts (notably Piera Aulagnier, 1979) insist on the dis-symmetry between the patient and the analyst or the infant and its carers, on the primary dependency and original helplessness—the term is Freud's (1950a [1895])—to which the analysand regresses as an effect of the process of psychoanalysis. Winnicott has pointed out that, alongside states of integration of the psychical and bodily Egos, a baby also experiments with states of non-integration—these are not necessarily painful and may be accompanied by the euphoric sense of being a limitless psychical Self, or indeed the baby may not wish to communicate these states because it feels too good or too bad. Little by little the infant acquires a sketchy understanding of human language, but this is limited to the second articulation and it is unable to use it to give out messages; primary articulation is beyond it; this mystery of sound, combined with its semiotic impotence, causes the child both pain and rage, like a psychical violence enacted upon it—Piera Castoriadis-Aulagnier (1975) has called that experience the "violence of interpretation"—not to mention the brutality of the physical and chemical attacks the child's body is exposed to or the "fundamental violence" (Jean Bergeret, 1984) of hatred, rejection, indifference, poor care and physical blows that may come from the people around it. This violent and increasingly intolerable dependence on a mother who is the "spokeswoman" (Castoriadis-Aulagnier, 1975) necessary to provide for its needs gives rise, in the baby's nascent psychical Ego, to the imago of the persecutory mother, accompanied by terrifying phantasies, and forces it to mobilise unconscious defence mechanisms which will curb, arrest or destroy the positive development I have outlined above. This dismantling process halts the dynamic which integrates sensations; projective identification prevents the feedback from forming itself into a loop; the multiple splitting scatters agglomerated parts of the Self and parts of objects into a nebulous space that is neither inside nor outside; and a belt of muscular rigidity, motor agitation or physical suffering creates a psychotic second skin, an autistic carapace or a masochistic wrapping which supplement the failing Skin-ego like a mask.

A second difference in approach is based on the fact that Brazelton studies behaviour, working with the stimulus-response model, whereas the psychoanalyst studies phantasies, which are themselves correlated with unconscious conflicts and particular arrangements of psychical space. Brazelton goes so far as to argue, rightly, that the many individual moments of feedback which occur between the baby and its carers constitute a dynamic or even economic system and create a topographical psychical reality that he calls "an envelope", without defining this term in any detail. It is an abstract notion that expresses the viewpoint of a fine-tuned but external observer. The baby, on the other hand, has a concrete representation of this envelope or wrapping, derived from what it experiences all the time with its senses, and that is the skin, a sense-experience intermixed with phantasies. These cutaneous phantasies clothe its nascent Ego in a figurative representation which is imaginary, of course, but which mobilises, to borrow an expression from Paul Valéry,[2] the deepest thing in us: our surface. They mark out the various levels of structuration of the Ego and show where it has gone wrong. The development of the other senses is referred back to the skin, the "originary" phantasised surface—in the sense of "originary" used by Piera Castoriadis-Aulagnier (1975), as the precursor and foundation of primary psychical functioning.

It is here that, as a psychoanalyst, I come up against a third difference in the interpretation of experimental findings. According to the cognitive psychologists, touch is not one of the first senses to develop. The senses of taste, smell, and hearing, whose existence from birth is proven, allow the baby to identify its mother (and consequently to identify *with* her) and also permit a rough differentiation between

---

[2]See *L'Idée fixe*: "*Ce qu'il y a de plus profound dans l'homme, c'est la peau*". "Et puis moelle, cerveau, tout ce qu'il faut pour sentir, pâtir, penser... *être profond* [...], ce sont des inventions de la *peau!*... Nous avons beau creuser, docteur, nous sommes... ectoderme" [*The most profound thing in man is his skin*. Our marrow, our brain, everything we need to feel, suffer or think... *to be profound* [...], all these are inventions of the *skin!*... However deep we dig, doctor, we are... ectoderm] (Paul Valéry, 1932, *Œuvres complètes*, Pléiade, volume 2, pp. 215–216, italics Valéry's).

things that are good and bad for it. Later, when the infant enters the world of intentional communication, echopraxes, echolalias, and echorhythmias are said to play a more decisive role than what I have proposed to call "echotactilisms"—meaningful exchanges of tactile contacts.

I have several objections to this minimisation of the role of the skin in the development of the psyche. In the embryo, if not in the neonate, the tactile sense is the first to appear (see pp. 13–14) and this is no doubt due to the development of the ectoderm, which is the common neurological source of the skin and the brain. As it is born, the event of birth gives the child the experience of being massaged over its whole body and rubbed all over its skin, as the mother's body contracts and it is expelled out of the enclosure of the vagina which has dilated to its exact dimensions. It is well known that these natural tactile contacts stimulate and trigger the respiratory and digestive functions; if that is not sufficient they are replaced by artificial contacts such as shaking, bathing, warm packs or manual massage. In turn, the development of activities and later communication though the senses of hearing, sight, smell, and taste is fostered by the way the baby's carers carry it, reassuring it by holding its body tightly against their own, support- ing its head or spinal column. This is clear from everyday language, in which we speak of "contact" in relation to all the senses—when we contact someone by telephone we hear them at a distance with- out seeing them; we may have good contact with someone whom we can see but not touch, etc.—thus the skin is the basic referent to which we spontaneously relate the various other sense data. Even supposing it does not chronologically predate all the other senses, touch has a structural primacy over them for at least three reasons. First, it is the only sense that is found all over the body. Second, it contains in itself several other distinct senses—warmth, pain, contact, pressure—whose physical closeness brings about psychical contiguity. Finally, as Freud (1923b) suggests, touch is the only one of the five senses that has a reflexive structure: a child touching parts of its body with its finger is experiencing two sensations at once—it is a piece of skin touching something and at the same time it is a piece of skin being touched. All other sensory reflexivities (hearing oneself make a sound, smell- ing one's own odour, seeing oneself in the mirror) are modelled on the reflexivity of touch and so, later on, is the reflexivity of thought.

Special features of the Skin-ego as an interface

At this point I can set out in detail my concept of the Skin-ego. The mothering environment is so called because it "surrounds" the baby with an external wrapping made up of messages and because it adapts itself with a certain flexibility—leaving some space between—to the internal wrapping of the surface of the baby's body, which is both the site and the vehicle of the transmission of messages: to be an Ego is to feel oneself capable of sending out signals that other people will hear.

This tailor-made wrapping completes the baby's individualisation through the recognition it receives in the confirmation of its individuality: it has its own style and character, different from everyone else yet fundamentally the same. To be an Ego is to feel that one is unique.

The gap between the inner and outer wrappings allows the Ego, once it is a bit more developed, to choose not to make itself understood, not to communicate (Winnicott). To have an Ego is to be able to turn in on oneself. If the external wrapping adheres too tightly to the child's skin (cf. the theme of the poisoned tunic in Greek mythology), the development of its Ego is stifled and it is invaded by one of the other Egos around it; this is one of the ways, highlighted by Harold Searles (1959), of driving another person crazy.

If the outer wrapping is too loose, the Ego lacks consistency. The inner layer tends to form a smooth, continuous, closed wrapping while the outer one has the structure of a mesh network (cf. Freud's "sieve" of contact-barriers, to which I shall return on p. 80ff). One pathology of the wrapping consists in an inversion of these structures, in which the outer layer, proposed/imposed by other people, becomes rigid, resistant and enclosing (the second muscular skin) and the inner layer turns out to be porous and full of holes (the sieve Skin-ego).

The double feedback observed by Brazelton results, in my opinion, in an interface, represented as a skin common to the mother and the child, with the mother on one side and the child on the other. This common skin keeps them attached to each other but has a certain symmetry that prefigures their later separation. "Plugged in" to each other through the common skin, the two partners communicate directly, with reciprocal empathy and an adhesive identification: it is a single screen that resonates with the sensations, affects, mental images, and vital rhythms of both.

Before the phantasy of the common skin is formed, the new-born baby's psyche is dominated by an intra-uterine phantasy, denying that the birth ever happened and expressing the typical desire of primary narcissism, to be back inside the mother's body—this is a phantasy of mutual inclusion and the fusion of primary narcissism, and the child more or less draws its mother along with it, for the birth has emptied her too of the foetus she was carrying. It is revived later in life in the experience of being in love, in which each of the lovers encloses the other in their arms while at the same time being enclosed by them. Autistic wrappings (see p. 270) express a fixation on the intra-uterine phantasy and an inability to progress to the phantasy of the common skin. More precisely, because of this failure—whether it is due to something wrong in the autistic child's genetic programming or inadequate feedback from its carers or an inability to create phantasies—it escapes, in a premature and pathological reaction of negative self-organisation, from the whole pattern of open-system functioning, takes refuge inside an autistic wrapping and withdraws into a closed system, like an egg that will not hatch.

The interface changes psychical functioning into an ever more open system, which leads the mother and child to function ever more separately. At the same time, the interface keeps the two partners in a state of reciprocal, symbiotic dependency. At the next stage, the common skin must be dispensed with, in the recognition that each of the two has their own skin and their own Ego—this cannot be achieved without resistance and pain. This is when phantasies of the flayed or stolen skin, the damaged or murderous skin, come into action (see Anzieu, 1984).

If the child manages to overcome the anxieties connected to these phantasies, it will achieve its own Skin-ego, through a dual process of interiorising

- the interface, which then becomes a psychical wrapping containing psychical contents (leading, according to Bion, to the formation of a thought-thinking apparatus); and
- the mothering environment, which becomes the inner world of thoughts, images and affects.

A precondition of this interiorisation is the establishment of what I have called the double taboo on touching (see Chapter Ten). The key phantasy, typical of secondary narcissism, is that of an invulnerable, immortal, heroic skin.

Fixation on any of these phantasies, especially on that of the flayed skin, along with the defence mechanisms that are mobilised to repress them, project them, convert them into their opposite or hyper-cathect them erotically, plays a particularly clear role in the two fields of skin conditions and masochism.

Summarising post-Kleinian research, Didier Houzel (1985a) describes increasingly complex stages of the organisation of psychical space, and these converge with the outline I have just given of the development of the Skin-ego. In the first stage—which Houzel, somewhat question-ably, calls "amorphous" and which is actually characterised by suckling of the breast/milk and intestinal fermentation—the infant experiences its psychical substance as liquid (hence the fear of being drained) or gaseous (hence the fear of explosion); frustration creates fissures in the protective shield, which is still developing, and these open up the risk of draining or explosion; the lack of internal consistency in the Self must be related, in my view, to the failure to achieve the first function of the Skin-ego, being supported by leaning against a "holding" object.

At the second stage, the appearance of the earliest thoughts (thoughts of absence or lack) makes it possible to tolerate dehiscences that open up in the wrapping as a result of frustrations. "Thought creates a kind of internal framework". Yet—I would add—these thoughts cannot be thought without the assured continuity of contact with the supporting object, which has now also become a containing object (cf. my notion of the skin-breast), and this continuity finds its expression in the phantasy of the common skin. Object-relations are based on adhesive identifica-tion (Meltzer, 1975). The Self, not yet properly distinguished from the Ego, is experienced as a sensitive surface which allows the constitution of an internal space distinct from external space. Psychical space is two-dimensional. "The significance of objects is experienced as inseparable from the sensual qualities that can be apprehended of their surfaces" (Meltzer, 1975, p. 225).

At the third stage, with access to three-dimensionality and projective identification, the internal space of objects appears. It is similar to but distinct from the internal space of the Self: in both these spaces thoughts can be projected or introjected; the inner world begins to be organ-ised, through phantasies of exploring the inside of the mother's body; the thought-thinking apparatus is set up; and "psychical birth takes place" (Margaret Mahler, cited in Frances Tustin, 1972).[3] Yet the state of symbiosis persists: time is frozen, repetitive or fluctuating, cyclical.

The next stage, which follows introjective identification with the good parents, joined together in the primal scene and phantasised as fertile and creative, brings about the acquisition of psychical time. Now there is a subject who has an inner history and can move from a narcissistic relation to an object-relation. The six other positive functions that I attribute to the Skin-ego (after the holding and containing functions) can now develop; and the negative function, the self-destruction of the container, becomes less threatening.

Two clinical examples

Case study: Juanito

A Latin-American colleague reported this case to me after she had heard me lecture on the Skin-ego. Juanito, who suffered from a congenital deformity, had had to undergo an operation soon after he was born. His mother had interrupted her domestic and professional activities to go with him but for several weeks she was only able to see him through a glass pane and could neither touch him nor speak to him. The operation was a success. By dint of draconian conditions, the convalescence went well. Back in his own country, the little boy acquired language normally, even somewhat early. But, as one might expect, he suffered major psychical after-effects, and so he was sent to a psychotherapist at the age of five or six.

The turning-point in Juanito's treatment was a session in which he tore off a huge strip of paper from the wall; the washable paper was pasted up for children to paint freely on and that piece was not yet marked. He cut the paper into small pieces, got undressed and asked his therapist to stick the pieces all over his body, apart from his eyes; he was insistent that she should both use up all the pieces and cover his entire body, without leaving any gaps (except to see through). In the next few sessions, he repeated this game of having

---

[3] *Translator's note:* Tustin's citation of Mahler is rather differently worded: "As she puts it, 'the child hatches from the symbiotic membrane'" (Tustin, 1972, p. 28).

his skin wrapped up completely by his therapist, and then he did the same thing himself to a celluloid doll.

In this way Juanito repaired the flaws in his Skin-ego caused by the lack of tactile and auditory contacts and bodily handling by his mother and other carers which had been unavoidable during his hospital stay. Keeping a visual link with his mother had preserved his emerging Ego; this explains why he had to keep his eyes wide open while his therapist was sticking the paper pieces on him. This intelligent little boy, who had a good mastery of language, had been able to put into words for her the two needs of his bodily Ego—the need to feel his skin as a continuous surface and the need to register all the stimuli he received from outside and integrate them into a *sensorium commune* (a common sense).

Case study: Éléonore

Colette Destombes, who is familiar with my interest in the Skin-ego, passed on to me the following sequence taken from the psychoanalytic psychotherapy of a little girl aged around nine years old, who was clearly failing at school. The child was apparently of normal intelligence and understood what the teacher was telling her, yet she was incapable of retaining it from one day to the next. She learned her lessons and then immediately forgot them. The same symptom was evident in the treatment, and this made it more and more difficult: the little girl would never remember what she had said or drawn in the previous session. She seemed genuinely upset by this: "You see—no one can do anything with me". Her therapist was on the point of giving up, believing there might be some underlying mental disability.

During one session, in which the symptom was more blatant than ever, she tried her last card, and said to the girl: "You know what, you've got a head like a sieve". The child's manner and tone changed completely: "How did you guess?" For the first time, instead of everyone telling her off, directly or indirectly, Éléonore had been given the right description of how she saw her Ego and her psychical functioning. She explained that this was exactly how she felt, that she was afraid other people would notice and did everything she could to hide the fact, exhausting her mental energies in the attempt. After this recognition and confession, she remembered her sessions. At the next meeting, she spontaneously suggested to her therapist that she should do some drawing. She drew a bag. Inside the bag there was a closed pen-knife, which she opened up in the drawings she made in the next few sessions.

Thus Éléonore had at last found someone who was able to understand her and to whom she could reveal the drive that was causing her problems. The bag was the wrapping of her Skin-ego, which was now continuous and could guarantee the continuity of her Self. The knife was her unconscious aggression, denied, closed up, turned back on herself, and which made cuts all over her psychical wrapping. Her hateful, destructive envy could flow out through these multiple holes without too much danger—split, fragmented, and projected into numberless pieces. But at the same time, through the same holes, her psychical energy was draining away, her memory getting lost, the continuity of her Self crumbling, and her mind could not contain anything.

From this point on, the psychotherapy went normally, though not of course without its ups and downs. The little girl had released her aggression and it became more and more open and violent as she attacked and threatened her therapist, but in a way that was now interpretable, a clear progression from the earlier phase of negative therapeutic response in which she had silently destroyed both the therapy and her own thought-thinking apparatus. The case study of Éléonore illustrates one common configuration of the Skin-ego that results from unconscious attacks of hatred against the containing psychical wrapping—the sieve Skin-ego.

PART II

STRUCTURE, FUNCTIONS, OVERCOMING

CHAPTER SIX

Two precursors of the theory of the Skin-ego: Freud and Federn

Freud and the topographical structure of the ego

Rereading Freud, I am struck, like most of his successors, by how many of the innovations they have suggested can already be found in germ in his work, either as ideas still in the form of images or as concepts prematurely sketched out and then abandoned. I shall try to show how an early description given in 1895 of what he would call in 1896 the "psychical apparatus"[1] anticipates the Skin-ego; it appears in the notion—which he did not return to and which remained unpublished in his lifetime—of "contact-barriers". I shall trace the development of his argument through to one of his very last descriptions of the psychical apparatus, in his "Note upon 'the mystic writing-pad'" (1925a), and I will attempt to illustrate his transition to a topographical model, increasingly free of anatomical and neurological references, which is premised implicitly and perhaps fundamentally on the idea that the Ego leans anaclitically on the experiences and functions of the skin.

---

[1]See the letter to Fliess of 6th December 1896, in Sigmund Freud, 1887–1902.

Doubtless because of his scientific training and cast of mind, Freud thought in terms of an "apparatus", a word that refers, in German as well as in French, to an assemblage of elements or organs that may be either natural or manufactured into a whole that fulfils a practical use or a biological function. In either case, the apparatus (as a material object) is organised in terms of an underlying system, an abstract entity that oversees the relations of the working parts, dictates how the whole thing will operate and enables it to achieve the desired effects. We may cite some examples (to give a few of Freud's own favourites): in the case of apparatuses invented by humans, an electrical or optical instrument; or, in the case of apparatuses within a living organism, the digestive or urogenital systems. It was one of Freud's innovations to study the psyche as an apparatus and to think of this apparatus as joining together different systems—i.e., as being a system of sub-systems.

The speech apparatus

In his first publication, *On Aphasia* (1891b), Freud coined the term and the concept of a "speech apparatus".[2] In a critique of the cerebral localisation model, which was dominant at the time, he explicitly bases his argument on the evolutionist views of Hughlings Jackson, arguing that the nervous system is a highly organised "apparatus" which, in its normal state, integrates "modes of reaction" corresponding "to earlier states of its functional development" and which, in certain pathological states, unleashes modes of reaction following a process of "functional retrogression" (Freud, 1891b, p. 87). The speech apparatus links together two systems—Freud refers to "complexes" rather than systems—that of word-presentations and that of what from 1915 he came to call thing-presentations, though in 1891 he used the terms "object associations" or "the object representation". The first of these "complexes" is closed (or enclosed), while the second is open.

I reproduce below Figure 8 of Freud's book with his commentary:

> The word-presentation is shown as a closed complex of presentations, whereas the object-presentation is shown as an open one. The word-presentation is not linked to the object-presentation by *all*

---

[2] See J. Nassif, *Freud, L'Inconscient* [*Freud: The Unconscious*] (Editions Galilée, 1977), Chapter Three for a full discussion of Freud's book on aphasia.

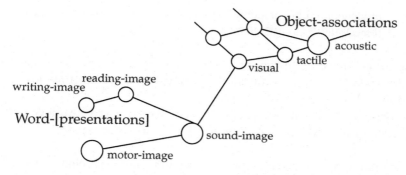

PSYCHOLOGICAL DIAGRAM OF A WORD-PRESENTATION

Figure 1.

its constitutive elements, but only by its sound-image. Among the object-associations, it is the visual ones which stand for the object, in the same kind of way as the sound-image stands for the word. The connections linking the sound-image of the word with object-associations other than the visual ones are not indicated.[3] (Diagram and commentary reproduced from Freud 1915e, Appendix C, p. 214)

The speech apparatus is clearly also based on a neurological model.

Our concept of the structure of the speech apparatus was based on the observation that the so-called speech centres border externally (peripherally) on parts of the cortex which are important for the speech function, while interiorly (centrally) they enclose a region not covered by localization which probably also belongs to the speech area. The apparatus of speech therefore presented itself to us as a continuous cortical area in the left hemisphere extending between the terminations of the acoustic and optic nerves and the origins of the motor tracts for the muscles serving articulation and arm movements. The necessarily ill-defined parts of the speech region which border on these receptive and motor cortical fields, have acquired the significance of speech centres from the point

---

[3]The object-associations (acoustic, visual, tactile, etc) constitute the *object-presentation*. In the last section of his article on "Das Unbewusste" [The unconscious] (1915e), Freud modifies his terminology: thereafter he speaks of *thing-presentation*, still in contradistinction to word-presentation, and reserves the term *object-presentation* for a combination of *thing-presentation* and *word-presentation*.

of view of morbid anatomy but not in respect of normal function.
(Freud, 1891b, pp. 102–103)

Lesions situated at this periphery cut off one of the elements associated
with speech from its connections with the rest, though this does not
apply to lesions situated at the centre.

This psychological model allows Freud to arrive at a clear idea of the
neurological model and to classify aphasia into three types:

• verbal aphasia, in which only associations between elements of the
  word-presentation are disturbed (as in the case of peripheral lesions
  which cause the complete destruction of one of the supposed speech
  centres);
• asymbolic aphasia, which cuts off the word-presentation from the
  object-presentation (here the peripheral lesion causes only a partial
  destruction);
• agnostic aphasia, which affects the recognition of objects, in which
  the agnosia indirectly disturbs the incentive to speak (this is a purely
  functional disorder of the speech apparatus following a lesion situated at the centre).

From Freud's theoretical research on the speech apparatus, I have
retained three aspects of his thought processes in particular: an effort to
detach the study of speech from a narrow one-to-one correlation with
anatomical and neurophysiological findings, looking instead for the
specifics of verbal thinking and psychical functioning in general; a need
to classify things into threes (the three types of aphasia are a prelude to
three instances of the speech apparatus); and an original and promis-
ing topographical intuition: that whatever functions as the "supposed
centre" is actually to be found at the periphery.

The psychical apparatus

In the *Studies on Hysteria* (1895d), co-authored with Josef Breuer, Freud is
still using the contemporary terms "organism" and "nervous system".[4]

---

[4]Thirty years later, in the last sentence of the 1925 re-edition of the book, he significantly
replaced "*Nervensystem*" [nervous system] by "*Seelenleben*" [psychical life].

In the same year, in his "Project for a scientific psychology", he distinguishes three systems within the "nervous system",[5] corresponding to three fictitious types of neuron—systems φ, ψ and ω, with the "contact-barriers" between systems φ and ψ playing a key role. The whole structure forms "the φ, ψ, ω apparatus" which itself is protected at the outer edge by a screen against quantities made up of "nerve-ending apparatuses".

In *The Interpretation of Dreams* (1900a), published in 1899 but dated 1900, Freud introduced the original expression "psychical apparatus".[6] He had already used the term in a letter to Fliess on 6th December 1896, explicitly connecting it to his earlier work on aphasia, specifically to the idea that memory belongs to a different psychical system from perception and that it registers events not once but several times over (the "rearrangement" of traces being actually a "retranscription" of them). This psychical apparatus is made up of three systems, which Freud generally calls *"Instanzen"* [agencies][7]—the conscious, the preconscious, and the unconscious—whose particular interactions derive from a topographical fact, namely that they are separated by two censorship agencies, and by a difference of purpose: they obey distinct principles of functioning.

The essential property of this apparatus—speech apparatus, φ, ψ, ω apparatus or psychical apparatus—is to establish associations, connections, and links. The term "association" appears frequently in Freud's monograph on aphasia, a difficult text in which it is not always easy to distinguish between his use of the term in the sense of nerve connections and the other use, so dear to British empiricist psychology, of the association of ideas.[8]

Freud's theories developed in tandem not only with his clinical interests but also with the therapeutic techniques he used with

---

[5] The published French translation uses the term *"système neuronique"* [neural system].

[6] Freud uses *"psychischer Apparat"* and *"seelischer Apparat"* [psychical or mental apparatus] interchangeably.

[7] In the *Standard Edition* Strachey explains his use of the term "agency" in the section "Notes on some Technical Terms [...]" which follows the General Preface (*S.E., 1*, pp. xxiii–xxiv).

[8] There is, as far as I know, no substantial study of the notion of association in Freud. Such a study could show how Freud moved from neurological and psychological concepts of the term to the fully psychoanalytic notion of free association. For a study of associative processes in groups, see René Kaës, *La Parole et le lien* [*Words and Links*] (1994).

neurotic patients. At the time of the speech apparatus he was practising electrotherapy and hypnotic counter-suggestion. The φ, ψ, ω apparatus belongs to the period in which he moved on from the cathartic method described in *Studies on Hysteria* to that of mental concentration, sometimes accompanied by pressing his hand on the forehead of the patient, who was awake. The conception of the psychical apparatus arises at more or less the same time as the word—and the notion—of "psychoanalysis", which establishes the free-association method and introduces the interpretation of dreams and similar unconscious formations as one of the mainsprings of treatment. I am struck by how well the double tree-structure in the psychological diagram of a word-presentation of 1891 (this volume, p. 77) could be used to configure the network of verbal free associations in the preconscious and how they are deployed in both directions—towards the conscious (where they become an open system) and towards the unconscious (where they form a closed system).

For thirty years, this double, asymmetrical tree-structure diagram remained one of the implicit models of Freud's conceptualisations and practice. The publication of *Beyond the Pleasure Principle* (1920g) and *The Ego and the Id* (1923b) marks his break with this structure: as a representation of the psychical apparatus, the double tree-structure gives way to the image and notion of a vesicle or wrapping. The focus shifts from conscious and unconscious contents to the psyche as container. The "Note upon the 'mystic writing-pad'" (1925a) completes the detailed description of this wrapping and implicitly confirms the anaclitic dependence of the Ego on the skin. In the interval, the manuscript Freud sent to Fliess in 1895 continued the epistemological reversal he had sketched out in his monograph on *Aphasia*—the psychical apparatus (which was soon to acquire this name) is more than a system for the transformation of forces, since the relative arrangement of its subsystems defines a psychical space whose particular configurations are still, in Freud's mind and imagination, very reliant on anatomical and neurological models but will eventually settle upon the topographical basis of the projection of the body surface, against whose ground sense experiences will emerge as figures of meaning.

The contact-barriers

In the "Project for a scientific psychology" (1950a), which Freud sent Fliess on 8 October 1895 and which remained unpublished until after his death, Freud develops a new idea, that of the "contact-barrier" (*Kontaktschranke*). He did not use this notion in any subsequent publications and Bion was the only psychoanalyst to take it up, with significant modifications.[9] It is a surprising concept—the paradox of a barrier that closes off movement from one side to another because it is in contact with both sides and thus partially permits movement from one side to another. Though he does not say this explicitly, Freud seems to be taking his inspiration from the model of electrical resistance. The concept belongs to the neurophysiological speculation he was so fond of as a young scientist and which he more or less abandoned for good when he discovered the Oedipus complex in October 1897. As early as 1884, Freud insists that the cell and the nerve fibres constitute a single anatomical and physiological unit, an argument that is a precursor of Waldeyer's neuron theory of 1891. Similarly, the notion of contact-barriers anticipates that of synapses, proposed in 1897 by Charles Sherrington. It was invented in response to theoretical necessities.

The scientific psychology that Freud dreamt of creating, at the time, on the model of the physicochemical sciences starts out from the two fundamental notions of quantity and the neuron. It is the science of physical quantities and the processes that affect them—for example, hysterical conversion or the hyper-intense ideas of obsessional neurotics. As for neurons, they obey the principle of inertia, which means that they tend to rid themselves of quantities. A hysterical attack is an example of the quasi-reflex abreaction of a considerable quantity of excitation of sexual origin that has not been discharged in any other way. "This discharge represents the primary function of the nervous system" (Freud, 1950a, p. 297). But the organism goes on to develop activities which

- are more complex than simple reflex responses to external stimuli;
- respond to the major internal vital needs (hunger, respiration, sexuality); and which
- can only be implemented by means of a prior store of quantity.

---

[9] In Chapter Eight of *Learning from Experience* (1962), Bion uses the term "contact-barrier" to refer to the border between the unconscious and the conscious. A dream is the prototype of this barrier, but it can also be found in a waking state. It is constantly in the process of formation and consists of a collection and multiplication of alpha elements, which may simply be massed together or bound by a certain cohesion or they may be ordered chronologically, logically or geometrically. The pathological counterpart to this is the beta screen.

This increasingly complex way in which vital needs are satisfied is called psychical life. It is based on the secondary function of the nervous system which is to "maintain a store of quantity". How does the system achieve this?[10]

While φ neurons are permeable (they transmit quantities received from the outside world, allowing the current to flow), ψ neurons are impermeable: they may be empty or full; the extremity which brings them into contact with each other is equipped with a contact-barrier that inhibits discharge, retains quantity or only lets it through "with difficulty or partially" (1950a, p. 299) and they are "the *contacts* [between one neurone and another], which in this way assume the value of *barriers*" (1950a, p. 298, parenthesis in original). The properties of the contact-barriers are numerous and crucial for psychical functioning.

1. They are retainers of quantity; or, to use Bion's term, "containers" of energy which is thus made available to the subject.
2. They are flexible and malleable organs: contact-barriers will allow a breach or "facilitation" [*Bahnung*], which means that the next time a smaller excitation can cross through them; they thus become gradually more permeable.
3. After a current has crossed through they re-establish resistance; even after a total facilitation has been established a certain resistance persists, which is the same in all contact-barriers; thus not all the available quantity circulates: a portion is retained. In this way they are the regulators of energy.
4. Consequently, they can share out energy, distributing the quantity they control along various paths of conduction: "a stronger stimulus follows different pathways from a weaker one [...] This is how the single φ path is relieved of its burden; the larger quantity in φ will be expressed by the fact that it cathects several neurones in ψ instead of a single one [...] Thus quantity in φ is expressed by *complication* in ψ" (1950a, pp. 314–315). As a special case of this general property, Freud goes on to point indirectly to Fechner's law, which states that sensation varies with the logarithm of the strength of a stimulus. A quantitative increase is expressed in qualitative changes which

---

[10] I am indebted to Jean-Michel Petot whose detailed study of the text has helped me to write the following section on contact-barriers.

offset increases in the original intensity and produce ever more complex sensory qualities.

5. There is a limit to the resistance of contact-barriers. They are removed temporarily, or even permanently, by the sudden appearance of heightened quantities. This occurs, for example, with pain, which, following a sensory stimulus of heightened quantity, sets in motion the φ system and is transmitted with "no obstacle" to the ψ system. This pain, "as though there had been a stroke of lightning" (1950a, p. 307), either leaves behind it permanent facilitations or does away entirely with the resistance of the contact-barriers (1950a, p. 307).

6. Yet "there is pain where the external quantity is small, and in such cases this is regularly linked with a breach in continuity: i.e., an external Q [quantity] which acts directly on the ends of the φ neurones and not through the nerve-ending apparatuses produces pain" (1950a, p. 307). Thus contact-barriers are second-line protections that presuppose, in order to work, the first-line intervention of "screens against quantity" ["Q-screens", *Quantitätsschirmen*] which, once broken, open the way for the contact-barriers to be quantitatively flooded. In fact:

> We discover […] that the φ neurones do not terminate at the periphery freely [i.e., without coverings] but in cellular structures which receive the exogenous stimulus in their stead. These "nerve-ending apparatuses", [using the term] in the most general sense, might well have it as their purpose not to allow exogenous Qs to make an undiminished effect upon φ but to damp them down. They would then have the significance of Q-screens, through which only *quotients* of exogenous Qs will pass.
>
> This accordingly tallies with the fact that the other kind of nerve-ending, the *free* ones, without end-organs, are by far the more common in the internal periphery of the body. No Q-screens seem to be needed there, probably because the $Q\acute{\eta}$s which have to be received there do not require to be reduced first to the intercellular level, but are at that level from the start. (1950a, p. 306, parentheses in original)

This is a dissymmetrical structure. Though Freud is not yet referring to a psychical wrapping, the latter is prefigured here, in the description of an interleaving of two layers, an outer one (the "screen against quantity", like the cellulose membrane of plants or the hide or fur of animals) and an inner one (the network of "contact-barriers", like the sense organs of the epidermis or the cortex). The inner layer is protected against exogenous quantities but not against endogenous ones.

7. The screen against quantities—which Freud calls the "protective shield against stimuli" [*Reizschutz*] from *Beyond the Pleasure Principle* (1920g) onwards—protects the nervous apparatus (which Freud soon begins to call psychical) against the intensity of excitations originating from the outside: it acts as a screen. On one side the contact-barriers receive the external stimuli that this screen has let through and on the other side they directly receive stimuli of internal origin (connected to the basic needs). Their function is no longer one of quantitative protection but of breaking up quantity and filtering quality. They are no longer structured like a screen but like a "sieve" [*Sieb*]. Joining together the two images of a screen and a sieve suggests a third, more modern image, that of a meshed network. Figure 13 in the manuscript of the "Project for a scientific psychology" (1950a [1895]), which Freud drew himself, sketches this configuration, explicitly described as a branching structure, and it appears to be a variant on the right-hand section of the word-presentation diagram of 1891.

Here is the passage from Freud's text referring to this figure:

> Here a special contrivance seems to be present, which once again keeps off Q from ψ. For the sensory path of conduction in

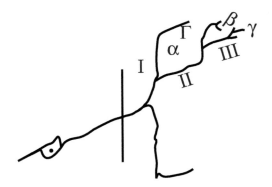

Figure 2.

φ is constructed in a peculiar fashion. It ramifies continually and exhibits thicker and thinner paths, which end in numerous terminal points—probably with the following significance: a stronger stimulus follows different pathways from a weaker one. For instance [1] Q$\acute{\eta}$ will pass only along pathway I and will transfer a quotient to ψ at terminal α. 2 (Q$\acute{\eta}$) will not transfer a double quotient at α, but will be able to pass also along pathway II, which is narrower, and to open up another terminal point to ψ [at β]. 3 (Q$\acute{\eta}$) will open up the narrowest path [III] and will transfer through γ as well. This is how the single φ path is relieved of its burden; the larger quantity in φ will be expressed by the fact that it cathects several neurones in ψ instead of a single one. (1950a, pp. 314–315)

All this concerns the processing of quantity. But the contact-barriers also have the function of processing quality; that is their proper filtering function. In addition to quantity, external stimuli have a "*characteristic*—'period'" (1950a, p. 313, note 2), which passes through the nerve-ending apparatuses, is conveyed by φ and ψ cathexes and, once it arrives at ω (the third type of neuron Freud invented to support his description of the perception-consciousness processes) becomes quality. This notion of periodicity serves three purposes: it is a tribute to Fliess, who distinguished between masculinity and femininity and identified critical moments of life according to their periodicity; it is the transposition to psychology of a phenomenon familiar to physicists; and it is a way to take into account the temporal variability of the psychical apparatus (I would add that it is also an intuitive acknowledgment of the role of rhythmic resonance or dissonance in the constitution of the Skin-ego or its flaws). Quantity, which forms a continuum on the outside is "first *reduced* and second *limited* owing to excision" (1950a, p. 313). Qualities, by contrast, are discontinuous, "so that certain periods do not operate as stimuli at all" (1950a, p. 313). "The quantity of the φ excitation is expressed in ψ by complication, its quality is expressed topographically, since, according to their anatomical relations, the different sense-organs are in communication through φ only with particular ψ neurones" (1950a, p. 315). This sixth function of contact-barriers could be summarised as follows: they serve to separate quantity from quality and to bring to consciousness the perception of sensory qualities, particularly those of pleasure and pain.

8. As a result of their properties relating to quantity, the group of ψ neurons, unlike the φ neurons, are able to register modifications and serve as a support to memory. Changes effected by the passage they undergo afford *"a possibility of representing memory"* (1950a, p. 299, italics in original). *"Memory is represented by the differences in the facilitations between the ψ neurones"* (1950a, p. 300, italics in original). "Now there is a basic law of *association by simultaneity* [...] which is the foundation of all links between the ψ neurones. We find that consciousness—that is, the quantitative cathexis of a ψ neurone, α—passes over to another, β, if α and β have at some time been simultaneously cathected from φ (or from elsewhere). Thus a contact-barrier has been facilitated through the simultaneous cathexis α–β" (1950a, p. 319).

Apart from the very special case of the experience of satisfaction, memory and perception are separate. As the basis for this separation Freud postulated two types of neuron, the one permanently modifiable— i.e., able to be breached or "facilitated" (the ψ neurons)— and the other essentially unable to change, always ready to receive new excitations, or only temporarily changeable, for they let in quantities but revert to their previous state as soon as the excitation has passed through (the φ neurons). Though this separation of memory and perception is not entirely an effect of the action of the contact-barriers, it would be impossible without them.

The meshed network of contact-barriers thus constitutes what I propose to call a surface of inscription; this is distinct from the screen against quantity but is attached to it, for its protection.

In conclusion, contact-barriers serve a triple function of separation: they keep the unconscious from the conscious, memory from perception, and quantity from quality.

Their topography is that of a dissymmetrical, double-facing wrapping (though at this point Freud had not yet proposed the idea of a wrapping), with a surface turned towards external excitations transmitted by the φ neurons and shielded by a screen against quantity, and an inner surface turned towards the "internal periphery of the body" (*Körperinnenperipherie*) (1950a, p. 306). Endogenous excitations can only be recognised if they are transformed into excitations of the other kind, i.e., projected into the outside world as visual, auditory, tactile representations, etc. (*cf.* the "day's residues" of the dream) and finally registered by the network of contact-barriers. It follows that drives can only be identified through their psychical representatives.

However, as Freud clearly notes, the psychical system is not autonomous: in early infancy it is subject to the initial state of helplessness [*Hilflosigkeit*] and the mother's intervention is needed as a source of psychical life.

The Ego as interface

In 1923, in Chapter Two of *The Ego and the Id*—the chapter itself carries the same title—Freud redefined the notion of the Ego and made it one of the key elements of his new conception of the psychical apparatus.

This definition is illustrated by a diagram, long ignored by Freud's French translators and other commentators on his work, which is based on a geometrical analogy. Both the diagram and the text of this analogy tend in the same direction: the psychical apparatus is no longer conceived as essentially economic (i.e., consisting of the transformation of quantities of psychical energy) and the topographical perspective has become more important: the old topography of conscious, preconscious, and unconscious is retained but it has been profoundly renewed by the addition of the Ego and the Id, superimposed upon it in the diagram. The psychical apparatus can now be represented from a topographical point of view and conceptualised in terms of a subjective topography.

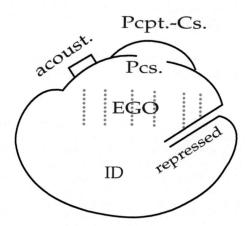

Figure 3.

The above abbreviations (taken from the *Standard Edition*) translate Freud's German terms, as below:

Pcpt.-Cs	Perception-Consciousness	W-Bw.	Wahrnehmung-Bewusstsein
Pcs.	Preconscious	Vbw	Vorbewusste
Acoust.	Acoustic [perceptions]	akust.	Akustische Wahrnemungen
Ego		Ich	
Id		Es	
Repressed		Vdgt	Verdrängte

This is how Freud presents this diagram in *The Ego and the Id*:

> We at once realize that almost all the lines of demarcation we have drawn at the instigation of pathology relate only to the superficial strata of the mental apparatus—the only ones known to us. The state of things which we have been describing can be represented diagrammatically […]; though it must be remarked that the form chosen has no pretensions to any special applicability, but is merely intended to serve for purposes of exposition.[11]
>
> We might add perhaps that the ego wears a "cap of hearing" [*Hörkappe*]—on one side only, as we learn from cerebral anatomy. It might be said to wear it awry.

> (*Gesammelte Werke* XIII [1923], p. 252; 1923b, pp. 24–25)

Comparisons of a topographical nature recur several times in Freud's text, above and below this diagram:

> We already know the point from which we have to start in this connection. We have said[12] that consciousness is the *surface* of the

---

[11] Commentators have been wrong, in my view, to take this caveat at face value. Freud laid too much emphasis on the role of pictograms as mediating between thing-presentation and verbal thinking based on alphabetical writing (if only in order to decipher the rebus of a dream) not to have "seen" in this diagram preconceptions he could not yet verbalise and which thus remained at the level of figurative thought. I have in fact tested the validity of this diagram by using it in the context of large-group psychodrama, in which it helped to create a group psychical apparatus (Anzieu, 1982a).

[12] Here Freud is referring to Chapter Four of *Beyond the Pleasure Principle* (1920g), in which he presents the crucial comparison of the psychical apparatus to the protoplasmic vesicle. The Pcpt.-Cs. System, which is analogous to the cerebral ectoderm, is described there as

mental apparatus; that is, we have ascribed it as a function to a system which is spatially the first one reached from the external world—and spatially not only in the functional sense but, on this occasion, also in the sense of anatomical dissection. Our investigations too must take this perceiving surface as a starting-point.

(*GW* XIII [1923], p. 246; 1923b, p. 19)

After this description of consciousness as an interface comes the articulation of the "shell" and the "kernel': the Ego is explicitly defined as a psychical "wrapping". This wrapping is not simply a containing sac; it plays an active role both in putting the psyche in touch with the external world and in collecting and transmitting information:

> We shall now look upon an individual as a psychical id, unknown and unconscious, upon whose surface rests the ego, developed from its nucleus the *Pcpt.* system. If we make an effort to represent this pictorially, we may add that the ego does not completely envelop the id, but only does so to the extent to which the system *Pcpt.* forms its [the ego's] surface, more or less as the germinal disc rests upon the ovum. The ego is not sharply separated from the id; its lower portion merges into it.[13]

(*GW* XIII [1923], p. 251; 1923b, p. 24, parenthesis in original)

Here Freud has no need to recall one of the basic principles of psychoanalysis—that every psychical phenomenon develops with constant reference to bodily experience. Going straight to the result, in such a condensed way that it may appear elliptical, he shows what bodily experience gives rise specifically to the Ego: the psychical wrapping derives anaclitically from the bodily wrapping. He explicitly mentions "touch" and the idea of the skin implicitly underlies the expression "surface [of] a person's own body":

---

forming its "crust". Its "situation [...] between the outside and the inside and the difference between the conditions governing the reception of excitations in the two cases have a decisive effect on the functioning of the system" (pp. 28–29). The conscious "crust" of the psyche thus appears to be what mathematicians nowadays call an "interface".

[13] Elsewhere Freud says that the Ego is an internal differentiation of the Id. Clinical experience certainly confirms the Freudian notion of an intermediate fusional space between the Ego and the Id—*cf.* Winnicott's transitional space.

Another factor, besides the influence of the system *Pcpt.*, seems to have played a part in bringing about the formation of the ego and its differentiation from the id. A person's own body, and above all its surface, is a place from which both external and internal perceptions may spring. It is *seen* like any other object, but to the *touch* it yields two kinds of sensations, one of which may be equivalent to an internal perception.[14]

(*GW* XIII [1923], p. 253; 1923b, p. 25)

It is thus clear that Freud's Ego, in its original form, corresponds to what I have proposed to call the Skin-ego. If we look more closely at the bodily experience on which the Ego leans anaclitically as it is formed, we might consider at least two other factors that Freud does not go into: the sensations of hot and cold, also derived from the skin; and respiratory exchanges, which occur alongside epidermal exchanges and may even be a particular variant of them. In relation to all the other sense registers, touch has a distinctive characteristic that not only places it at the origin of the psyche but allows it to provide the latter permanently with what might also be called the mental backcloth, the ground upon which psychical contents are inscribed as figures, or again the containing wrapping that makes it possible for the psychical apparatus to have contents. From the latter point of view, to borrow the terms of Bion (1967), I would say that first there are thoughts and then there is a "thought-thinking apparatus"; moreover, I would add that the transition from thoughts to thinking, i.e., to the formation of the Ego, is based on a double anaclitic process—on the container-content relation which the mother brings to her child, as Bion himself observes, and on what seems to me the decisive thing: the relation of containing exogenous excitations, a relation that the infant has experienced through its own skin, initially stimulated, of course, also by the mother. Indeed, tactility provides both an "internal" and an "external" perception. Freud alludes to the fact that I feel an object touching my skin at the same time as I feel my skin touched by the object. As is well known and easy to observe, the baby soon begins to explore this bipolarity actively: it deliberately touches parts of its body with its finger, puts its thumb or

---

[14] The italics on "seen" and "touch" are Freud's own.

big toe in its mouth, thus testing out simultaneously the complementary experiences of being object and subject. We may assume that the doubling intrinsic to tactile sensations lays the foundations for the reflexive doubling of the conscious Ego, again leaning anaclitically on the sense of touch.

Freud skips the logical link I have just re-established and goes straight for the conclusion: "The ego is first and foremost a bodily ego [*ein körperliches*]; it is not merely a surface entity [*Oberflächenwesen*], but is itself the projection of a surface" (*GW* XIII [1923], p. 253; 1923b, p. 26). From 1927, the following footnote was added, with Freud's permission, to this passage in the *Standard Edition*: "I.e., the ego is ultimately derived from bodily sensations, chiefly from those springing from the surface of the body. It may thus be regarded as a mental projection of the surface of the body, besides, as we have seen above, representing the superficies of the mental apparatus" (1923b, p. 26, note 1). The last line of Chapter Two of *The Ego and Id* repeats this essential point in a more condensed form: "[the conscious ego] is first and foremost a body-ego [*Körper-Ich*]" (*GW* XIII [1923], p. 255; 1923b, p. 27). In other words, consciousness appears on the surface of the psychical apparatus; better still, it is that surface.

Refinements to the topographical model of the psychical apparatus

Freud returns to the 1923 model, with a number of amendments, in 1932–1933, in "The dissection of the psychical personality", Lecture XXXI of the *New Introductory Lectures on Psycho-Analysis* (*GW* XV [1933], p. 85; 1933a, p. 78):

The two principal changes that appear here have significant consequences. The first is the introduction of the *Superego*, which is located *inside* the Ego in place of the "cap of hearing" which in 1923 was at the same place but on the outside. In both cases, the Superego is on the periphery of the Ego, though initially attached to the outer face and later to the inner one. Although Freud does not make this explicit, only suggesting it in both the text and the diagram, the extra-territorial or internal-peripheral locations of the Superego correspond to different phases of development of the psychical apparatus and also to distinct psychopathological forms; they thus call for differing forms of interpretation in psychoanalytic therapy. Let us also note

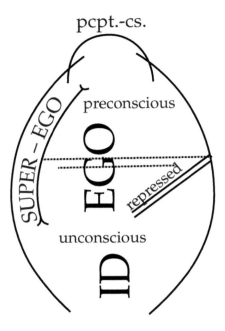

Figure 4.

another aspect of the topographical status of the Superego: it occupies only a circular arc on the edge of the psychical apparatus—this leads, to continue Freud's intuition, to the possibility (and the logical necessity) of describing a different type of psychopathological organisation, in which the Superego tends to make itself coextensive with the whole surface of the Ego and to substitute itself for the latter as a psychical wrapping.

The second change to be observed in the new diagram is that the wrapping, which completely surrounded the psychical apparatus in 1923, is now open at the base. The opening is a concrete representation of the continuity of the Id and its drives with the body and its biological needs, but at the cost of creating a discontinuity in the surface. It confirms the failure of the Ego to form itself into a total wrapping for the psyche—a failure that Freud had already noted in 1923. This suggests that the Id has an antagonistic and doubtless more ancient tendency to offer itself too as a total wrapping. This double tension (between the continuity and discontinuity of the psychical surface, and between the respective propensities of the Superego, the Ego, and the Id to constitute that surface) resolves itself into a multiplicity of clinical configurations, demanding interpretative strategies that are appropriate to the excess or lack of continuity or discontinuity and to the expansiveness of one or other agency. These points are not explicitly made in Freud's text but they seem to me to be implied *in potentia* in his new model.

In the course of this discussion, I have pointed to a number of characteristics of the psychical apparatus which Freud was able to highlight in 1925 owing to a new technological invention—the "mystic writing pad" or magic slate. Let me summarise these characteristics:

- the double-layered structure of the Ego: the celluloid surface layer stands for the protective shield (*cf.* a shell, hide or fur) and the lower layer made of waxed paper stands for the sensory reception of exogenous stimuli and the inscription of their traces on the wax tablet;
- the differentiation, within the Ego, between (conscious) perception as a sensitive and vigilant but non-retentive surface—like the celluloid layer—and (preconscious) memory, which registers and preserves impressions—like the wax tablet;
- the endogenous—i.e., drive-based—cathexis of the Ego system by the Id: this cathexis, which is "periodic", both "kindles and extinguishes" consciousness, condemning the latter to discontinuity and thus giving the Ego its earliest representation of time.

I propose to develop this latter intuition of Freud's by suggesting that the Ego acquires its sense of temporal continuity to the degree that the Skin-ego has been formed as a wrapping which is flexible enough in interactions with other people and good enough at containing what then become its psychical contents. What we call borderline cases essentially suffer from problems with their sense of the continuity of the Self, whereas the problems of psychotics are related to their sense of the Self's unity and those of neurotics to their sexual identity. The corresponding topographical configurations need to be identified and clearly described, using the models provided by Freud's two essays, *The Ego and the Id* and "Note upon the 'mystic writing pad'" and adding to them later developments and other adaptations necessitated by clinical practice.

Federn: Ego-feelings and feelings of fluctuation
in Ego boundaries

Federn's originality

For every psychoanalyst there are one or two areas which prove particularly essential to their self-analysis. For Sigmund Freud it was his
nocturnal dreams, or rather the account he gave of them to himself or
to Fliess by day, in writing; in this way he would first reconstruct and
then, through free association, deconstruct them. The dream is the royal
road to a knowledge of the unconscious—Freud made this assertion
because it was particularly true for him. In Vienna, about thirty years
after Freud rose to prominence, Paul Federn (1871–1952) set in motion a
series of discoveries by investigating his own experience of transitional
states—not dreams, experienced in a sleeping state, not parapraxes
which are committed in a waking state, but transitions between sleep
and waking, and more broadly between different levels of wakefulness
in the Ego. What body images are formed or deformed in the psyche
at these moments? What sense of itself does the psychical Ego experience? How is it distinguished from, or confused with, the bodily Ego?
Federn observed his own hypnagogic hallucinations at the moment of
falling asleep or waking up each day or while undergoing more exceptional experiences like a pre-operative anaesthetic, or even—though he
does not explicitly refer to this—creative regression; he compared this
with the accounts of his patients, not only when they were in analogous
situations but also when they were under hypnosis or during critical
times of depersonalisation or alienation; the combination of these two
bodies of material gradually opened up a different road for Federn—
less "royal" perhaps—towards a psychoanalytic understanding and
treatment of the psychoses.

Freud considered such an enterprise impossible; for that reason,
Federn was unable to devote himself to it until after the master had
died and he had emigrated to the United States. Freud had focused
on comparing dreams to the neuroses. Yet a nocturnal dream is a
hallucination—a temporary psychosis. How this hallucination is prepared and gradually comes into being following progressive phases of
entry into sleep, what kind of dissociation it presupposes both within
the Ego and between the Self and the outside world, and by what stages
the subject emerges out of it on waking—this is the extraordinary area

in which Federn chose to analyse his own experience between 1924 and 1935.[15] He sensed how a human being can become psychotic if what Bion later called the psychotic part of the personality comes to dominate their psychical functioning, and how they might later become normal again if the non-psychotic part is restored and affirmed. Back in Vienna, Victor Tausk had already shown great interest in extending psychoanalytic theory to the psychoses. In his "On the origin of the 'influencing machine' in schizophrenia" (1919) Tausk had intuited the crucial distinction between the psychical Ego and the bodily Ego. But he was more interested in madness than hallucination and in how a person entered a psychotic state rather than how they might emerge from it. This preoccupation was no doubt rooted in his personal problems, which led him eventually to a horrible suicide in 1919, a few months after the article was published.

As a thinker, Paul Federn was concerned with boundaries. He thought of a boundary not as an obstacle or a barrier but as a condition that makes it possible for the psychical apparatus to establish differences inside itself, between what is psychical and what is not and between what arises from the Self and what comes from others. He anticipated the physico-mathematical concept of an interface. The separation derived from this concept is necessary in order to keep local regimes distinct. The form of the interface changes in relation to the nature of regions and the nature of their regimes. Some changes may be "catastrophes" (René Thom defined seven mathematical types of these). On the basis of these interface effects, it became possible, again according to Thom, to develop a general science of the origin, development,

---

[15] Federn published his article on Ego feeling simultaneously in English and German in 1926; his articles on narcissism, on the variations of Ego feeling in dreams and on waking appeared between 1927 and 1935. In 1952 they were collected, together with later articles on the treatment of psychosis, in a volume entitled *Ego Psychology and the Psychoses*; citations are taken from this text, repr. 2012. Federn was interested in a very special type of affect, the Ego feelings, which are psychical states rather than affects. In parallel, another Viennese psychiatrist, who turned to psychoanalysis later, Paul Schilder (1886–1940) was working on disturbances in the consciousness of the Self (1913) and on the neurological notion of a body schema (1923); after his hasty emigration to the United States in 1930, he published his well-known article "The body image" in 1934 (repr. Schilder 1935). The investigations of these two scientists complement each other, though neither was aware of the other's work: Schilder highlights unconscious representations while Federn focuses on preconscious feelings.

and transformation of forms—morphogenesis. Federn anticipated this epistemological model, in particular the aspects relating to the structure of the Ego and the Self, and in this he was following the lead of Freud who in 1913, as we have seen, described the Ego as having the structure of a double-facing surface and elevated it to the status of a psychical agency with its own specific principles of functioning. Freud's second topography provided Federn with a framework within which he could achieve his own discoveries, a framework he could lean on while also questioning its boundaries. To sum up his fidelity to Freud's thinking: he conserved but also complemented it.[16] Freud was above all interested in the kernel or core of things—the unconscious as the core of the psyche and the Oedipus complex as the core of upbringing, culture, and neurosis. In parallel to Schilder who at the same moment was developing the notion of the body image, Federn directed his attention towards the outer shell, the periphery of things. Freud enumerated the primary and secondary psychical processes; alongside these processes, Federn studied the states of the Ego, for without a knowledge and interpretation of the latter any psychoanalytic treatment of narcissistic personalities would remain incomplete or ineffective. But he did so in accordance with Freud's own model, outlined in the latter's article "On Narcissism: An introduction" (1914c).

In Federn's view, the boundaries of the Ego are perpetually changing: they vary between individuals and, within the same individual, from one time of day or night to another and from one stage of life to the next; and their contents change as well. This idea makes sense, I believe, in relation to psychoanalytic treatment: during a session, the psychoanalyst needs to pay attention not only to the content and style of the patient's free association but also to the fluctuations of their Ego; analysts have to be sensitive to the moment when these fluctuations occur,

---

[16] Federn was one of the first small group that formed around Freud from 1902. Initially known as the "Psychological Wednesday Society", it became the Vienna Psychoanalytic Society in 1908. Along with Eduard Hitschmann and Isidor Sadger, Federn was one of the few founder members who remained in the Society until it was dissolved by the Nazis in 1938 at the time of the Anschluss. When Freud became ill with cancer it was to Federn that he handed the vice-presidency of the Vienna Psychoanalytic Society and when he emigrated he entrusted the original manuscript of the Minutes of the Psychoanalytic Society to him. Federn took it with him into exile in the United States and kept it, intending to publish it later; this was carried out by his son Ernst in collaboration with Herman Nunberg.

in order to help the patient's Ego to develop a sufficient awareness of the modifications of its boundaries—not least, one that is capable of surviving the end of the treatment. How timely or effective an interpretation may be depends on this; according to Federn, speech gains its effect by bringing two borders of the Ego into a certain relation, and this in turn creates modifications in the libidinal economy: "mobile" instinctual cathexes can replace "static" ones.

Ego feelings

According to Federn, Ego feeling is already present from the beginning of life, but in a vague form with little content. I would add that the feeling of the boundaries of the Ego is even more uncertain: there seems to be a primary feeling of a limitless Ego which can also be experienced later in depersonalisation or in certain mystical states. I have described this sense of blurred boundaries in the regressive dissociation that seizes the individual mind in a state of "gripping shock" in the first phase of a creative activity, or in the regressive fusion of the collective "group illusion" (Anzieu, 1980a). Psychoanalytic research on the couple in love has shown, indeed, that the two partners attach themselves to each other at the very points where their own psychical boundaries are uncertain, inadequate or defective.

Thus there is an Ego feeling which the subject is not aware of in a normal state of functioning but which reveals itself when something goes wrong. Ego feeling is primary, continuous, and variable. The Ego, which Freud made into an entity, certainly exists: human beings have a subjective sensation of it—a sensation, not an illusion, for it corresponds to a reality that is itself subjective. The Ego is both subject (we refer to it by the pronoun "I") and object (we call it our "Self"): "the ego is both the vehicle and the object of consciousness. We speak of the ego, in its capacity as the vehicle of consciousness, as 'I myself'" (Federn, 1952 [2012], p. 103).

This Ego feeling comprises three constitutive elements: a sense of unity across time (i.e., continuity), a sense of unity across space at the present moment (more precisely: proximity) and lastly a sense of causality. Federn endows the Ego with a dynamism and flexibility that Freud does not. But like Freud he gives a topographical representation of the Ego: the Ego feeling is its kernel and—except in cases of serious pathology—it is constant. The feeling of the Ego's boundaries constitutes its peripheral organ and, by contrast to what is felt to be its kernel, the latter in a normal state is a feeling of the constant fluctuation of boundaries.

For the Ucs. system, time does not exist—this explains the sense of an Ego having nether beginning nor end, of being immortal. The Cs. system, on the other hand, feels that the Ego has a temporal unity, which is what enables it to believe that what happens to us follows chronological order (this creates the flow of time from "before" to "now", and the traditional order of storytelling). In preconscious functioning, the sense of the Ego as unified across time is very variable; it may be at least partially preserved; in dreams, the sense of chronological order generally holds up, apart from the occasional dream consisting only of a "flash image"—this explains how the many characters in a dream reflect different aspects of the subject's Self and how creative artists often use dreaming as an instrument of discovery through its deconstruction of past knowledge and conscious states. If the sense of the Ego's continuity across time disappears from waking life, this causes phenomena of depersonalisation and *déjà-vu*.

As far as its content is concerned, Ego feeling includes both a mental and a bodily feeling. In normal life one is not aware of this duality, for the two are present together; so it is difficult to distinguish them unless one pays attention to processes, like waking or falling asleep, where they are separated—the problem being how to stay alert in psychical states that are typified by a drop in wakefulness. In these cases, too, there is a third feeling, a sense that the borders between the psychical Ego and the bodily Ego are fluctuating. When we are awake we feel that the psychical Ego is located inside the bodily Ego. Based on the periodicity of bodily processes, the bodily Ego acquires an objective ability to estimate time (this is conscious and preconscious: it allows us, for instance, to wake up at a particular hour); by contrast, the intensity of the psychical Ego in dreams combined with the absence of time in the unconscious explains the abnormal experience of speed and duration that we find in a dream-state. The mental feeling of the Ego (or the feeling of the psychical Ego) follows the rational formulation "I think therefore I am". It ensures the subject's continuity and sense of having a consistent identity. It is often associated with the Superego and remains a purely mental phenomenon—for the Superego, which has no access to mobility, can influence attention but not volition. For example, obsessional ideas and impulses derive from the Superego and are accompanied by the feeling—which varies according to the level of unconscious cathexis—that they are just about to achieve a motor discharge which they never reach in reality (hence the acuteness of the mental Ego of an obsessional neurotic). The mental Ego feeling is of an "inner Ego". This feeling fluctuates: mental processes may cease to be perceived as belonging to the inner psychical Ego (in other words, may cease to be recognised as mental); in hysterical neurosis they are converted into bodily phenomena and in psychosis they are projected onto external reality.

The bodily feeling of the Ego is "a unified feeling of libido cathexes of the motor and sensory apparatus" (Federn, 1952 [2012], p. 29). It is "a compound feeling" (p. 29): it includes many different feelings but cannot be reduced to any one of them—for example, sensory and motor memories concerning one's own person or the unity of perception of one's own body in relation to somatic organisation.

The feeling of the Ego borders

Human beings have the unconscious feeling of a border between their psychical Ego and their bodily Ego. Moreover, they have the unconscious feeling of a border between the Ego and the Superego. Let us see, with Federn, how the feelings of these boundaries occur in transitional states.

Falling asleep dissociates, on the one hand, the mental and bodily Ego feelings and, on the other, the Ego and the Superego:

> [...] it is usually possible to observe that in a withdrawal of cathexes with sudden falling asleep, bodily ego feeling disappears sooner than mental ego feeling or superego feeling. The body ego (for the sake of brevity I shall sometimes use the term "ego" instead of "ego feeling") can disappear entirely while falling asleep and can be freshly invested and awakened by the "mental" ego which has remained awake. In this way, we can succeed in postponing sleep voluntarily. It is probable that with most people, the superego loses cathexis before the ego. (Federn, 1952 [2012], p. 30)

In the case of a normal *waking-up* process, (i) the bodily and mental Egos wake simultaneously—the mental Ego is just a moment ahead, but without any sense of strangeness—we discover with pleasure that we are at the beginning of a new day; and (ii) the Superego does not wake up until after the Ego. Conversely, when one wakes out of a dream the mental Ego wakes up first, the bodily Ego feels dissociated from it and one may even hallucinate one's own body as an alien presence.

With *fainting* we find the most extreme dissociation of the two feelings: this dissociation lies behind the illusion of the separate existence of the body and soul.

Normal dreams, recollected as complete and lifelike, are of two kinds:

a. the majority lack any bodily feeling: the Ego of the dream is reduced to the mental Ego; libido has been withdrawn from the body and has regressed to the Id, not towards the bodily Ego; in the course of this regression, the Ego encounters object-presentations which are activated by the libidinal cathexis to the point of creating the illusion of reality; as vivid as the dream is, dreamers have no feeling of their own body;

b. sometimes, on the other hand, there is no mental Ego feeling and the vivid sensations are bodily ones; these are the "typical dreams" of flying, swimming or being naked; the dreamer is represented by themselves and the only objects that may occur in these dreams are fragmentary ones: what is vivid (in colour or brightness) is the detail of background, landscape or character—in other words, external reality.

Case study: Edgar[17]

In a dream, there is not enough libidinal cathexis for both the desired object and the dreamer's own body to be represented at the same time; if both the mental and bodily feelings were cathected, the dreamer would wake up.

> A patient who did not suffer from depersonalization in waking life has reported to me a remarkable example of the distinction between the mental and the bodily ego. He had an unusually complete and vivid sexual dream with very vivid object-presentation and ego feeling of a pleasurable sexual nature. The dream was

---

[17] I have given this name to Federn's unnamed patient.

enacted in his bedroom but not in his bed. He woke up suddenly and found himself in bed in a state of complete depersonalization; he felt that his body was lying beside him and that it did not belong to him. His mental ego awakened first. Bodily ego feeling had not awakened along with the mental ego because the libido available for narcissistic use is essential for the awakening of bodily ego feeling, and in the foregoing dream all the libido had invested the very vivid presentation of the object. This unusual occurrence clearly shows that the cathexis of the ego stands in a compensatory relation to cathexis of a sexual object. (Federn, 1952 [2012], p. 36)

Feelings of fluctuation in Ego boundaries

Let us now turn to the variations in the libidinal cathexis of the feeling of Ego boundaries and the consequences that arise from them—*feelings of strangeness* or *ecstasy*.

Whenever there is a change in ego feeling cathexis, we sense the "boundaries" of our ego. Whenever an impression impinges, be it somatic or psychic, it strikes a boundary of the ego normally invested with ego feeling. *If no ego feeling sets in at this boundary we sense the impression in question as alien.* So long as no impression impinges upon the boundaries of ego feeling, we remain unaware of the confines of the ego. Psychic and bodily ego feeling can both be active or passive. (Federn, 1952 [2012], p. 69)

Ego feeling is the original narcissistic cathexis of the Ego. At first it has no object. Later, when the libidinal object cathexes have reached the border between the Ego and the outside world or have cathected it and then been withdrawn, secondary narcissism appears.

The extent of the state of cathexis which constitutes the ego varies; its boundary at any given moment is the ego boundary and, as such, enters consciousness. When an ego boundary is charged with intense libidinal feeling but is not apprehended as to its content, the result is a sense of ecstasy; when, on the other hand, it is merely apprehended and not felt, a sense of strangeness supervenes. (Federn, 1952 [2012], p. 104)

When the Ego's external border loses its cathexis, external objects are still clearly perceived or may even interest the subject but they feel alien, unfamiliar, and even unreal—which may lead to a loss of the sense of reality. As the patient gradually gets better, an increase in libidinal cathexis at the boundary makes objects seem warmer, more glowing. An object is felt to be real (without need of reality-testing) when (i) it is excluded from the Ego and (ii) the impressions it makes impinge on a well cathected Ego border.

The repression of Ego states

Repression is brought to bear not only upon phantasmatic representations, but also upon Ego states. Thus the unconscious part of the Ego seems to be made up of stratified layers of Ego states which may be awakened by hypnosis, for example, or dreams—or indeed, I would add, the regression of creativity—along with their related cohort of experiences, memories and attitudes.

When there is a deficiency in Ego cathexis, a highly developed and well organised Ego cannot maintain a sufficient cathexis of all its borders, so it is at risk of being invaded by the unconscious and its false realities. Since returning to an earlier state of the Ego requires less expenditure of Ego cathexis it can be used as a defence. In such a case, the Ego borders are reduced to those of the earlier state. This is what causes the mind to be invaded by false realities and to lose the faculty of thought—the essential characteristics of schizophrenia.

The way to treat a psychotic, according to Federn, is by helping them not to squander their mental energy and learn instead to conserve it. This does not mean removing regressions but creating them; the therapist should not take a history, for recalling earlier psychotic episodes might cause a relapse. It means strengthening the weakened Ego border between psychical reality and external reality: false realities need to be rectified and the patient has to be shown how to use reality-testing correctly. The patient has to be made to recognise the triple status of their body—as a part of the Ego, as a part of the external world, and as forming the border between the Ego and the world.

CHAPTER SEVEN

The functions of the Skin-ego

W hat follows is based on two general principles. The first is specifically Freudian: every psychical function develops by leaning anaclitically on a bodily function, whose workings it transposes to the mental plane. Though Jean Laplanche (1970) advocates reserving the concept of anaclisis for the way the sexual drives lean on the organic functions of self-preservation, I favour a broader use: because the psychical apparatus develops by breaking away in successive steps from its biological base, these breaks on the one hand make it possible for it to escape from biological laws while on the other making it necessary for it to seek the anaclitic basis of all psychical functions in the functions of the body. The second principle, also known to Freud, goes back to Hughlings Jackson: the development of the nervous system in the course of evolution presents a peculiarity not found in any other organic system: the most recent organ, which is the closest to the surface—the cortex—tends to take charge of the system, bringing the other neurological sub-systems under its overall control. This is also the case with the conscious Ego, which tends to occupy a position within the psychical apparatus on the surface, in contact with the outside world, where it controls the functioning of the apparatus. We know, moreover, that the skin (the surface of the body) and the brain (the surface of the nervous system) derive from the same embryonic structure, the ectoderm.

For a psychoanalyst like me, the skin is of crucial importance: it provides the psychical apparatus with the representations that constitute the Ego and its principal functions. This observation fits, in turn, into the framework of the general theory of evolution. The difference between humans and the other mammals does not lie only in the greater size and complexity of the brain; in humans the skin also loses its hardness and its covering of fur. Body hair scarcely remains, except in a few places—on the cranium, where it serves as a further layer of protection for the brain, and surrounding the bodily orifices of the face and trunk, where it increases their sensitivity, even sensuality. As Imre Hermann (1930) noted, the infant's drive to cling to its mother becomes more difficult to satisfy in humans, which condemns the young of that species to early, intense and prolonged terrors of losing protection and lacking a supporting object, and gives rise to what has been called "original helplessness". To compensate for this, the attachment drive has become all the more important in human babies because their infancy lasts so much longer than that of other species. This drive finds its objects in tracking signals—in the mother and then in the family group that substitutes for her—smiles, softness of touch, the physical warmth of being embraced, the variety of sounds heard, the firmness with which the baby is carried, being rocked, the availability of food, the attention and presence of others: all these elements provide the baby with clues both about the nature of external reality and how to deal with it and about the affects felt by the partner, which respond to its own affects. Here it is no longer a matter of satisfying the vital needs of self-preservation (nourishment, breathing or sleep) upon which sexual or aggressive desires are constituted anaclitically, but of communication (pre-verbal and infra-linguistic), upon which linguistic exchange will in due course be anaclitically supported.

These two registers often work together—for example, suckling gives the baby the opportunity for tactile, visual, aural, and olfactory communications. But we know that a purely material satisfaction of vital needs, if it systematically lacks those affective and sensory exchanges, can lead to "hospitalism" or autism. It has also been observed that as the baby grows, there is a concomitant increase in the proportion of attention given by it and its carers to communication for communication's sake, independently of activities of self-preservation.

In its original form, communication—in reality but even more in phantasy—is a direct, unmediated communication of skin to skin.

In *The Ego and the Id* (1923b) Freud showed that it is not only defence mechanisms and character traits that are derived, anaclitically and through transformation, from bodily activities, but also psychical agencies: the psychical drives that make up the Id are derived from biological instincts; what he later called the Superego "has acoustic roots"; and the Ego is initially formed on the basis of the experience of touch. I believe we need to add to this a pre-existing, more ancient, perhaps even primal topology, which is the feeling of the existence of the Self—a Self that corresponds to the wrapping of sound and smell, a Self surrounded by an Ego differentiated on the basis of tactile experience, a Self onto whose outside both exogenous and endogenous stimuli are projected. Freud's secondary topology (the Id, the Ego with its appendage the ideal Ego, and the Superego together with the Ego-Ideal) comes into being when the visual wrapping—notably as a result of the primary taboo on touching—replaces the tactile wrapping as the essential anaclitic support for the Ego; when (mainly visual) thing-presentations become associated in the developing preconscious with word-presentations (supplied by the acquisition of speech); and when the subject is able to differentiate between the Ego and the Superego, on the one hand, and between external stimulation and drive-based excitation, on the other.

In my original article on the Skin-ego (1974), I assigned three functions to it: as a containing and unifying wrapping around the Self; as a protective barrier for the psyche; and as a filter of exchanges and for the recording of the earliest traces, the function that makes representation possible. Three configurations correspond to these three functions—the sac, the screen, and the sieve. The work of Francis Pasche (1971) on the *Le Bouclier de Persée* [*The Shield of Perseus*] led me to consider a fourth function, that of a mirror of reality.

The eight functions of the Skin-ego

I am now going to establish a more systematic parallel between the functions of the skin and the functions of the Ego; in each case, I shall attempt to show in detail how the organic and the psychical correspond, what kinds of anxiety are linked to the pathology of that function, and how the disorders of the Skin-ego that we meet with in clinical practice are configured. The order of functions given below does not follow any rigorous classificatory principle, and my list has no claim to being exhaustive; it remains open-ended.

1. Just as the skin fulfils the function of supporting the skeleton and muscles, the Skin-ego fulfils the function of *maintaining* the psyche. This function is exercised biologically by what Winnicott (1962a, pp. 59–60) calls *"holding"*, i.e., by the way the mother supports the baby's body.[1] The psychical function is formed through interiorising the mother's holding. The Skin-ego is a part of the mother—especially her hands—which has been interiorised and now maintains the psyche in a functional state, at least while the baby is awake, just as the mother keeps its body in a state of unity and solidity. The baby's ability to hold itself up physically allows it to achieve a sitting position, then to stand and then to walk. Being supported externally against the mother's body teaches the baby how to support itself internally on its spinal column, the solid body ridge which allows it to stand upright. One of the anticipatory kernels of the "I" is the image-sensation of an inner phallus that is maternal (or, more generally, parental), and this gives the mental space which is being formed a primary axis, a sense of verticality and the struggle against gravity, and lays the ground for the subject's experience of having a personal psychical life. By leaning against this axis, the Ego can implement the most archaic defence mechanisms, such as splitting and projective identification. But it can only feel truly secure in leaning against this support if it is sure that its body has zones of close, stable contact with the skin, muscles and palms of its mother (and other people in its primary caring environment) and also that, at the periphery of its psyche, it is reciprocally encircled—in what Sami-Ali (1974) has called "mutual inclusion"—by its mother's psyche.

Blaise Pascal, who lost his mother when he was very young, theorised particularly well, first in physics, then in psychology and religious apologia, the horror of the inner void which has long been attributed to Nature, the lack of the support-object that the psyche needs in order to find its centre of gravity. In his paintings, Francis Bacon portrays liquefying bodies, whose skin and clothes provide a superficial unity

---

[1] *Translator's note*: Anzieu's reference is to Winnicott 1962a, but this is more clearly defined in Winnicott 1962c pp. 43–45 and 49.

but which lack the dorsal spine that holds up the body and thought: they are skins filled with substances that are more fluid than solid, which corresponds closely to the body image of an alcoholic.[2]

What matters here is not the phantasmatic incorporation of the nourishing breast but the primary identification of a support-object which the infant can cling to and be held by; it is the drive to attachment or clinging that is satisfied rather than the libido. The body of the child cleaves face-to-face to that of the mother and this is linked to the sexual drive, which is satisfied orally by suckling and through that manifestation of love, the embrace. Adult lovers usually regain this kind of holding when they satisfy their sexual drives at the genital level. Conversely, primary identification with the support-object presumes another spatial arrangement which can be found in two complementary variants: James Grotstein (1981), a Californian disciple of Bion's, described them first—the child's back against the stomach of the supporting person (what he calls the "Background Object": Grotstein, 1981, p. 77ff) or the child's stomach against the other person's back.

In the first variant, the child leans its back against the support-object, who moulds themselves around it, and feels protected from behind, for its back is the only part of its body it cannot touch or see. The nightmare, which children often have when they are running a fever, of a surface falling into folds or warping, tearing or filling with humps and hollows, expresses in figurative form an attack on the reassuring representation of a common skin with the support-object. The dreamer may interpret this defective surface as a heap of snakes, but it would be a mistake to understand that solely as a phallic symbol. A nest of snakes writhing together has a different meaning from a single snake rearing up. Grotstein cites the dream of a little girl, reported to him by her mother, who was in analysis with him:

> The daughter apparently awakened in the middle of the night seeing snakes everywhere, including the very floor on which she

---

[2]See my two monographs, *De l'horreur du vide à sa pensée: Pascal* [*From the horror of the void to its thought: Pascal*] and *La peau, la mère et le miroir dans les tableaux de Francis Bacon* [*Skin, the mother and the mirror in the paintings of Francis Bacon*], reprinted in *Le Corps de l'œuvre* [*The Body of the Creative Work*] (Anzieu, 1981a).

was walking. She ran to her mother's bedroom and mounted her mother with her back to the mother's abdomen. This was the only place where she could find relief. Although the mother, not the child, was the patient, her associations to the event soon established that she had identified with her child. She was the little girl who wished to lie down on top of me in order to get the "backing", protection, and "rearing" which she felt deprived of by her own parents. (Grotstein, 1981, p. 79)[3]

The second position, that of the child lying with its front against the back of the person fulfilling the role of support-object, brings it the sensation-feeling that the most precious and fragile part of its body, its tummy, is safe behind the protective screen, the original shield against stimuli, provided by this other body. Usually this experience begins with one or other parent (or even with both parents); it may continue for quite a while longer with a brother or sister whose bed the child shares (until he entered analysis with Bion, Samuel Beckett could only overcome his terror of insomnia by falling asleep up against the body of his older brother). Similarly, one of my patients, who had been raised by violent and quarrelsome parents, found her inner security up to the age just before puberty by falling asleep against the body of her younger sister, who shared her bed. Whichever of the two was the more frightened would "make a chair" (that was their expression), to receive and hold close the reassuring body of the other. For a whole phase of her analysis, her transference implicitly invited me to make a chair for her in this way: she would demand that I take turns with her in producing free associations, and confess my thoughts, feelings, and fears; she offered to come close to me physically, not understanding why I refused to let her sit on my knee. I first had to analyse the hysterical seductiveness with which she made these demands as a defensive ploy of sexualisation, before we could move on to talking about her terror of losing the support-object.

Grotstein reports another significant kind of example: "Frequently I have heard dreams from analytic patients in which they were driving

---

[3]I am grateful to Annick Maufras du Chatellier for introducing me to this text and for having translated it into French for me.

a car from the back seat. The associations to these dreams almost invariably led to a notion of having a defective backing and consequently, difficulty with autonomy" (1981, p. 79). He even makes an untranslatable pun: "the object *behind* can also be felt to be *underneath*; it therefore becomes the paradigm for the commonly used word *understanding*" (ibid., p. 80; italics in original).

2. The function that corresponds to the skin covering the whole of the body and having all the external sense organs set in it is the Skin-ego's function of *containing*. This function is mainly carried out by the mother's *handling* of the baby. The image-sensation of the skin as a sac is awakened in the new-born child by the daily bodily care provided by the mother, which is appropriate to its needs. The Skin-ego as a psychical representation emerges from the interplay between the mother's body and the child's as well as from the mother's reactions to the baby's sensations and emotions; these reactions are both gestural and vocal, since at that time the sound wrapping supplements the tactile wrapping, and they are circular, for the echolalia and echopraxes of the one imitate those of the other, and this allows the infant to experience these sensations and emotions for itself, little by little, without feeling destroyed by them. René Kaës (1979a, and see this volume, p. 42 note 1) distinguishes two aspects of this function by using two different terms. The container [*contenant*], properly so-called, which is stable and immobile, offers a passive receptacle for the baby to deposit its sensations/images/affects and keep them neutralised and preserved. The containor [*conteneur*] corresponds to the active aspect, Bion's "maternal reverie", projective identification, the exercise of the alpha function, which elaborates, changes and restores to the child its sensations/ images/affects in a representable form.

Just as the skin is wrapped around the whole body, so the Skin-ego aspires to enwrap the whole psychical apparatus; this ambition will later prove to be exorbitant but at the beginning it is necessary. At that time, the Skin-ego is conceived as a shell and the instinctual Id as a kernel, each of these terms having need of the other. The Skin-ego cannot function as a container unless it has instinctual drives to contain, to localise in bodily sources and later on to differentiate. A drive can only be felt as an impulse, a motor force, if it comes up against boundaries and specific points of insertion into the mental space in which it is deployed and if its source is projected into areas of the body with their own individual excitability. This complementarity of the shell and the kernel is the basis of the sense of a continuous Self.

If the containing function of the Skin-ego fails, two forms of anxiety result. The anxiety of an instinctual excitation that is diffuse, scattered, unlocalised, unidentifiable, and impossible to calm expresses a psychical topography consisting of a kernel without a shell; individuals with this problem try to create a substitute shell out of psychical pain or psychical terror, wrapping themselves in suffering. In the other case, the wrapping does exist but without continuity, pitted with holes. This is the sieve Skin-ego: thoughts and memories are difficult to retain and they drain away—as in the case of Éléonore (see above, pp. 71–72). The subject has a great fear of having an inside that is emptying itself out, and especially that the aggressivity needed for any self-affirmation is leaking away. These psychical holes may be based anaclitically on the pores of the skin: the case study of Gethsemane (see pp. 199–210) shows a patient who perspired during sessions and thus let loose on his analyst a foul-smelling aggression which he could neither hold back nor work through, with the result that his unconscious representation of a sieve Skin-ego was never interpreted.

3. The surface layer of the epidermis protects its sensitive layer (where the free nerve-endings and the Meissner tactile corpuscles are found) as well as the organism in general against physical attacks, some forms of radiation and excessive stimuli. As early as 1895, in the "Project for a scientific psychology" (1950a [1895]), Freud recognised that the Ego has the parallel function of a protective *shield against stimuli*. In the "Note upon the 'mystic writing-pad'" (1925a), he makes clear that the Ego—like the epidermis, though Freud does not specify this—presents a double-layered structure. In the "Project" of 1895, Freud implies that the mother plays the role of protective shield for the baby, and she continues to do so (I would add) until the child's growing Ego finds in its own skin a sufficient anaclitic support to take over this function. Generally speaking, the Skin-ego is a potential structure at birth and it is realised as the relationship between the baby and its primary care environment unfolds; the remote origin of this structure seems to go back to the first appearance of living organisms.

The excesses or deficiencies of the protective shield offer a great variety of figurative representations. Frances Tustin (1972) describes two body images that belong, respectively, to primary and secondary autism: an amoeboid Ego (in which none of the functions of the Skin-ego—support, containment, protective shield or the double-layer structure—have been acquired) and a hard crustacean Ego, in which a rigid carapace takes the place of the missing container and prevents the Skin-ego functions that should develop later from being triggered.

The paranoid terror of psychical intrusion appears in two forms—(i) persecution: someone is stealing my thoughts or (ii) the influencing machine: someone is putting thoughts into my head. In both cases, the functions of protective shield and container do exist, but inadequately.

The terror of losing the object who fulfils the role of auxiliary protective shield is at its most extreme when the mother has given the child to her own mother (its maternal grandmother) to bring up, and if this grandmother has looked after it so perfectly, from both a qualitative and quantitative point of view, that it has experienced neither the possibility nor the necessity of creating its own anaclisis. Drug addiction may then appear to be a solution, by building a barrier of smoke or fog between the Ego and external stimuli.

The subject may attempt to supplement the protective shield by leaning on the dermis rather than the epidermis; this is Esther Bick's "muscular second skin" or Wilhelm Reich's "character armour".
4. The membrane of organic cells protects the cell's individuality by distinguishing between foreign bodies to which it bars entry and substances that are similar or complementary to it and to which admission or association are permitted. Through its surface appearance, colour, texture, and odour, human skin presents a considerable range of individual differences. These may be narcissistically or indeed socially hypercathected. They allow us to distinguish, among other people, those whom we love and are attached to and to assert ourselves as an individual with our own personal skin. In turn the Skin-ego performs the function of *individuating* the Self and making it feel unique. The terror of the "uncanny", described by Freud (1919h), is related to a perceived threat to the Self's individuality of its borders being undermined.

In schizophrenia, the whole of external reality—which is poorly distinguished from internal reality—is considered dangerous to absorb, and it is only by the extreme expedient of losing all sense of reality that the Self can maintain its oneness.

5. The skin is a surface containing pouches and cavities in which the sense organs—other than those of touch, which are set in the epidermis itself—are housed. The Skin-ego is a psychical surface which links together sensations of various kinds and makes them stand out as figures against the original background of the tactile wrapping: this is the *intersensorial* function of the Skin-ego, which leads to the formation of a "common sense" (the *sensorium commune* of medieval philosophy) whose basic reference point is always the sense of touch. If this function is deficient there is a terror of the body falling apart, or more precisely being dismantled (Meltzer, 1975); in other words, a fear of the various sense organs working anarchically, independently of each other. Later I will illustrate the decisive role played by the taboo on touching in the progression from the containing tactile wrapping to the intersensorial space which prepares the ground for symbolisation. In neurophysiological reality, the integration of information derived from the various sense organs is carried out by the encephalon; thus, intersensoriality is a function of the central nervous system or, more broadly, of the ectoderm (from which the skin and the central nervous system develop simultaneously). In psychical reality, by contrast, this role is unknown and instead there is the imaginary representation of the skin as a backcloth, an original surface upon which sensory interconnections are deployed.

6. The baby's skin is the object of a libidinal cathexis on its mother's part. Feeding and other care are generally accompanied by pleasant skin-to-skin contacts that pave the way for auto-erotic experience and make skin pleasures the habitual backcloth to sexual pleasure. The latter become localised at certain erectile zones or certain orifices (outgrowths or pouches) where the surface layer of the epidermis is thinner or direct contact with the mucous membrane produces an effect of increased excitation. The Skin-ego fulfils the function of a surface for *supporting sexual excitation*, a surface on which, if a person's sexual development is normal, erogenous zones can be localised, the difference between the sexes can be recognised and this complementarity can be desired. The exercise of this function may be sufficient in itself, as the Skin-ego attracts libidinal cathexis to its whole surface, becoming a total wrapping of sexual excitation. This configuration is at the

root of the childhood phantasy, no doubt the earliest sexual theory, that sexuality consists entirely in the pleasure of skin contact and that pregnancy results simply from embracing and kissing. If there is no satisfactory means of discharge, this wrapping of erogenous excitation may change into a wrapping of anxiety (see the case study of Zénobie, pp. 243–250).

If the cathexis of the skin is more narcissistic than libidinal, the wrapping of excitation may be replaced by a gleaming narcissistic wrapping, which is believed to make its owner invincible, immortal, and heroic.

If the support of sexual excitation is not fully secure, once the individual grows into an adult they will not feel safe enough to engage in complete sexual relations leading to mutual genital satisfaction.

If the sexual outgrowths and orifices are the site of painful rather than erogenous experiences, this may increase the representation of the Skin-ego as full of holes, raise the level of persecution anxiety and redouble the tendency to develop sexual perversions in order to turn pain into pleasure.

7. The function of the Skin-ego in ensuring *libidinal recharging* of psychical functioning, maintaining internal energy tension and distributing it unequally among the psychical sub-systems (*cf.* the "contact barriers" in Freud's "Project" of 1895) corresponds to the skin as a surface that is perpetually subject to sensorimotor stimulation by external excitations. Failures in this function may produce two opposite kinds of anxiety: a fear that the psychical apparatus might explode under the pressure of too much excitation (for example, an epileptic seizure, *cf.* Hervé Beauchesne, 1980) or Nirvana anxiety (the fear of what would happen if the desire to reduce tension to zero were fulfilled).

8. Since it contains the tactile sense organs—touch, pain, heat-cold, and dermatoptic sensitivity—the skin provides direct information about the external world, which is later cross-checked by the "common sense" with audial, visual information, etc. The Skin-ego fulfils the function of *registering* tactile sensory traces, in what Piera Castoriadis-Aulagnier (1975) calls a pictogrammic function or what Francis Pasche (1971) identifies with the shield of Perseus reflecting back a mirror-image of reality. This function is reinforced by the mothering environment insofar as it plays the role of "object-presentation"

(Winnicott, 1962)[4] for the young baby. This function of the Skin-ego develops on a dual basis, biological and social. Biologically, the first pattern of reality is imprinted on the skin; socially, the individual who belongs to a particular social group is marked by cuts, scarification, skin-painting, tattoos, make-up, hairstyles, and the supplementary layer of clothing. The Skin-ego is the original parchment that acts as a palimpsest, preserving the crossed-out, scratched-through, over-written drafts of an "original" pre-verbal writing made of traces on the skin.

An early form of anxiety related to this function is the fear of being marked all over the surface of one's body and Ego by indelible and shameful inscriptions derived from the Superego—blushes, rashes, eczema, symbolic wounds according to Bettelheim (1954)—or by the infernal machine of Kafka's "In the penal colony" (1914–1919) which engraves, in Gothic letters carved into the skin of the condemned man, the article of the penal code that he has transgressed, until he dies of it. The converse fear is of the inscriptions being erased under the weight of overload or of losing the ability to retain traces, for example in one's sleep.

Attacks against the Skin-ego

All the functions described above are in the service, first, of the attach-ment drive and, second, of the libidinal drive. But is there not also a negative activity of the Skin-ego, in the service of Thanatos, which aims at the *self-destruction* of the skin and the Ego? Developments in immun-ology, triggered by the study of resistance to organ transplants, give us a lead here, so far as living organisms are concerned. Elements of incompatibility between the donor and the recipient have confirmed that no two human beings on earth are exactly alike (apart from iden-tical twins) but they have also helped us to grasp the importance of the molecular markers of "biological personality". The more similar these markers are in the donor and the recipient the more likely the transplant is to succeed (Jean Hamburger); and these similarities arise from the existence of a plurality of different groups of white corpuscles

---

[4] *Translator's note*: Anzieu does not specify whether he is referring to 1962a or 1962b.

which apparently are markers not just of the corpuscles themselves but of the whole personality (Jean Dausset).

Biologists have found themselves resorting—without realising they were doing it—to notions (such as the Self, the Not-Me) analogous to those that some of Freud's successors coined to complete his second topology of the psychical apparatus. In many illnesses, the immunological defence system may suddenly start up without rhyme or reason and attack an organ of the person's own body as though it were a transplant. This is an auto-immune activity, in other words (etymologically) the activity of a living organism directing an immunological or immune reaction against itself. The cellular army is meant to reject foreign tissues—what biologists call the "non-Self"—but sometimes it is blind enough to attack the "Self", even though it respects the latter totally in a state of health; this is what causes auto-immune diseases, which are often very serious.

As an analyst, I am struck by the analogy between this auto-immune response and the negative therapeutic response of turning the drive against oneself, along with other attacks against linking in general and psychical contents in particular. I note also that the distinction between the familiar and the strange (Spitz) or the me and the not-me (Winnicott) has biological roots at the very level of the cell, and my hypothesis is that the skin, the body's wrapping, forms an intermediate reality between the cellular membrane—which collects, sorts and transmits information as to whether ions are foreign or not—and the psychical interface of the Ego's Pcpt.-Cs. System.

Specialists in psychosomatic illness have described how in the structure of allergies the signals of security and danger are reversed: instead of being protective and reassuring, what is familiar is seen as bad and thus shunned, while unknown things, instead of seeming disturbing, are attractive; this leads to the paradoxical reaction of allergy sufferers, and also of drug addicts, who avoid what might do them good and are fascinated by what will harm them. The fact that the structure of allergies often takes the form of an alternation between asthma and eczema allows us to describe in detail the configuration of the Skin-ego that is at stake here. Originally, the thing is to mitigate the inability of the Skin-ego-sac to delimit an internal psychical sphere in terms of volume, i.e., to move from a two-dimensional representation of the psychical apparatus to a three-dimensional one (see Didier Houzel, 1985a). The two conditions correspond to two possible modes of approaching the surface area of this sphere—from the inside and from the outside. Asthma is an attempt to feel the wrapping of the bodily Ego from within: asthmatics fill themselves up with air to the point where they are able to feel the borders of their body from below and are assured of the expanded limits of the Self; in order to maintain that sensation of an inflated Sac-self, they hold their breath in, at the risk of blocking the rhythm of respiratory exchange with the environment and suffocating. This can be seen in the case study of Pandora (see pp. 126–131). Eczema is an attempt to feel the bodily surface area of the Self from the outside, with the skin's painful lacerations, rough feel, humiliating appearance, and at the same time a wrapping of warmth and diffuse erogenous excitations.

In the psychoses, especially schizophrenia, the paradox of allergic conditions reaches its peak. Psychical functioning is dominated by what Paul Wiener (1983) has called the anti-physiological response. Trust in the natural functioning of the organism is destroyed or has never been acquired. What is natural is experienced as artificial; what is living is perceived as mechanical; what is good for life and in life is felt to be mortally dangerous. By a circular reaction, this paradoxical psychical functioning distorts the perception of bodily functioning and that reinforces the paradox. The paradoxical configuration that underlies the Skin-ego in these cases means that fundamental distinctions—between sleeping and being awake, between dream and reality, between animate and inanimate—are never acquired. The case study of Eurydice (Anzieu, 1982b) provides a limited example of how this works in a patient who is not psychotic but who feels threatened by mental confusion. One of the psychoanalyst's essential tasks in treating such patients is to restore their trust in the natural and successful functioning of the organism (provided that it finds an echoing response from its environment that meets its needs), though this task is arduous and repetitive on account of the patient's unconscious efforts to paralyse the analyst entrapped in the paradoxical transference (see Anzieu, 1975b) and drag them down into their own failure.

In my view, unconscious attacks against the psychical container, which may lean anaclitically on organic auto-immune phenomena, originate in parts of the Self that are fused to representatives of the Id's innate self-destructive drive, banished to the periphery of the Self and encysted into the surface layer which is the Skin-ego; here they eat away at the Skin-ego's continuity, destroying its cohesiveness and undermining its functions by inverting their aims. The imaginary skin that covers the Ego becomes a poisoned tunic, suffocating, burning, and disintegrating. One may call this a *toxic* function of the Skin-ego.

Other functions

This list of eight psychical functions of the Ego, corresponding to biological functions of the skin, provides a grid against which to test facts; it remains open to further development and improvement.

In relation to other skin functions that I have not yet mentioned,[5] one could suggest correspondences to further functions of the Self:

- the function of storage (e.g., of fats) can be compared to the function of memory; but, as Freud insists, this arises in the preconscious area of the psychical apparatus and does not belong to its "surface", which is characterised by the Pcpt.-Cs. System;
- the function of production (e.g., of hair or nails) can be compared to the production of defence mechanisms by the zone (itself, once again, preconscious or even unconscious) of the Ego;
- the function of emission (e.g., of sweat or pheromones) can be compared to the preceding function, since projection is one of the Ego's most archaic defence mechanisms; but it should be articulated with the particular topological configuration that I have called the sieve Skin-ego (*cf.* the case studies of Éléonore, pp. 71–72, and Gethsemane, pp. 199–210).

One could also compare certain tendencies (if not actual functions) of the Skin-ego with certain structural characteristics of the skin that are no longer functional. For instance, the fact that the skin has the largest surface area and is the heaviest of all the body's organs corresponds to the Ego's claim to envelop the whole of the psychical apparatus and weigh the most heavily in its functioning. Similarly, the tendency of both the inner and outer layers of the Skin-ego and the various psychical wrappings (sensory, muscular, rhythmic) to be interleaved can be seen as analogous to the enmeshing (described on pp. 17–18 above) of the layers that make up the epidermis, the dermis and the hypodermis. The complexity of the Ego and the multiplicity of its functions

---

[5] I am grateful to my colleague François Vincent, who is a psycho-physiologist, for having drawn my attention to these other functions.

might equally be likened to the existence of many major differences of structure and function between one point on the skin and another—for example, the density of the different types of gland or sensory corpuscles, etc.

A case of perverse masochism

Case study: Monsieur M.

The rather exceptional case of Monsieur M., which was reported by Michel de M'Uzan (1972, 1977) before the publication of my first article on the Skin-ego (1974), did not indicate psychoanalytic treatment and was simply the object of two private conversations with that colleague. Following my discussion of the eight functions of the Skin-ego, however, I can reinterpret it retrospectively by showing how almost all the functions I have listed (which will thus be indirectly validated) are damaged in serious cases of masochism, and how the subject resorts to perverse practices in order to restore them.

For Monsieur M., who was, not coincidentally, a radio electrician, the function of maintenance was artificially secured by inserting pieces of metal or glass all over his skin (thus creating a second skin that was not muscular but metallic), especially needles into the testicles and penis; by placing two steel rings at the tip of his prick and the root of his balls; and by cutting thongs out of the skin of his back so that he could be suspended from butcher's hooks while being sodomised by a sadist—a realisation of the mytheme of the hanged god, which we saw earlier (p. 53), in the Greek myth of Marsyas.

Failures of the containing function of the Skin-ego were visible not only in the innumerable scars of old burns and cuts found all over his body, but by flattening down certain outgrowths (the right breast torn off, the little toe of the right foot cut off with a metal saw), blocking up certain cavities (the navel filled with molten lead) and artificially enlarging certain orifices (the anus, the opening of the glans). The containing function was restored by the repeated creation of a wrapping of suffering, through the great variety, ingeniousness and brutality of instruments and techniques of torture: a perverse masochist has to keep the fantasy of ripped skin perpetually alive in order to re-appropriate the Skin-ego.

In such a case, the function of protective shield is abused to the point of no return, where the danger becomes fatal to the organism. Monsieur M. always pulled back safely from that point (he succumbed neither to a serious illness nor to madness) but his young wife, with whom he shared the discovery of these masochistic perversions, died of exhaustion as a result of the tortures she had undergone. Monsieur M. raised the stakes very high in thus dicing with death.

The function of individuating the Self is only achieved through suffering that is both physical (torture) and moral (humiliation); and the systematic insertion of non-organic substances under the skin and ingestion of repulsive matter, such as the partner's urine or excrement, show how fragile this function is: the distinction between one's own and other people's bodies is endlessly called into question.

Intersensoriality is unquestionably the best respected function, which explains why Monsieur M. was so well adjusted both professionally and socially.

The Skin-ego's functions of sexual excitation and libidinal recharging were also maintained and activated, but only at the price of the extreme sufferings outlined above. When Monsieur M. emerged from his sessions of perverse practices he was neither downcast nor depressed, nor even simply worn out: they invigorated him. He achieved orgasm not through penetration or being penetrated but at first through masturbation and later only through watching perverse scenes (for example seeing his wife undergoing the brutality of a sadist) while his whole skin was also being stimulated by torture. "The whole surface of my body could be stimulated by pain". "I ejaculated when the pain was at its height [...]. After that, it just hurt, that's all" (M'Uzan, 1977, pp. 133–134).

The function of registering traces was hyperactive. His whole body, apart from his face, was covered with innumerable tattoos; for example, on his buttocks it said "Fine pricks welcome here"; on his thighs and belly, "Long live masochism", "I am a living shite", "Use me like a female, you'll love it", etc., (ibid., p. 127). All these markings bore witness to a particular identification with women's anatomy, accompanied by an erogenisation of the whole surface of the skin and an invitation to others to enjoy orgasms by means of various orifices (the mouth, the anus) through which he himself had none.

Lastly, what I have called the toxic—i.e., the self-destructive—function of the Skin-ego reaches its peak. The skin becomes the source and the object of destructive processes. But the split between the life and death drives is only fleeting, whereas with psychotics it is definitive. At the point where the game with death was about to turn suicidal, the sadistic partner stopped the torture, libido made a "wild" recovery and Monsieur M. had his orgasm.

At least, he always had enough psychological flair to choose such partners: "The sadist always bottles out at the last moment", he confided (ibid., p. 137); and Michel de M'Uzan comments: "That's his wish for omnipotence talking". I would add to this: to the perverse masochist, seeking destructive omnipotence is the only way to accede to a phantasy of erotic omnipotence, which is needed in order to experience pleasure: no, the skin has not been totally torn off, the functions of the Skin-ego are not irreversibly destroyed and recovering them *in extremis* at the very moment of losing them produces a "jubilatory assumption" that is just as clear in its narcissistic economy as what Lacan describes in the mirror phase, but much more intense—because it is felt in both the body and the psyche.

I have shown, I hope, that these well-known defence mechanisms—the splitting of the drive, reversal, and turning against the self, the narcissistic hypercathexis of impaired psychical and organic functions—only work this effectively if they occur in an individual Skin-ego which has provisionally acquired its eight basic functions and which repeatedly relives the phantasy of the torn-off skin and the drama of losing almost all those functions in order to experience more intensely the joy of recovering them. The phantasy of having a skin of one's own, which is essential in order to develop psychical autonomy, is fundamentally fraught with guilt because of the prior phantasy that having one's own skin must mean one has taken it from someone else and that it is really best to let that person take it back in order to give them pleasure and ultimately to have pleasure oneself.

Wet wrappings

The pack

The "pack" is a technique in the treatment of seriously ill psychotics; it is based on the practice of wrapping in wet sheets used in French psychiatry in the nineteenth century but it also has analogies with the African ritual of therapeutic burial and the icy baths of Tibetan monks. It was introduced in France around 1960 by the American psychiatrist

Michael Woodbury and he added another aspect of treatment to the actual physical binding in cloths—the technique of keeping the patient closely surrounded by the group of medical staff. This addition offers an unpremeditated confirmation of the hypothesis put forward from the beginning of this study: the Skin-ego has a dual anaclisis—a biological one based on the surface of the body and a social one based on the support of a united group of people attentive to what the person is going through at that moment.

The nursing staff wrap the patient, wearing underclothes or naked, according to preference, in pieces of wet, cold cloth. First they bind each of the four limbs separately, then the whole body, including the limbs but not the head. The patient is then immediately wrapped in a blanket which allows them to warm up again, more or less quickly. They remain lying down for three-quarters of an hour and are free to choose whether or not to verbalise what they are feeling—in any case, according to staff who have tried it themselves, the sensations and emotions experienced during the pack are so intense and extraordinary that words can barely express them. The nurses touch the wrapped-up patient with their hands, questioning them by their gaze, and respond to anything they say; they are eager and anxious to know what is going on inside the patient. The pack creates such a powerful group feeling that it arouses jealousy among other staff members. This endorses another of my theories, which is that the bodily wrapping is an unconscious psychical organising factor in groups (Anzieu, 1981b). After a relatively brief period of anxiety arising from the sense of being entirely surrounded in coldness, the wrapped-up person experiences a feeling of omnipotence, of physical and psychical completeness. I believe this is a regression to the original limitless psychical Self, whose existence is hypothesised by a number of psychoanalysts and which is said to correspond to a dissociation of the psychical from the bodily Ego, similar to that experienced by members of a group or by mystics or creative artists (see Anzieu, 1980a). This sense of well-being is short-lived, but it lasts longer each time the pack is repeated (the complete treatment, like its psychoanalytic model, may take years, at a rate of three sessions per week).

The pack gives the patient the feeling of a double bodily wrapping—a thermal wrapping (first cold, then warm, due to peripheral vasodilation resulting from the contact with coldness) which controls the body's internal temperature and a tactile wrapping (the wet, tightly bound cloths that adhere to the whole skin). This temporarily reconstitutes the patient's Ego as separate from all others and at the same time continuous with them, which is one of the topographical characteristics of the Skin-ego. Claudie Cachard (1981), a practitioner of the pack, has referred in this connection to "membranes of life" (see also Diane de Loisy, 1981).

The pack may also be used with psychotic children and with deaf-mute children, whose only access to significant communication with other people is through touch. The pack offers them an "emergency wrapping" that gives structure and takes the place, for a while, of their pathological wrappings. Through this experience, they can give up part of their defensive use of agitated movement and loud noises, and feel unified and immobile. Yet at first they resist being wrapped up: the attempt to immobilise these children completely arouses in them mortal panic and exceptional violence.

Three observations

The experience of the pack leads me to make three observations. First, an infant's body seems to be programmed to experience a containing wrapping; if the right sensory materials are not available, it must find a way of experiencing it with whatever else is at its disposal—this explains the pathological substitute wrappings made of incoherent noises or motor agitation, which are meant not to bring about a controlled discharge of instinctual energy but to ensure the adaptive survival of the organism. Second, the paradoxical resistances one finds among carers and educators derives from the difference in levels of structuring between their bodily Ego and that of the child, and their fear of falling into a regressive state where that difference disappears and mental confusion results. Third, therapy based on "emergency wrappings" (packs, massages, bioenergetics or encounter groups) has only a temporary effect. It is the extreme version of a phenomenon that can be identified in normal people who periodically feel the need to use physical experiences to reconfirm their basic sense of having a Skin-ego. It also illustrates the necessity, in severe cases of deprivation, of developing compensatory substitute configurations.

CHAPTER EIGHT

Disturbances of basic sensori-motor distinctions

In this chapter, I shall examine just one basic sensorimotor distinction, the distinction between respiratory fullness and empti- ness. Other oppositions will be analysed in Part III. The reader may also wish to consult my article "Sur la confusion primaire de l'animé et de l'inanimé. Un cas de triple méprise" [On primary confusion between the animate and the inanimate: a case of triple misunderstanding] (Anzieu, 1982b).

On the confusion of respiratory fullness and emptiness

Prometheus stole fire from heaven to give it to the human race. In revenge, the gods of Olympus sent Pandora, a woman of striking beauty, charm, seductive speech, and manual skill, whom they had cre- ated after the image of goddesses and adorned with every gift and every guile, to be the wife of his brother Epimetheus. The latter entrusted to his wife's keeping, instructing her never to open it, an earthenware jar filled with air in which all the evils of the world were enclosed. Pandora was curious: she opened the lid, the evils flew out and ever since their breath has spread throughout the earth. This myth, after which I have named the patient whose case I am about to report, surely has much to teach us about certain patients who feel the need to hold back the breath in their lungs for fear it may spread a hatred that would destroy everyone around them. Originally, this hatred is directed at their mother who, depressed and silent when they were very young, failed to provide them either with vital respiratory exchange or with the flow of speech that is carried on the air.

We know, indeed, that the respiratory reflex is triggered at birth by the baby's experience of having its whole body massaged by the contractions of the womb and the grasp of the vagina; maintaining this reflex depends on the repetition of the full-body stimulation of breastfeeding or daily care. Respiratory exchange with the physical environment is dependent on tactile exchange with the human environment. This dependency is transformed through the exchange of sound, which uses the air as a support for words. A concept of "respiratory introjection", using this term in different ways which I do not intend to go into here, was developed by Otto Fenichel in 1913 and later by the Kleinian Clifford Scott. A function of primal communication is supported anaclitically on the respiratory function of self-preservation, at the time that the Skin-ego is beginning to be formed. To quote one of the findings of Margaret Ribble (1944) from her study of six hundred infants: in the new-born baby, "breathing is shallow, rapid, and frequently irregular" (Ribble, 1944, p. 629). It is automatically and definitively stimulated by sucking and physical contact with the mother: "Infants who do not suck vigorously seldom breathe deeply and regularly. Those who are not held in the arms sufficiently, particularly if they are bottle-fed babies, also develop gastro-intestinal disorders. They become air-swallowers and frequently develop what is popularly known as colic. They may have trouble with defecation, or they may vomit frequently" (ibid., p. 631).

A detailed, but unfortunately very old, review of the research of psychoanalysts and specialists in psychosomatic medicine on respiratory disorders can be found in an article by Jacques-Alfred Gendrot and Paul-Claude Racamier entitled "Fonction respiratoire et oralité" [Orality and the respiratory function] (1951). Doubtless for reasons of psychoanalytic orthodoxy, the authors stress the link between the nervous system's regulation of the two functions of breathing and digestion; they privilege the oral relation over that of tactile exchanges and neglect to take into account the effect of early flaws in the bodily pre-Ego (which I prefer to call the Skin-ego) in causing respiratory problems. On the other hand, they make a wise distinction between problems of respiratory absorption and expulsion. They show that an inability to breathe out is related to an interiorised bad object: "The asthmatic is condemned to be unable to expel what he has taken in aggressively" (1951, p. 470). In all cases of respiratory retention, they point out an urge to remain full and a terror of emptying out.

In a study that is more theoretical than clinical, *Le Stade du respir* [*The breathing phase*] (1978), Jean-Louis Tristani takes Freud to task for neglecting respiration in his theoretical reflections, though he is well aware of it in his clinical observations (Dora's nervous cough; the primal scene misunderstood both as panting and as suckling;[1] and his reference to crying as leading to the first inter-human bond in the "Project" (1950a) of 1895). Tristani proposes several interesting hypotheses:

• Along with feeding, breathing is one of the self-preservation drives and thus one of the Ego drives, upon which the sexual drives will later lean (though Tristani fails to describe the nasal mucus as an erogenous zone).
• Whimpering is to breathing what sucking is to the orality of feeding.
• The vital dilemma "It's me or you" underlies certain severe respiratory problems (Tristani quotes a psychotic patient of François Roustang's who said "I breathe in as little air as possible so as not to take it from my parents; I must suffocate so that they can breathe").
• There are two types of confusion between the respiratory and digestive systems. Inhaling corresponds to oral ingestion and exhaling to anal expulsion, but inhaling and exhaling take place through the same orifice, which alternates as entry-point and exit-point (the respiratory function is circular, consisting of a coming-and-going, whereas the digestive function is linear, with entry and exit at opposite ends of the body). The first type of confusion is vomiting, in which the digestive system acts on the model of respiration: the mouth ingests and then expels what it has eaten as though it were breathing food. The second type of confusion is aerophagy: in this case the respiratory system functions like digestion: it eats, swallows,

---

[1] *Translator's note*: Anzieu here implies an effective wordplay between the near-homonyms "halètement" [panting] and "allaitement" [suckling], which of course cannot represent an equivalent in Freud's German original.

and digests air—which causes stomach aches or colic. In fact there are two respiratory orifices, the nose and the mouth; one can breathe through either of them, or make the air follow a circuit, entering by one and leaving by the other, as is seen, for example, in inveterate smokers.

Case study: Pandora

Pandora sent me a letter which was a cry for help. She was desperate: if psychoanalysis could not do anything for her, there was no way forward. She felt alienated from her own life; she was very frightened of her suicidal temptations. She had terrible nightmares, in which she knew she was about to be killed and did nothing to prevent it, or in which she was raped, suffocated or drowned.

On her first visit, I beheld a tall, beautiful woman. She looked round my office, with its walls covered in bookshelves, files heaped up everywhere and fairly low ceilings. She said she felt hemmed in by this room, that it "lacked volume", though of course, in a different sense, the place had rather too many volumes; in this way she presented me right from the start with her problem, which concerned the fundamental distinction between emptiness and over-fullness. She concluded that "it could never work" with me. She was perceptibly short of breath, but did not put this into words. I responded immediately with a quite lengthy interpretation which was a construction. I put it to her that in my office she was reliving her first encounter with a person from whom she had once expected everything; if she felt constricted, this was because the person who looked after her when she was small either did not give her enough free space or missed something essential in her desires, thoughts or anxieties; and so she herself had long been trying to find limits within which she could recognise and find herself. At these words, her breathing relaxed. She confirmed my interpretation: both the two attitudes I had described were true—the first was her grandmother's, the second her mother's. At the end of our interview, she decided to enter treatment with me. I offered her a course of face-to-face psychoanalytic psychotherapy once a week for an hour and she accepted. During these sessions, Pandora would remain silent and immobile for a long time; her gaze was averted, but every so often she would suddenly look up, to reassure herself that my eyes were fixed upon her and I was still paying attention. If I got tired or fell silent and stopped communicating my theories about what was wrong with her—anxiety dreams, conflicts at work, romantic problems that cropped up during the week—or if I stopped looking at her or thinking about her, she would jump up and leave, slamming the door behind her. I inferred from this that her mother must have been indifferent, giving her neither a word nor a look. She confirmed that her mother fed and cared for her satisfactorily, with the help of her own mother (Pandora's maternal grandmother), but added that the rest of the time her mother did not communicate with her, would turn her back on her and spent hours standing in silence on the balcony of the flat, gazing into space. It appeared that Pandora's fear nowadays, in moments when she was in thrall to a powerful desire to destroy herself (by taking an overdose, using her uncle's revolver or cutting her genitals with sharp bits of glass), reproduced her terror, long ago, that her mother would drag her down into the void: this is what Bion (1967) calls the "nameless dread" or, in André Green's terms (1984, Chapter Six), the identification with "the dead mother" and pursuit of union with her in a mutual accomplishment not of the life drives but of the Nirvana principle.

Pandora challenged me to understand her, and tried to trap me in the following dilemma: if I was silent, waiting for her to contribute material that would get me on the right track, this showed that I was incapable of guessing what was obvious to her; if I spoke up, she blamed me for always missing the point. We did get into a working relationship eventually, however, as little by little she accepted that we could breathe and talk together.

Whenever Pandora had been unable to speak for a whole session, she would phone or write to me afterwards to explain. I later came to realise that for her air was a medium that carries bad parts of the Self which are split off and projected, and so she found it easier to write than speak. I always replied to her letters, either by letter or orally at the next session. As for me, little by little and through trial and error, I went on with the vital task of creating a "bath" of interpretations to immerse her in, and here and there I got things right. Whenever I did, she acknowledged it at once and, by recounting a memory, a dream or a recent disappointment, she gradually set out the cumulative series of traumas that had scarred her early childhood and caused her to create a happy imaginary world in which she could live, while glaring through a kind of windowpane at the real world, knowing at any moment she might have to intervene by defying or deriding it. More and more frequently, in our sessions, she manifested moments of breathlessness.

Physiologists consider laughter, sobbing, and vomiting to be modified breathing movements. By observing patients in psychotherapy we can confirm the importance of these responses as three different modalities of respiratory identification. In treating Pandora, I encountered the first two of these and I also suspected her of hiding the third—vomiting—from me. Let's begin with laughter. Often, at the end of a session in which Pandora had succeeded, with the help of my interpretations, in overcoming successively an asthmatic problem with her breathing and a speech block, she would burst out laughing and say (for example) that she felt very alive, that all those blockages did not stop her from enjoying her body, her friendships, and her artistic hobbies, that I had let her make a fool of me, etc.—and I generally joined in this laughter, equally relieved to see she had recovered a normal breathing pattern. Here one could see how a patient may identify with the other person who reflects back to them an image of "natural" psychophysiological functioning, giving them confidence that they too can function naturally. Now for sobbing.

During a session in which I focused my analytic work on certain of her defence mechanisms—withdrawing communication, keeping absolutely still, bottling up affects—Pandora referred to a scene of conflict with her father that she had already recounted briefly and without emotion. I pointed out to her that she was simply reporting the facts and not her feelings. Suddenly she began to cry and was soon close to sobbing. She recovered the two emotions at play—the intense humiliation that had overwhelmed her and a sense of wickedness resulting from the parricidal impulse that had suddenly and powerfully entered her consciousness. This affective recollection was accompanied by an intensification of the transference. Pandora accused me of cruelty, making her relive these unbearable emotions and forcing her to break a fundamental family rule: children were not allowed to cry. Nothing could be more dangerous, then, than the free association required by psychoanalysis, for it brought wicked impulses into the open air where, like the contents of the jar released by the Pandora, they were free to spread far and wide and inflict their evil spells on everyone. Some patients go so far as to sob aloud. In my experience, this reaction is connected to the activation of a dual phantasy—that psychoanalysis can only do them harm and that the air is the medium for murderous desires to be spread abroad.

Little by little, Pandora's treatment progressed and a proper psychotherapeutic process took shape. But our sessions remained difficult. Here is an example of a "session" which was exceptional in two ways—first, by its dramatic intensity, and second because I had to conduct it outside the classical psychoanalytic framework. One Sunday morning, Pandora phoned me from her holiday home. Her voice was almost inaudible. Before she left she had told me that she had just become pregnant—she and her husband were very happy with this news (the progress of her treatment having enabled her to marry and become a mother). Exhausted by her condition and acting on advice to get plenty of sun and fresh air, she was taking advantage of a fortnight's break from work. But since the previous day she had been suffering from an asthma attack which was getting worse all the time. Her respiratory anxiety was redoubled by an anxiety about what to decide for the best: she had been told to avoid the drugs she usually took for these attacks, as they might endanger the baby's health or even its life; but if she did not take them, her own life was at risk—she was suffocating. Her doctor had left this decision up to her, advising her to go to hospital and maybe even think about terminating the pregnancy. She was distraught. I kept having to ask her to repeat what she said, as I could barely hear her. Then I offered an interpretation of the structure of the dilemma—"the mother or the child", "either she survives and the other person dies, or the other lives and she will die"—as being linked back to her own relationship with her mother: "If I live, I will cause my mother to die". Pandora corrected me: "It was just the opposite. For years, I vowed to disappear in place of my mother, who was always talking about dying. I thought that if anyone had to die, it should be me and that I must die so that she could live". Thus, not breathing was a way to leave the air available to her mother. We now launched into a session by phone. I told her this, making clear that I was at her disposal (by contrast to her mother, who had not been). Remembering what a difficult birth she had

had, and linking it to the future birth of her child, I put it to her that as a mother now expecting a much-desired child, she nevertheless felt compelled to repeat her mother's resistance to having a baby she did not desire. Pandora replied: "There's some truth in that. At night, I find myself thinking that I won't even manage to do as well as my mother, I won't even be able to give birth". Then I asked her to tell me in detail what she knew about her own birth. She said she could not possibly speak at this length. I went on encouraging her, pointing out that it was just after she had told me she was incapable of carrying through a pregnancy, as her mother had, that she said she could not possibly communicate with me. In a more audible voice, Pandora said: "I'll try".

She proceeded to give a very full account, contrary to her usual habit, giving me fresh details of the event which she had only referred to before in a roundabout way. She had been born with the cord around her neck, was given up for dead, had turned black and they had had to shake and slap her repeatedly before she began to breathe at last. This speech was actually a dialogue, in which I echoed each one of her sentences back to her; in other words, got her going, in my turn, with shakes and stimulation which were the verbal equivalent of the tactile stimuli she had lacked early in her life (though I did not communicate this similarity to her). I pointed out that her breathing was perfectly capable of functioning and only needed the right impetus to start it off, and that the fact she had survived was a clear proof that she had been and still was capable of breathing, both then and now.

As our conversation went on, I began to relax (I'm sure I don't need to say that her phone-call had worried me profoundly) and I could feel her relaxing too. While continuing to pour out my interpretations aloud to her, my thoughts turned to myself, and I phantasised that I was a mother giving birth to her baby daughter and giving her air to breathe.

After an hour, I asked Pandora how her breathing was— "Better"—whether we could stop—"Yes"—and what she was going to do—"I have made my decision: I will go into hospital but I won't take any medicine that might harm the baby".

There were two or three more crises during her pregnancy, in which again she felt she could not carry it to term, but I now knew enough elements of the story to be able to pick up, develop, and complete my interpretations in the following way: she was obeying her mother's curse telling her she could not be a wife and mother; she knew she was committing *lèse-majesté* by wanting to be her mother's equal, stealing away her fertility; she was afraid of being defenceless against the temptation to reject her child as her mother had rejected her as a baby. These persecutory episodes were triggered by dreams whose existence I was soon able to sense in advance, so that I could draw them out of her and interpret their content.

The birth was straightforward. Pandora experienced a true honeymoon with her baby, whom she breastfed, occasionally inter-cut by sudden storms in which she feared the worst disasters; but by dint of persisting with our psychotherapeutic work we cleared these away each time. She also had more asthma attacks, but they were less intense and less serious. I now had a whole grid of interpretations to tackle them. Her transference developed from paranoid mistrust and schizoid withdrawal to a half-narcissistic, half-oedipal seduction and the gradual, though far from smooth, progress towards a transference love directed, through me, towards the paternal imago.

This fragment of a case-study illustrates a particular psychogenetic point: if the mother fails to cathect her new-born baby libidinally and narcissistically and this is expressed in an avoidance of physical con-tact, the child will be predisposed to respiratory problems, because the respiratory system will not have been properly aroused at birth or through stimulation of the baby's skin over the first few weeks. My description of Pandora's case also illustrates a point of technique. Psychoanalysts avoid touching their patients and being touched physi-cally by them,[2] apart from the traditional hand-shake. But they must find words that mean the same, symbolically, as an act of touching and can exercise the functions of the patient's bodily and psychical Egos which, in the past, did not receive enough stimulation to develop. Restoring

---

[2] In certain extreme cases, a minimal level of touching may be allowed, exceptionally and as a transitory measure, in order to rebuild the anaclitic support of the Ego on the skin; the patient may, for example, lay their head on the analyst's shoulder for a moment at the end of the session (*cf.* the treatment of Mme Oggi, as reported by Raymond Kaspi, 1979).

primary tactile communication in this symbolic form can help a patient regain the confidence that it is possible to have communication—not with everyone, which would be a delusion of omnipotence and inter-changeability, but with certain carefully chosen and suitably invited interlocutors. In actual fact, the repetition compulsion tends to cause fragile individuals to attach themselves to partners who reproduce the deficiencies, traumas, and paradoxes of their early environment and who thus extend the pathologies they originally experienced. I have suggested that this process can be called "negative attachment". The task of the psychoanalyst is not to fill the patient's narcissistic gaps nor to supply a real love-object but to help develop in the patient enough knowledge of themselves and other people to be able to seek, find, and maintain (outside the analysis) relationships with personalities capa-ble of satisfying their bodily needs and their psychical desires. Mental health, Bowlby said, consists of choosing to live with people who do not make us ill...

CHAPTER NINE

Impairments of the structure of the Skin-ego in narcissistic personalities and borderline cases

The structural difference between narcissistic personalities and borderline cases

Since the 1960s there has been a problem in nosology, clinical practice, and psychoanalytic technique concerning whether it is possible to distinguish between "narcissistic disturbances of the personality" (themselves quite often confused with "character neuroses") and "borderline cases" (which in turn are sometimes confused with "pre-psychotic" cases). In the USA, there was a lively debate between Heinz Kohut (1971), who supported this differentiation, and Otto Kernberg (1975), who opposed it.

Briefly summarised, the debate seems to be as follows.[1] Borderline cases are subject to regressions similar to transitory psychotic episodes

---

[1] In France, a detailed account of the debate can be found in two studies by Jean Bergeret (1974, pp. 52–59 and 76; 1975, pp. 283–285). Bergeret's position is closer to Kohut's than to Kernberg's. He shows that a borderline state cannot be considered as a "neurosis" (even a narcissistic one) and that the extent of narcissistic deficiency increases from the narcissistic personality to the borderline case and then to the pre-psychotic case (this term referring in fact to a case of psychosis that has not yet been decompensated). In the view of Bergeret, the true disorder of primary narcissism is psychosis; the true disorder of

in which recovery, always possible though often difficult, requires the patient to encounter an auxiliary Ego—either in their life or in their psychoanalytic sessions. This auxiliary Ego maintains the normal operation of the psychical functions that have been disrupted or even temporarily destroyed by unconscious attacks from the hateful parts of the patient's own psyche, which the latter thinks of as external to the Self. In borderline states, the feeling of a continuous Self is easily lost.

Narcissistic disturbances of the personality affect a more advanced feeling, that of the cohesion of the Self. This is related to a failure of the Self to develop properly. According to Kernberg, the Self is derived from early object relations that have been interiorised. For Kohut, it results from the internal vicissitudes of narcissism, which follows a line of development somewhat separate from the object relation, passing through the particular structure of relations to "Self-objects". In these relations, the differentiation between Self and objects is deficient: they are cathected narcissistically (whereas object relations are cathected libidinally); they can be psychoanalysed by recognising two kinds of specifically narcissistic transference—mirror transference and idealising transference. Patients suffering from narcissistic disturbances retain fairly autonomous psychical functioning and do not lose the ability—except at moments of acute narcissistic wounding, but these pass off, especially if another person behaves empathetically towards them—to tolerate delayed satisfaction of desire, to bear moral suffering or to identify with the object.

Kernberg, by contrast, distinguishes a large range of borderline states, according to the seriousness of the character pathology involved. These various degrees of borderline state also include associated narcissistic disturbances, which are themselves very varied, ranging from normal narcissism through forms of narcissistic personality and narcissistic character neuroses to pathological narcissistic structures, defined by the libidinal cathexis of a pathological Self—the grandiose Self, which is a fusion of the ideal Self, the ideal object and the current images of the Self. The function of the grandiose Self is to defend against the archaic images of an internal fragmentation of a destructive

---

secondary (relational) narcissism is the borderline state; neurosis does of course include narcissistic failures but it is not in itself a "disorder of narcissism". I am indebted to Jacques Palaci for his help in disentangling these points.

Self and a persecutory object, which feature in early object-relations, cathected both libidinally and aggressively.

The topographical perspective into which my concept of the Skin-ego fits could bring a further argument to bear on the difference between narcissistic personalities and borderline states. The "normal" Skin-ego does not cover the whole of the psychical apparatus and it has two faces, external and internal, between which there is a space available for some free play. Both the incomplete covering and the space between tend to disappear in narcissistic personalities. These patients want to feel that their own psychical wrapping is enough and that they do not need the common skin with another person which signals and provokes a dependence on them. But they do not quite possess the means to fulfil this ambition: their Skin-ego has begun to form but it is still quite fragile. It needs strengthening. Two operations are required. The first consists in getting rid of the space between the two faces of the Skin-ego, between external stimuli and internal excitations, between the image the person gives of themselves and the image reflected back to them; their wrapping becomes solid, turning into a centre, even a double centre, of interest: for both the person themselves and for others, it tends to envelop the whole of the psyche. Thus extended and solidified, the wrapping creates certainty but lacks flexibility and the most minor narcissistic wound will tear a hole in it. The other operation aims to reinforce this cemented personal Skin-ego from the outside with a symbolic maternal skin, like Zeus's aegis, or the dazzling gladrags worn by young, often anorexic models, which recreate their narcissism for a brief moment in the face of the unconscious threat that the psychical container is crumbling away. In the narcissist's phantasy, the mother does not share the common skin but gives it away to the child, who puts it on triumphantly: this generous gift from the mother (she strips off her own skin in order to give her child protection and strength in life) confers a potential blessing: the child imagines itself called to a heroic destiny (which may indeed lead it to achieve great things). The double wrapping—its own plus that of its mother—is gleaming and ideal; it provides the narcissistic personality with the delusion of being invulnerable and immortal. In the psyche it is represented by the phenomenon of the "double wall", which I shall illustrate in a moment. In the masochistic phantasy, the cruel mother only pretends to give her skin to the child; it is actually a poisoned gift and her evil plan is to get back the child's singular Skin-ego, which will stick to it, by tearing it away, causing the child agony, in order to restore the phantasy of the common skin and the dependence that goes with it; the child would then get back its mother's love at the cost of losing its independence and in exchange for consenting to moral and physical wounds.

In narcissistic personalities, whose Skin-ego is organised as a double wall, the relationship of container to content is preserved and the psychical Ego remains integrated in the bodily Ego. The activity of thought—and indeed creative psychical work—remain possible.

By contrast, in borderline states, the damage is not limited to the periphery: the whole structure of the Skin-ego is affected. Its two faces form one, but this single face is twisted in the manner of the strip described by the mathematician Moebius, to which Lacan was the first to compare the Ego:[2] this is what causes them difficulty in distinguishing between what comes from the inside and what comes from the outside. One part of the Pcpt.-Cs. system, normally located at the interface between the outside world and inner reality, has come unstuck from that position and been changed into an external observer (borderline patients feel that they are witnessing the functioning of their body and mind from the outside, like disinterested spectators on their own lives). But the part of the Pcpt.-Cs. system that survives as an interface ensures that the subject is sufficiently adapted to reality not to become psychotic. The production of phantasies and their circulation among those close to the subject is lessened. As regards the affects that constitute the existential core of the person, the difficulty of containing them due to the twisted nature of the Skin-ego sends them from the centre to the periphery, where they take over some of the places vacated by the centrifugal shift of part of the Pcpt.-Cs. system; here they become unconscious and encysted and break down into fragments of hidden Self whose disruptive return to consciousness is dreaded like ghostly apparitions. This leads to a second paradox resulting from the Moebius-strip structure: just as the outside becomes an inside and then an outside again, over and over, so the poorly-contained content becomes a container that contains poorly. Finally, the central place of the Self, deserted by those primary affects that were too violent—distress, terror,

---

[2] According to Lacan, the Ego normally has this structure, which perverts and alienates it. In my experience, this Moebius-strip configuration is specifically typical of borderline states.

hatred—becomes an empty space and the anxiety of this central inner emptiness is what such patients complain most about, unless they have managed to fill it with the imaginary presence of an object or an ideal person (a cause, a master, an impossible passion, an ideology, etc.).

A literary example of a narcissistic personality

By way of illustration of the narcissistic personality, I shall take not a case-study but a literary allegory, in the form of a novella, *La Invención de Morel* [*The Invention of Morel*], by the Argentine writer, friend and collaborator of Borges, Adolfo Bioy Casares. The narrator has taken refuge on a desert island and confides to his diary what he has been told:

> The island [...] is the focal point of a mysterious disease that attacks the outside of the body and then works inward. The nails drop off the fingers and toes; the hair falls out, the skin and the corneas of the eyes die, and the body lives on for one week, or two at the most. The crew of a ship that had stopped there were skinless, hairless, without nails on their fingers or toes—all dead, of course—when they were found by the Japanese cruiser *Namura*. (1992 [1940, 1964] p. 10)

In the end—in every sense of the word—this disease of the bodily wrapping reaches the narrator as well. On the penultimate page of his journal, he notes:

> I am losing my sight. My sense of touch has gone; my skin is falling off; my sensations are ambiguous, painful; I try not to think about them.
>   When I stood in front of the screen of mirrors, I discovered that I have no beard, I am bald. I have no nails on my fingers or toes, and my flesh is tinged with rose. (ibid., p. 102)

This corrosion occurs in two stages, first attacking the epidermis, then the dermis.

This confirms my idea of the existence of a double psychical skin, one outside and one inside, whose relationship I shall elucidate presently. This ever-deeper attack on the skin forms the leitmotiv around which Bioy Casares's novella composes its variations. The first variation: after suffering a miscarriage of justice, the narrator has escaped from a life sentence and taken refuge on this small abandoned island, which becomes his eternal prison. He presents himself as a persecuted man, flayed alive in perpetuity. The frustrations and traumas that befall him in this inhospitable place constantly impinge on his fragile Skin-ego. In the second variation, the island itself is described as an inadequate symbolic skin, which fails to cover, contain or protect its inhabitant; the tides submerge him, the swamps drag him down, the mosquitoes exasperate him, the trees are mouldering, the swimming pool is crawling with snakes, toads, and water-insects, the vegetation is consumed in its own profusion and the foodstuffs he finds in what he calls the museum—in fact it was once a hotel—have all gone bad. A third version of this theme of cutaneous decomposition gradually encroaching on the inner life of both body and mind takes a philosophical-theological form. What preoccupies the narrator's thoughts, when he is not absorbed in the immediate struggle for survival, is the question of eternal life: can consciousness, which is the inner life of the body, survive after death without even a partial survival of the surface of the body? How can the destruction of that surface be kept within bounds?

This attack on first the outer and then the inner Skin-egos is compared, in Bioy Casares' novella, to the experience of the uncanny, when the narrator suffers an error of perception and disturbance of belief. He thought he was safe from pursuit on his desert island. But from the first page of his journal—and this is why he decides to keep one—he goes from surprise to terror. The island suddenly rings out to the sound of old tunes pouring forth from an invisible phonograph. The "museum" is populated by servants and weird, snobbish holidaymakers dressed in the fashion of twenty-odd years earlier. The swimming-pool, which had appeared unusable, comes alive with their frolics; they take strolls around the upper part of the island. He keeps out of their way, but hears and notes down snatches of their conversations. While the island seems inhospitable and its constructions strange to the narrator, the relaxed behaviour of these men and women shows that they feel perfectly safe there. At first he is afraid they will see him, apprehend him and turn him over to the authorities. But none of them seem bothered about him. Later he will be seized by a much more fundamental anxiety: despite many blunders which ought to have called attention to him, despite his attempts to make contact with a woman he falls in love with, who looks like a gypsy and keeps her distance from the group, and despite the fact that they really are alive, these apparitions show nothing but indifference towards him. "Her composure was not altered; she ignored me, as if I were invisible" (ibid., p. 28). The more familiar they become to him, the stranger they seem. He believes in their existence. Yet these "ghosts" do not believe in his, to the point where he feels terrified, cornered, caught between murder or madness.

The narrator eventually realises that the crisis of belief is his. "Now it seems that the real situation is not the one I described on the foregoing pages; the situation I am living is not what I think it is" (ibid., p. 58). In fact he is witnessing a scene in which Morel, the day before he set sail for home, explained his invention to the others. Unbeknownst to them, on this island which he has equipped with three kinds of apparatus (to capture their images, save them and project them) Morel has been filming and recording them, not only in sight and sound, like cinema or television, but also images of touch, heat, smell and taste. If, as the British empiricist philosophers maintain, consciousness is simply the sum of our sensations—and this is, I believe, presupposed by Morel's reasoning—then images that reproduce the sensory totality of an individual will acquire a soul. Not only will a member of the audience seeing them projected experience each particular individual as real but the actors who are filmed in this way will experience one another as alive and conscious during the projections. Morel, the woman he has loved in vain and all the people who were with them during that week on the island will therefore live for eternity. Each high tide will recharge the engines hidden safely in the basements of the museum and trigger the life-size projection of the film of their stay on the island. Thus the apparitions that so frightened the narrator were nothing but the images or ghosts of real beings, the spectres of people who existed, no doubt, twenty years earlier, when he was a child—idols, in other words.[3] Morel's invention is doubly allegorical. It is a literary allegory—after all, is a novel not a machine to fabricate characters by endowing them with qualities so tangible that the reader believes they are real people? And it is a metapsychological allegory: with its three types of apparatus for

---

[3] The ancient Greeks explained our ability to see objects by the fact that an invisible film-like layer detaches itself from them and carries their form to the eye which receives their impression. An "idol" (from the verb *idein*, to see) is the immaterial double of the object that makes it possible for us to see it.

perceiving, recording and projecting, Morel's machine is a metaphorical variant of Freud's psychical apparatus—the Pcpt.-Cs system is split in two, the recording corresponds to the preconscious, and the unconscious is… forgotten. By contrast to the fragility of human skin, which can be eaten away or riddled with holes, Morel's machine represents the utopian idea of an incorruptible skin. The narrator, whose Skin-ego is so fragile, is fascinated by the ideality of that film-like surface and, rather than loving real beings, he prefers to adore their idols—which is true idol-worship.

Morel's machine filmed Morel and his companions for a week and it will project episodes from that week over and over again. But in order to be able to transfer their living, conscious characteristics into the projected images, the recording robbed the real people of them. "And then I happened to remember that some people are afraid of having their images reproduced because they believe that their souls will be transferred to the images and they will die. […] the theory that the images have souls seems to demand, as a basic condition, that the transmitters lose theirs when they are photographed by the machines" (ibid., p. 94). Through an "imprudence" (ibid., p. 92), as he puts it, but more through a logical necessity inherent in his belief, the narrator decides to test this out on himself. He places his left hand in front of the recording apparatus and soon afterwards his real hand withers away; but the image of his hand, fully intact, is preserved in the museum archives where, every so often, he goes to see it projected. This shows him exactly how Morel and his friends died—from having been recorded for all eternity. Morel's cynicism had made him the only one of the group who knew this and desired it: "Such a monstrosity seems to be in keeping with the man who, following his own idea, organizes a collective death and determines, of his own accord, the common destiny of all his friends" (ibid., p. 94). The delusion of immortality is accompanied—this does not surprise me—by the group delusion: with the help of Morel's invention,

> Man will select a lonely, pleasant place, will go there with the persons he loves most, and will endure in an intimate paradise. A single garden, if the scenes to be eternalized are recorded at different moments, will contain innumerable paradises, and each group of inhabitants, unaware of the others, will move about simultaneously, almost in the same places, without colliding. (ibid., pp. 82–83)

The narrator, who is Morel's double, takes his invention and this delusion to its logical conclusion. He is in love with the immortal Faustine, but she can no longer perceive him. So, after enormous efforts, he learns how to control the machine. He projects all the scenes in which Faustine is present and re-records them, putting himself into the picture as though he were walking beside her and engaging her in an amorous conversation. He is certain to die of this; already his skin is beginning to drop off. But he puts this new footage into the projection machine, in place of the old film, and it will now be projected eternally. His journal and his life end with the wish that someone might invent an even more perfect machine, which could make him enter Faustine's consciousness—a machine capable of deleting all differences between perception and phantasy, between a representation coming from the outside and one from the inside.

The phantasy of the double wall

Delusions of immortality, the group delusion, the delusion of love, the delusion that characters in a novel are real people—all these are part of the problematics of narcissism. And the necessity of hypercathecting the narcissistic wrapping in such ways appears to be the defensive counterpart to the phantasy of a fleshless skin: faced with the danger of constant attacks from both outside and inside, one must replenish and refurbish a Skin-ego which is insecure in its two functions of protective shield and psychical container. The topographical solution consists of closing the gap between the external and internal faces of the Skin-ego and imagining the interface as a double wall. As long as this solution remains "imaginary" in the fullest sense—i.e., it produces an image of oneself that is false but reassuring—the patient remains in the terrain of neurosis, but if the solution consists of a real transformation of the Skin-ego, it leads to autism, or psychogenetic mutism, as Annie Anzieu has attempted to explain in her article "De la chair au verbe" [From flesh to the word]:

> The external cutaneous wrapping of the body actually is "pierced" by the organs of the senses, the anus and the urethral orifice. One could hypothesise that the sensitivity of these orifices, each orientated towards the outside of the body by the object that uses it as a passageway, causes confusion in the very young child: the internal

contact of the body and its contents with the cutaneous wall that holds it in is not differentiated from cutaneous contacts with objects in the external world. This is as much as to say that the child is penetrated by visual images, sounds, and smells and becomes itself their container and passageway, just as it does for faeces, urine, milk or its own crying. The internal wrapping may also be attacked and punctured by object-perceptions. Certain states of anxiety can turn this phantasmatic phenomenon into a sense of permanent persecution, which violates and agitates the infant's physical insides, so that it defends itself by shutting all the orifices it can control, by any means possible. (A. Anzieu, 1978, p. 129)

It is curious, indeed, to note that the narrator of *The Invention of Morel*, who fails to differentiate between the outer and inner surfaces, experiences the delusion of a double wall. After he discovers, through a basement window, the hermetically sealed underground room where the machines are kept, he manages to get inside by breaking a hole with an iron bar. More than the sight of the machines, which are standing idle, he is struck by "ecstatic, prolonged amazement: the walls, the ceiling, the floor were of blue tile and even the air itself (in that room where the only contact with the outside world was a high skylight obscured by the branches of a tree) had the deep azure transparency of a waterfall's foam" (ibid., p. 17). Once he has discovered what Morel's intention was, he goes back to the machines to try to understand and master their workings. They begin to move; he examines them; but in vain, for he is unable to gain access to the mechanism. He gazes round the room and suddenly feels disorientated.

I looked for the opening I had made. It was not there. [...] I stepped to one side to see if it persisted. [...] I held out my arms and felt all the walls. I bent down to pick up some of the pieces of tile I had knocked off the wall when I made the opening. After touching and retouching that part of the wall repeatedly, I had to accept the fact that it had been repaired. (ibid., pp. 87–88)

He tries using the iron bar once again but the pieces of the wall that he has knocked out join up again immediately. "In a vision so lucid it seemed ephemeral and supernatural, my eyes saw the blue continuity of the tile, the undamaged and whole wall, the closed room" (ibid.,

p. 89). There is absolutely no way out: he feels hounded, the victim of a spell, seized by panic. Then he understands:

> These walls [...] are projections of the machines. They coincide with the walls made by the masons (they are the same walls taken by the machines and then projected on themselves). Where I have broken or removed the first wall, the projected one remains. Since it is a projection nothing can pierce or eliminate it as long as the motors are running. [...] Morel must have planned the double-wall protection to keep anyone from reaching the machines that control his immortality. (ibid., pp. 89–90)

For a more in-depth study of the narcissistic wrapping and its role for the personality of the aviator, the hero and the creative artist, I recommend the reader to consult an article by André Missenard, "Narcissisme et rupture" [Narcissism and rupture] (1979).

Disturbances of belief and borderline states

Belief is a vital human necessity. One cannot live without believing that one is alive. One cannot perceive the outside world without believing it is real. One can only be a person if one believes in one's identity and continuity. One cannot be in a state of wakefulness without believing one is awake. Of course, these beliefs, which keep us joined to our being and at home in our own life, are not the same thing as knowledge. If we test them in terms of truth or falsity, they appear debatable; and philosophy, literature, religions, and psychological science have gone to considerable trouble either to try and justify them or to prove them futile.

People who possess these beliefs naturally have to question them. But a person who does not possess them has to acquire them before they can feel their own being and well-being. Without these beliefs, people suffer and complain of lacking them. This is evident from the clinical treatment not of narcissistic personalities but of borderline states—depressions or certain psychosomatic breakdowns (i.e., states in which there is either a frequent or a lasting deficiency of the psychical container). One theory that helps us to understand how the failure of belief works is provided by Winnicott (1966). In his view, the psychical Ego develops through anaclisis but also through differentiation and splitting from the bodily Ego. In human beings there is a tendency to integrate, to "achieve a unity of the psyche and the soma, an experiential identity of the spirit or psyche and the totality of physical functioning" (Winnicott, 1966, p. 112). This tendency, which is latent from the start of an infant's development, is either strengthened or undermined by interaction with its environment. After the earliest, non-integrated state, what follows is integration: the psyche locates itself in the soma and takes possession of the psychosomatic unity that Winnicott calls the Self. This moment, let us add, marks the start of the child's threefold belief—in its continuous existence, its conscious identity and the natural functioning of its body. This belief, which is the basis for the earliest pleasure in being alive, obeys the pleasure principle. But one of the characteristics of that principle (as Bion has shown) is that the aim to avoid unpleasure becomes stronger than the pursuit of pleasure, under certain circumstances: when the child's innate endowment is weak or the environment is not good enough or it has suffered excessive or cumulative traumas in early life. In these cases it will set up a defensive dissociation to protect against the pain of powerlessness, frustration or distress, even to the point of damaging its basic beliefs and losing, entirely or in part, its original pleasure in being alive. Thus, according to Winnicott, psychosomatic dissociation in adults is a regressive phenomenon which makes use of the residues of the early splitting between psyche and soma. The split between the psychical and the somatic guards against the danger of total destruction that the psychosomatic patient would feel they risk if they believed themselves to be a unified person in whom the body and mental life are one since, if either of those two conjoined aspects were attacked, the entirety of the person would be destroyed. This split cuts its losses, sacrificing one aspect to preserve the other. If, at least at first, this defence is respected by carers, the patient can feel secure enough internally to allow the tendency to integration to emerge and become active. But if the belief is lost, as a result of the splitting, then the fear of emptiness sets in.

Case study: Sébastienne

Unlike the narcissistic personality featured in Bioy Casares's novella, Sébastienne was a borderline case, and I was able to improve her condition through a second, face-to-face analysis, following the unhappy outcome of her first, couch-based treatment at the hands of a "psychoanalyst" who was miserly with his interpretations and given to foreshortened sessions. She presented to me in a state of serious depression, revived by the treatment she had just broken off and intensified by the violent loss of idealisation towards her first analyst. Here are some extracts from her last session before the summer break, which she dreaded because it had reawakened her fear of a break in the continuity of the Self:

> Something's happening, something's getting off the ground, and then… splash! Just when I'm beginning to believe in it, just my luck, the holidays… And what does that mean anyway, thinking "Just when I'm beginning to believe in it", right at the start of the holidays? I'm scared. Who am I talking to? What's going on? Someone's doing something to me, what is it? Last time, when you talked to me about that thing from my childhood [this refers to the distressing experience of sexual games forced on her by an older half-brother, in which she would stop herself from feeling pleasure and withdraw from her body], I felt it was all a big lie. You were making me say something I didn't know, something where I couldn't find myself [I had spoken of her mind spinning in the face of the sensations she must have felt inside her at that time]. But there's more, worse stuff. Telling you this, I'm saying it without really saying it, I hate myself, I hate you. I'm sick of this […] Why do I stay? Probably because I need you to be somewhere different from the place I'm projecting you into so hard right now. So I could still talk to you. So you would still answer me and I could go on living.

Her feelings of guilt were superficial but her shame was deep, connected to a Skin-ego that was not fulfilling its function as a protective shield, so that there was a risk that the sensations, emotions and drives she wanted to keep hidden would become visible to other people. Falling into inner emptiness is a way of disappearing from potential prying eyes. Excitation was not associated with oedipal phantasies; not only did its sexual meaning go unrecognised but it was experienced as something purely mechanical, without meaning of any kind. All attempts to discharge it, i.e., to resolve it in a quantitative way, ended in failure—both masturbation during her adolescence and coitus nowadays gave her orgasms but these did not relieve the tension she continued to feel throughout her body. This was because sensation had undergone a qualitative transformation: the pleasurable quality of the sensations had been dissociated from them and split into multiple scattered fragments which were no longer pleasurable. Sébastienne agreed that what predominated in her over the pleasure principle was the principle of avoiding unpleasure at all costs, and that she preferred to give up the pursuit of pleasure in order to divert her libido from object-cathexis and invest it in the narcissistic aims of the Ego and in protecting the Self. This predominance belongs, according to Bion, to the psychotic part of the psychical apparatus, the part that is not contained by the environment or by thought. Emptying oneself of sensory qualities is a way, if not of ridding oneself completely of unpleasant things (for a feeling of un-ease still remains), at least of holding them off beyond the Pcpt.-Cs. system. This emptying forms a kind of *cordon sanitaire*, which the psyche puts in place of the comprehensive wrapping of containment that a failing Skin-ego cannot provide. Once she had achieved this emptying out of sensory qualities (without affecting her other bodily and intellectual functions), Sébastienne went on living, but without believing she was alive, without believing in the possibility of functioning naturally. Her life seemed to pass her by. She observed from a distance the mechanical functioning of her body and mind, which three years of analysis with me had essentially restored. She expressed a growing hatred for me, on three counts: first, she was angry at this improvement because it condemned her to function automatically, without pleasure, and diminished her intuitive skills, which had formerly been excellent; second, her libido, rekindled by the treatment, was redirected towards objects and had recathected her erogenous zones, which threatened the balance she had achieved by emptying herself out, to which she was still attached; and lastly as the transference developed it no longer allowed her to seek in me the anaclitic support of a sufficiently understanding environment and was now confronting her with the threatening image of the seductive and persecutory male penis. At the same time, and contradictorily, the hope of finding a different way of functioning, based on the pleasure principle and capable of making her happy, was emerging: the summer holidays arrived just when she was beginning "to believe in it". I then had to interpret her repetition compulsion—the fact that she was expecting or even provocatively anticipating the return of the disappointment she had felt long ago at those early encroachments and at her mother's paradoxical demands—the latter had been both generous and over-stimulating in her bodily care and very loving towards her daughter, but had suddenly taken on a rigid, moralising and negative attitude in the face of the needs of her Ego.

> But there was more to it than that. The mother, who was a religious atheist, if I dare put it this way, dedicated herself to social welfare. During her frequent absences, she left Sébastienne in the charge of a neighbour, a sturdy peasant woman, simple and dedicated, who carried out the housework energetically with her right hand while holding the little girl more or less tightly to her with her left hand. This woman also wore a huge leather apron which was covered in grease and was never washed, on which the baby's feet, clad in woollen bootees, slithered around. Thus her fear of losing her mother was exacerbated by her desperate quest for something to lean on physically, for a fundamental structure to hold on to, and the fear of losing the supporting object. It took me quite some time to make a connection in the transference with her repetition of the flaw that was handicapping the first function of her Skin-ego: in fact I had the unpleasant feeling that however dedicated I was, however cleverly I interpreted, my patient was slipping through my fingers.
>
> For a long time I had been intrigued by Sébastienne's physical posture: she would sit in the seat opposite mine but her body did not face mine; she turned towards her right, making an angle of about twenty degrees away from me, and she stayed in this position throughout the session: when she talked or listened to me, only her left eye would look my way. I told myself that she was setting up an "oblique" line of communication with me; indeed, she often took my interpretations in a skewed way; when I talked to her, I felt like a billiards player who has to aim at the red ball not directly but off the cushion. In fact this posture was over-determined: from the oedipal point of view, it protected her against having to relive the sexual confrontation with her elder half-brother; from the narcissistic point of view, it allowed her to express with her body that twisting of the Skin-ego like a Moebius strip that I described above as being typical of borderline states. Twisting the interface of the Pcpt.-Cs. system in this way caused her to misread the emotional and gestural signals of people around her, which in turn led to an aggravation of misunderstanding and frustration, then to an outburst of rage, which exhausted both her and them.

Sébastienne came to the decision that her psychoanalysis was finished the day she sat in front of me with her face turned directly towards me, not in profile, so that she could say to my face the two things she had to tell me: on the one hand, she had to break off this analysis because it was costing her too much time and money, reopening too many old wounds and hatreds, prolonging her past by bringing it into the present and causing her to put off actually starting to live; and on the other, her mind was no longer twisted, her spine had recently clicked back into place, she now felt able to cope with her reactions of disappointment and hatred by seeing them for what they were and getting out of them by her own efforts.

Other patients of mine have confirmed that it is possible for the Ego and the Self to come back into shape suddenly as a result of reestablishing a non-skewed communication with the other person in the transference. In the treatment of narcissistic personalities, restoring the containing function of the Skin-ego is usually enough. As the example of Sébastienne shows, the treatment of borderline cases requires more than this: the restoration of three other functions of the Skin-ego—holding, protection against stimuli, and libidinal recharging.

CHAPTER TEN

The double taboo on touching, the condition for overcoming the Skin-ego

There are four reasons behind my hypothesis of a taboo on touching. The first is historical and epistemological: Freud did not discover psychoanalysis—the set-up of the treatment, the oedipal organisation of the neuroses—until he had implicitly imposed this taboo on his own practice (though without theorising it).

The next reason is psychogenetic: the earliest prohibitions a family imposes on a child, once it enters the world of (locomotor) movement and (infra-verbal and pre-linguistic) communication, are essentially to do with tactile contacts; and these exogenous, variable and multiple prohibitions form the basis for an internalised taboo which is relatively permanent, autonomous and not single but double, as I shall go on to show in detail.

The third reason is structural: if, as Freud put it, the Ego is fundamentally a surface (that of the psychical apparatus) and the projection of a surface (that of the body), and if therefore it functions, at first, in the structural form of a Skin-ego, how could it move on to another system of functioning (that of thought, which belongs to a psychical Ego differentiated from the bodily Ego and articulated with it in a different way) if not by giving up, as a result of the double taboo on touching, the primacy of the pleasures of the skin and then the hand and by transforming concrete tactile experience into basic representations, to serve as the background against which systems of sensory correspondence can be set up (initially at a figurative level, which maintains a symbolic reference to contact and touch, and later at a purely abstract level, freed from that reference)?

And finally a polemical reason: the boom in the last few decades of so-called "humanistic" or "emotional" psychotherapies, the competition with "encounter groups" which recommend or even insist on bodily contact among participants and the threat these pose to the rigour of psychoanalytic technique, with its rule of abstinence from touching, all this calls for a response from psychoanalysts that goes further than either deaf and blind indifference or angry contempt, or indeed an impassioned conversion to the "new methods"—which often are simply modifications or variants on pre-psychoanalytic techniques of "suggestion".

According to the modes of organisation of the psychical economy, what are the effects of tactile stimulation—narcissistic restoration, erogenous excitation or traumatic violence? What comprises the play of tactile interactions in primary communication? In what kinds of case might it be thinkable or even necessary to bring back that play, and in what kinds might it be useless or even harmful? What stimulating or inhibiting consequences for later sexual life arise from the success or failure of the psychical apparatus to create a Skin-ego for itself and then overcome it in favour of a thinking Ego? Why is it that today's psychoanalytic theory tends to lose sight too often of the Freudian (and clinical) finding that psychical life is grounded in sensory qualities? These are the interrelated questions that arise from the necessity of recognising the taboo on touching.

A taboo on touching implied in Freud's work[1]

In his practice of animal magnetism, Mesmer entered into a "rapport" with his patients, touching them with his hand, look or voice until he had induced a state of emotional dependency, anaesthetised consciousness and susceptibility to stimulation; once they were in this state, he

---

[1] The present draft of this sub-section takes account of a number of points made by Gérard Bonnet (1985) in relation to my article of 1984 on the double taboo on touching.

could produce a cathartic jolt either by the direct contact of his hand on their body or by the indirect contact of a magnetised oak tub touched with an iron rod. Later on, the hypnotist would merely mime touch by passing a hand to and fro in front of the eyes of the patient, who was sitting or lying down and who then fell into an induced sleep. In order to apply his technique of counter-suggestion for hysterical symptoms better, Charcot would ask the patients he was hypnotising to close their eyes. It was the warmth, insistence, and firmness of the hypnotist's voice that demanded sleep and banished the symptom. Yet Charcot's hand was still medical as it palpated the hysterogenic zones and seemed experimental when it thus triggered hysterical attacks before an invited audience. With its extensions in the form of the voice and occasionally also the eye—an eye that does not only gaze, a voice that does more than speak; rather, a look and a discourse that envelop, seize and caress; in other words, an eye and a voice endowed with tactile powers—the hand of the hypnotist (generally a man) exerts a real or symbolic function of suggestion and when exercised upon adults (most commonly young women, still more commonly hysterics), it also enacts a complementary function of seduction—a secondary gain (or rather loss) of the operation.

In the ten or twelve years before he analysed his own dreams and discovered psychoanalysis, Freud the hypnotherapist was a man of the eye and the hand rather than a man of words. One incident, which shed a retrospective light on the misadventure of Breuer with Anna O., alerted him to the particular dangers of seduction. An agency nurse whom Freud had cured of her symptoms through hypnosis jumped up to kiss him and was about to throw herself into his arms. Freud neither succumbed nor took fright: he discovered, as he tells us, the phenomenon of the transference. What he does not tell us, since it goes without saying, is that psychotherapists must eschew any physical closeness with their patients. For all that, while bodily intimacy was prohibited because of the risk of eroticisation, the hand continued to examine painful points on the patient's body—Frau Emmy von N.'s ovaries, Fräulein Elisabeth von R.'s thigh—where excitation had gathered after failing to be discharged in pleasure. Then, when Freud abandoned hypnotic sleep in favour of psychical analysis, his hand moved up from the hysterogenic zones where somatic conversion takes place towards the head, where unconscious pathogenic memories are active. He invited his patients to lie down, close their eyes and concentrate on memories (visual memories, of course, but equally well auditory ones, in which phrases are recorded in the body by symbolisation) and on the corresponding emotions that appeared in response to being asked where their symptoms had come from. If there was resistance—nothing occurring to the patient's mind—Freud resorted to pressing his hand on their forehead, declaring that as soon as he took it away the desired repressed images would appear. Thus, if they wanted to be delivered, all the patient needed to do was say what they could see and hear inside themselves. However limited and localised, this was still suggestion. And it still carried the same latent sexual charge, as witness a dream reported by one of my patients. This young man dreamt that I received him for his session not in my office but in a place he took to be my country house and that I adopted a very friendly attitude towards him. I sat down in a large rattan armchair and invited him to sit on my knee. Things moved fast: I kissed him on the mouth, gazed into his eyes, laid my hand on his forehead and murmured in his ear: "Tell me whatever this makes you think of". The patient woke up, furious at my behaviour, or rather my misbehaviour, totally forgetting the fact that he was the author of the dream.

While he was still practising hypnotherapy, the patient from whom Freud learned most about the essential characteristics of what would later become the analytic framework is of course Frau Emmy von N. As early as 1st May 1889, she was adjuring him: "Keep still!—Don't say anything!—Don't touch me!" (1895d, p. 49), a command she repeated many times afterwards. Another patient, Irma, whom Freud shared with Fliess, induced in him on 24th July 1895 the first dream of his self-analysis. In the dream, he was examining her throat, breasts and vagina and noted that the recurrence of her symptoms was connected to a "thoughtlessly" (1895d, p. 107) administered "injection" of a medicine whose ternary composition is related to sexual "chemistry". The medical examination of a patient's body and its algogenic or hysterogenic zones must of necessity be physical. The psychoanalytic examination of erogenous zones can only be mental and symbolic. Freud (1900a) heeded the warning. He gave up the technique of "mental concentration", invented the term psychoanalysis and, basing the set-up of the treatment on the two rules of non-omission and abstinence, suspended all tactile exchange with the patient, replacing it by the use of verbal exchanges alone—even this being asymmetrical because the patient is required to speak freely while the analyst speaks only on certain occasions. This asymmetry is even greater as far as sight is concerned: the analyst can see the patient but the patient cannot and must not see the analyst (even after Freud was no longer insisting on the patient's eyes being closed).

In this situation, his patients—and Freud himself, in tandem with them—began to dream more and more. The systematic analysis of those dreams (his and theirs) led him in October 1897 to the momentous discovery of the Oedipus complex. Thus the essential role of the incest taboo could not be explicitly set out until the taboo on touching had been implicitly recognised. On this point, the personal history of Freud's discovery recapitulates the universal history of childhood. The taboo on touching as an act of physical violence or sexual seduction precedes, anticipates, and makes possible the oedipal taboo, which forbids incest and parricide.

The verbal exchange that defines the field of psychoanalytic treatment is effective only because it resumes, on a newly symbolic plane, what had earlier been exchanged in the visual and tactile registers. This is illustrated in a footnote to Freud's *Three Essays on the Theory of Sexuality* (1905d), in which a three-year-old boy in an unlit bedroom complains that he is afraid of the dark and asks his aunt to say something; when she objects that this would not help because he could not see her, the child answers: "That doesn't matter [...] if anyone speaks, it gets light" (1905d, p. 224 note 1). In another passage about various types of sexual preliminaries involving touch or sight, Freud also remarks: "The same holds true of seeing—an activity that is ultimately derived from touching" (1905d, p. 156). The tactile is only foundational provided that, at the right moment, it is forbidden. The prescription of having to say everything has as its inseparable corollary the proscription not just against action but more specifically against touching. The tactile prohibition on both the patient and the analyst is underscored by a visual prohibition imposed particularly on the patient: the latter must not try to "see" the analyst outside sessions or try to have any "contact" with them.

The psychoanalytic framework dissociates the scopophilic drive from its bodily support, the sense of sight (in order to know one must give up the wish to see) and the drive to grasp from its bodily support, the hand (one must put one's finger on the truth rather than on a body, i.e., move from the pleasure-pain dimension to that of true and false). This allows those two drives—as well as the epistemophilic drive—to constitute, to borrow an expression from Bernard Gibello (1984), "epistemic objects" rather than libidinal ones.

This prohibition was particularly justified for Freud by the fact that his clientele consisted almost entirely of hysterical girls and young women, for whom vision was eroticised (showing themselves off or staging sexual phantasies) and who pursued physical closeness (being touched, caressed or embraced). For these patients it was essential to create enough distance to set up a relationship of thought, a psychical space, the addition to the Ego of a part that could observe itself. Freud encountered other difficulties with obsessional neurotics, in whom the psychoanalytic setting favours object-relations "at a distance" (as Maurice Bouvet was later to call it), a splitting of the psychical and bodily Egos, the eroticisation of thought, a phobic fear of contact, a fear of contagion, and a horror of being touched.

The difficulty seems to be greater still with those categorised as borderline cases or narcissistic personalities. Their experiences are more often algogenic than erogenous; the avoidance of unpleasure motivates them more than the pursuit of pleasure; they adopt a schizoid position, which maximises the remoteness of the object, the withdrawal of the Ego, hatred of reality and a flight into the imaginary. Freud declared them impossible to analyse because they cannot commit themselves to a psychoanalytic process dominated by transference neurosis and the progress of symbolisation. With them, therefore, more adjustments of the psychoanalytic set-up were needed. These patients might be seen face to face, which allows a dialogue to develop that is visual, posturally tonic, facially gestural, and respiratory: the prohibition on sight is lifted while the prohibition on touching is maintained. The work of analysis focuses not on interpreting phantasies but on reconstructing traumas, on exercising psychical functions that have suffered deprivation; these patients need to introject an adequate container Skin-ego that stands as a total background surface on which erogenous zones can eventually emerge as figures. The psychoanalytic technique I use consists of restoring the wrapping of sound which is itself the backing of the primary tactile wrapping; showing the patient that they can "touch" me emotionally; forming symbolic equivalents for deficient tactile contacts by "touching" them with words that are true and full or even with meaningful gestures that work as simulacra. What is maintained is the taboo on undressing, displaying oneself naked, touching the psychoanalyst's body or being touched by their hand or any other part of their body;

this is the minimum level required by psychoanalysis. No one is forced to practise psychoanalysis and there is every reason to choose the type of psychotherapy that works best for each case. But if psychoanalysis is indicated and one has decided to engage in it, then one must respect its spirit and its letter—in this case, the taboo on touching. It is dishonest of certain body therapists to invoke the name of psychoanalysis to endorse their methods when they fail to observe one of its essential rules.

Christ's explicit prohibition

The prohibitions "invented" by Freud (in the sense of uncovering a buried treasure from its hiding-place) were already known before him; the collective consciousness of many cultures had registered their existence: Sophocles and Shakespeare turn the oedipal taboo to their dramatic purpose; Diderot describes it too. When he named it, Freud leaned upon the "obscure perception" of psychical reality that can be found in myths, religions, and great works of visual and literary art. It must be the same for the taboo on touching. Naturally it is modulated differently in each culture but it is present in pretty much all of them. Is there not one legend in which it is announced explicitly?

During a visit to the Prado Museum in Madrid, I paused, disturbed and intrigued, in front of a canvas by Correggio, painted when he was thirty, around the years 1522–1523. The painting owes its originality to an undulating effect in the rhythm of the composition, which sweeps through the two bodies, their clothes, the trees and clouds, and the light of day dawning in the background. All the fundamental colours except purple are here: white in the metal of the garden tools, black in the shadows, the man's brown hair, and his blue garment, which leaves his torso bare and pale—but is it actually a man?—and the woman, blonde, with pallid skin, in a broad golden dress and a half-glimpsed red cloak flung behind her, while the sky and vegetation offer every shade of yellow and green. He is no longer a man but not yet a God. It is Christ, victorious over death, who stands forth on the day of his resurrection, in the Garden of Golgotha, preparing to ascend to the Father, the index-finger of his left hand pointing towards the sky, his right hand lowered, with fingers raised and spread out, in a sign of prohibition, but with a hint of tenderness and understanding, intensified by the harmony of the rhythm of the bodies and the echoes of the tones in the landscape. Kneeling at his feet is the Magdalene, her face in supplication, shattered with emotion; her right hand, which Christ's gesture has repulsed, bent backwards towards one hip while her left hand holds back a panel of her cloak, or rather is holding itself back by grasping that fold of cloth. The viewer's attention is focused on the triple exchange of looks, gestures, and words which we intuit from the movement of the lips; it is an intense exchange and the painting renders it wonderfully. The title given by the painter to his canvas is the phrase spoken by Christ at this moment: "Noli me tangere".

This is a quotation from John's Gospel, XX: 17. The day after Easter, following the Sabbath rest, Mary of Magdala—her second forename, "Magdalene", derives from the village on the shores of the Sea of Galilee where she was born—enters the action. Alone, according to John, accompanied either by another Mary, the mother of James and Joseph, according to Matthew (XXVIII: 1), by a third woman, Salome, according to Mark (XVI: 1) or by a whole group of women according to Luke (XXIV: 1–12), she "cometh [...] unto the sepulchre, and seeth the stone taken away from the sepulchre" (John XX: 1). She is afraid that the body has been stolen, and alerts Simon-Peter and John, who go into the tomb and discover it is empty; they guess that Christ is risen. The two men go back, leaving her alone and weeping in the cemetery garden. She sees two angels who ask her questions, and then a shadowy figure whom she takes for the garden keeper and who repeats what the angels have said: "Woman, why weepest thou? Whom seekest thou?" (John XX: 15). She asks the supposed gardener where he has laid the body; and "Jesus saith unto her, Mary. She turned herself, and saith unto him, Rabboni; which is to say, Master" (John XX: 16). At this moment, Jesus pronounces the words that concern us: "Noli me tangere", and then he charges Mary Magdalene, the first person to whom he has appeared after his resurrection, to go and tell his disciples the good news.

The translation of Christ's words, which are in Latin in the Vulgate, is both simple and difficult. Simple because taken word for word it means "Do not touch me'; difficult if one wants to understand it in spiritual terms. "Do not hold me back" is the formulation agreed upon by the French translators of the so-called ecumenical Bible, published by Cerf, with the following footnote: "Jesus means to convey to Mary that the change which is taking place in him as he prepares to ascend to his Father will entail a new type of relationship". I note therefore that the taboo on touching, in its initial Christian formulation, is linked sometimes to separation from the beloved object—"Do not hold me back"—and sometimes to the abandonment of gestural language in favour of a spiritual communication based on words only—"Do not touch me" implying "Only listen and speak". The resurrected Jesus is no longer a human being whose body can be felt; he becomes again what he was before the incarnation: pure Logos. Bonnet (1984) observes that by laying down the taboo on touching the New Testament can be opposed to the Old Testament, which prioritises the taboo on representation.[2]

The Latin *tangere* has the same range of meanings, both corporeal and affective, as the French verb "toucher"—from "to place one's hand on" to "to move emotionally". Furthermore, though the authors of all four gospels refer to the encounter of Mary of Magdala with the resurrected Christ, only John reports the prohibition pronounced by Jesus. It is no coincidence, doubtless, that the prohibition on touching is directed against a woman, not a man. Of course it is a sexual prohibition, creating an inhibition of the libidinous aim and the "sublimation" of sexual love for a partner into desexualised love for one's neighbour in general. It is also a taboo on touching: the quotation from the gospels that I have been commenting on tends to confirm Freud's analogy between religion and obsessional neurosis.

Nonetheless, Christ's prohibition on touching is no simple matter. It is caught up in several contradictions, and what follows is far from the least of them: no sooner is it pronounced than it is transgressed, as we can see in the next section of John's text. Christ appears on the evening of his resurrection to a secret gathering of his male disciples. But Thomas Didymus, who is not at that meeting, refuses to believe in the resurrected Christ unless he has seen him with his own eyes and touched his wounds with his fingers. "And after eight days again his disciples were within, and Thomas with them" (John XX: 26). Jesus reappears and says to Thomas: "Reach hither thy finger, and behold my hands; and reach hither thy hand, and thrust it into my side" (John XX: 27). Thus Thomas, a man, is invited to touch what a woman, Mary Magdalene, had to be satisfied with only glimpsing. Once Thomas is convinced, Jesus adds: "Because thou hast seen me, thou has believed: blessed are they that have not seen, and yet have believed" (John XX: 29). The commentators have nothing to say about the fact that this conclusion confuses touch

---

[2] *Translator's Note*: Here, Anzieu does not specify which Bonnet text (1981 or 1985) he has in mind.

with sight. By contrast, they are definite about this: "From now on, faith rests not on sight but on the testimony of those who have seen". The underlying epistemological problem could be expressed in these terms: is truth visible, tangible, or audible? I point in passing to a question which I do not have the competence to deal with: is the taboo on touching more typical of Christian civilisations than others? It is a fact, certainly, that the practice of psychoanalysis has spread particularly in countries of Christian culture: what it has in common with that culture is the conviction that communication by language is spiritually superior to communication between bodies.

Touch: three problematics

Tradition has confused three different New Testament women under the name of Mary Magdalene.

Mary of Magdala is a sick woman suffering from possession whom Jesus cures by removing from her "seven demons" (Luke VIII: 2; Mark XVI: 9); after this she accompanies him everywhere, together with the group of holy women and the twelve male disciples.

Mary of Bethany anoints Jesus's feet and hair with a costly perfume at the dinner given by her and her sister Martha in celebration of the resurrection of their brother Lazarus. Judas deplores this waste and Martha complains that her sister has left her to do all the work. Jesus replies that in embalming his body in advance Mary is anticipating his coming death—and, it is understood, his resurrection—and that by sitting at his feet and listening to his words she has chosen the better part (John XII: 3; Luke X: 38–42).

An unnamed female sinner, also from Bethany, enters the hall during a banquet given by Simon, a Pharisee, in honour of Jesus who cured him of leprosy; she bathes Jesus' feet in her tears, wipes them with her hair and covers them with kisses, spreading perfume on them; the host is surprised that Jesus has not guessed that this "woman [...] that toucheth him" is a prostitute, and Jesus replies that she has honoured him better than he has, she has shown great love and thus he pardons her sins (Luke VII: 37–47). Tradition has, for no philological or theological reason, identified this repentant courtesan with Mary of Magdala; in doing this it has followed the popular belief that any act of touching between two people of the opposite sex necessarily has a sexual connotation.

In fact these three women from the gospels represent three different problematics of touch—the problematic of sexual seduction, by the female sinner; the problematic of acts of bodily care as constituting the Skin-ego and auto-eroticism, by Mary of Bethany; and the problematic of touch as proof that the touched object exists, by Mary of Magdala.

The oedipal prohibition (you must not marry your mother; you must not kill your father) is derived metonymically from the prohibition on touching. The taboo on touching prepares the ground for the oedipal taboo by providing it with a presexual foundation. In psychoanalytic treatment it becomes possible to understand at what particular cost—through what difficulties, failures, counter-cathexes or hypercathexes—this derivation has been effected in each case.

The prohibitions and their four dualities

Every prohibition is dual in nature. It is a system of tensions between opposing poles; these tensions in the psyche develop force-fields which inhibit some functions and cause others to change their form.

First duality: The taboo relates to both the sexual and the aggressive drives. It channels the pressure of the drives, defines their bodily sources, reorganises their objects and aims, and structures the relations between the two major families of drives. It is clear how this applies to the oedipal taboo. The taboo on touching is similarly concerned with the two basic drives: do not touch inanimate objects in case you break them or they hurt you; do not use excessive force against parts of your own or other people's bodies (this prohibition aims to protect the child against aggression, whether its own or that of other people); do not constantly touch your body or other people's bodies in the areas sensitive to pleasure, for you will be overwhelmed with an excitation you are incapable of understanding or satisfying (this prohibition aims to protect the child against its own and other people's sexuality). In both cases, the taboo on touching puts the child on its guard against an excess of excitation and its consequence, the surging of the drive.

In the taboo on touching, sexuality, and aggression are not differentiated structurally: they are both expressions of instinctual violence in general. The incest taboo, on the other hand, distinguishes between them and places them in a relation of inverse symmetry rather than similarity.

Second duality: Every prohibition has a double face, one turned outwards (which receives, accommodates and filters the interdictions communicated by other people) and one turned towards inner reality (which deals with the representational and affective representatives of instinctual currents). The intra-psychical taboo leans anaclitically on external proscriptions but these are the occasion rather than the cause of establishing it. The cause is endogenous—the psyche's need to differentiate itself. The taboo on touching helps to create a border or interface between the Ego and the Id. The oedipal taboo completes the creation of a border or interface between the Ego and the Superego. The two censorships proposed by Freud in his first theory (one between the unconscious and the preconscious, the other between the preconscious and the conscious) could, I believe, be redeployed in this context.

The earliest interdictions related to touch that are imposed on a child serve the principle of self-preservation: don't put your hand in the fire, don't touch knives or the rubbish or medicines, for this would put your body, or even your life, in danger. Their correlatives are prescriptions of touch such as: don't let go of my hand when you're leaning out of the window or crossing the road. Interdictions refer to external dangers while prohibitions refer to internal ones. Both assume that the child already understands the distinction between inside and outside—without this the taboo makes no sense—and the taboo itself reinforces that distinction. Any prohibition is an interface separating two areas of psychical space, each with its own psychical qualities. The prohibition on touching separates the area of the familiar, which is protected and protective, from the area of the unfamiliar, which is disturbing and dangerous. This taboo is, in my opinion, the true creator of the change that occurs around the ninth month of life and which Spitz has reduced to the simple distinction between familiar and unknown faces. The primary form of the taboo on touch—you must not cling to your parents' bodies—assumes that the child has a separate body that can explore the outside world. But in addition (and this is a more advanced form) it is told: don't touch unfamiliar objects without taking precautions, for you don't know what harm they might do. The prohibition invites the child to touch things other than those that are familiar and familial in order to get to know them. But the interdiction teaches the child to be forearmed against the dangers of ignorance and impulsiveness: you can't touch just anything in any old way. Picking up an object is fine if you want to see how it works—but not putting it in your mouth and swallowing it because you like it, or smashing it and putting what you imagine are the hateful pieces inside your tummy. The taboo on touching helps to differentiate orders of reality that are confused in the early tactile body-to-body experience of infancy: your body is different from other bodies; space exists independently of the objects that populate it; animate objects behave differently from inanimate objects.

The oedipal taboo reverses what is learned from the taboo on touching: whatever is familiar (in the original sense of familial) becomes dangerous in relation to the dual instinctual investments of love and hatred: danger resides now in the twin risks of incest and parricide (or fratricide) and the price to be paid is castration anxiety. On the other hand, under certain conditions, the little boy will have the right—even the duty—to do battle against men outside his family, clan, and nation, and to choose a wife from outside his family.

Third duality: Every prohibition is constructed in two phases. The oedipal taboo, as Freud envisaged it, with its focus on the threat of genital castration, restricts love relations on the basis of different sexes and generations. An earlier, pregenital version of the Oedipus complex set out by Melanie Klein precedes and prepares for it: here we have the anti-cannibalistic prohibition against eating the desired breast or the phantasy of destroying the children-faeces and the father's penis inside the mother's belly; and the child's belief that weaning is a punishment for its desires to devour. The taboo on touching likewise has a dual starting-point. Indeed we need to distinguish between two structures of tactile experience: (i) contact in the form of an embrace, which involves a large portion of the skin and includes pressure, warmth or coldness, comfort or pain, kinaesthetic and vestibular sensations, a contact that has connotations of the common skin phantasy; and (ii) the touch of the hand, which supports the infant's body and to which, later on, touch tends to be limited, once the child has mastered the gestures of pointing and grasping objects and been taught that skin-to-skin contact is too childish or erogenous or brutal and therefore must be limited to highly controlled manifestations of love or muscular prowess. Thus, interleaved with each other, there are two prohibitions: the first against full-body contact—the conjoining, fusion or confusion of bodies—and the second, more selective, against touching with the hand: touching one's own genital organs or, more generally, touching the erogenous zones and their products or touching people and objects in a violent way; for touch is now restricted to operational ways of adapting to the outside world and the pleasures it brings can only be preserved as long as they are subordinated to the reality principle. It varies from one culture to another which of these two taboos on touching is emphasised or minimised. The stage of a child's life at which each is presented and how far they extend are very variable. But there is scarcely any society in which they cannot be found. Sanctions applied to transgressions are equally variable. They range from corporal punishment to the threat of it, or simply moral disapproval expressed in a raised voice.

The primary taboo on touching transposes the effects of biological birth onto the psychical plane. It imposes a separate existence on the living person who is becoming an individual. It forbids the return to the womb, a return that can only now be experienced in phantasy—though this prohibition is not established in an autistic child, who continues to live psychically inside its mother's body. The interdiction is communicated implicitly by the mother through acts of physical distancing: she moves away from the child or moves it away from her, by withdrawing the breast, turning her face away when the baby is trying to grab it or putting the baby in its cot. If the mother fails to put the interdiction into action, there is always someone else around to be the spokesperson of the prohibition, this time in a verbal form. Either the father, her mother-in-law, a neighbour or the paediatrician will remind the mother that she has a duty to separate herself physically from the baby, so that it can get to sleep, not be over-stimulated, not get into bad habits, learn to play on its own, walk instead of always being carried, so that it can grow up and leave those around it some time and space to live their own lives. The primary taboo on touching is specifically opposed to the attachment or clinging drive. The corresponding threat of physical punishment may be phantasised as a flaying that leaves bare the surface of the common skin between the baby and the mother (or her substitute, who may be the father)[3]—and we have already seen how this image of flaying is echoed in many mythologies and religions.

The secondary taboo on touching applies to the drive to mastery: not everything can be touched, grasped or mastered. This interdiction

---

[3] The "new fathers" of the last generation who have willingly taken on an equal share of the feeding and care of the baby—apart from pregnancy and breastfeeding—have been a great help to the mother and get a lot of pleasure themselves, but they complicate the task of the infant, who has to extricate itself from two dual relationships rather than only one, and this may delay or weaken the formation of an internalised prohibition.

is expressed in verbal or gestural language. When the child is about to reach for something, someone in the family says "no," either in so many words or by a movement of their head or hand. The implicit meaning is: you don't just grab, you ask first and you have to accept the risk of a refusal or a delay. The meaning of this prohibition becomes explicit as the child acquires sufficient mastery of language; indeed it encourages the development of that mastery: you don't point to interesting objects, you call them by their names. The threat of physical punishment that corresponds to the secondary taboo on touching might be expressed in familial and social discourse in the following terms: the hand that steals, strikes or masturbates will be tied up or cut off.

Fourth duality: Every prohibition is bilateral in nature. It applies to the person issuing it as much as to the person it is addressed to. However strong the incestuous and hostile oedipal desires of parents towards their children on the brink of sexual maturity, they must not act on these desires. In the same way, if it is to achieve the effect of restructuring psychical functioning, the taboo on touching must also be respected by the child's parents and educators. Repeated, serious breaches result in a cumulative trauma which, in its turn, will cause major psychopathological consequences.

Case study: Janette

This was the case with Janette, who had been a patient of mine, sometimes in psychoanalysis, sometimes in psychotherapy, for over thirty years. Throughout these years I had to face her very intense persecution anxiety. She felt safe neither in her body nor in her home. She would invade mine by phoning me at any time of the day or evening, weekday or weekend, demanding immediate meetings, or by refusing to leave my office at the end of some sessions. As we gradually established a regular psychotherapeutic framework and reconstructed the principal traumas of her childhood and adolescence, she was able, little by little, to form a Skin-ego, find a professional occupation that gave her independence from her parents and devote her leisure-time to composing literary texts in which she could work on expressing her conflicts in a symbolic form. Transposing into a fictional character the experience of verbal exchange that she had acquired with me, she described the words of that character as hands that held her, retained her, contained her, gave her back a face and enabled her to acknowledge her suffering: a hand that reached out towards her from far, far away above an abyss, a hand that finally succeeded in grasping hers like a bridge across time (though in reality we had had no bodily contact apart from the traditional handshake), a hand that warmed both her hands and then let go, while at the same time the character's voice gently explained that he had to leave but he would come back and, watching him go, she was able, for the first time in many years, to weep at length. Another important passage concerned the ending of a short story in which the heroine, returning home at night, was knocked down by a car. As she lay dying, a voice beside her kept her alive a while longer, saying four times over in four different versions: "Don't touch her". Then she passed into the sun—the sun of death representing the psychical death of my patient as a result of so many attacks, but also the sun of truth. What she, in her defenceless state, had never been able to express, except indirectly by giving out the signs of madness—that she was not to be touched—was at last stated clearly, calmly, powerfully, as an indestructible law of the psychical universe, which might occasionally be broken and thus hidden from sight, but whose fundamental structuring reality could not be undermined.

From the Skin-ego to the thinking ego

Here, two points must be appended: the taboo on touching promotes the restructuring of the Ego only if the Skin-ego has been adequately achieved; and the latter survives, after that restructuring, as a backcloth to the functioning of thought. To introduce my argument on these two points, I shall summarise a science-fiction story by John Varley, "The Eyes of the Night".[4] An American drop-out, weary of industrial civilisation, is wandering through the Southern states. He arrives by chance in an astonishing community which, he discovers, is made up almost entirely of deaf-blind people. Its members marry and reproduce; they grow or manufacture everything they need and limit their contact

---

[4] It is the last in a collection of short stories entitled *The Persistence of Vision* (1978). I am grateful to Françoise Lugassy for having brought this text to my attention.

with the outside world to a few essential exchanges. The traveller is welcomed by a girl of fourteen, naked like all the inhabitants of this settlement, which enjoys a warm climate. She is one of the few children born with sight and hearing and she learned to speak before her parents, who have the sensory handicaps, migrated to this place. She acts for the young man as an interpreter between his language, English, and the tactile language used by the community. The settlement is criss-crossed by a system of pathways marked out with tactile signs. Information is exchanged through the sense of touch and the extreme sensitivity of the natives allows them to use vibrations in the environment to detect the arrival of strangers or the occurrence of unexpected events. Meals, taken seated closely side by side in a single refectory, are the occasion to gather and exchange news. Later in the evenings, before each family withdraws to its own private area, in a huge space which is both living-room and dormitory, other non-verbal communications take place which are more intense, personal, and emotional. Each person clasps a partner or several partners, body to body, to ask questions or give answers, pass on impressions or feelings, in an unmediated, directly comprehensible form. This is why the inhabitants have to be naked. This is their implicit philosophy: if the sensitivity of the body's surface was cultivated in early life and its development has not been hampered by either clothing or moral prejudices, then it possesses considerable power, the power of suggesting one's emotions, thoughts, desires, and plans directly to other people. Naturally, if a third person wants to know what two people are saying to each other, he or she connects to them by placing a hand or a part of the body on theirs. The speakers can fend off this intervention temporarily if it is unwanted. Naturally also, if what the two people are communicating has to do with love, they end up quite naturally making love, in a close and joyful union—which the visitor's fourteen-year-old bilingual interpreter, who is far from naïve, invites him to join. The freedom and reciprocity with which, from puberty onwards, everyone gives themselves to other people, leaves no place—this at least is the theory of this community—for frustration or jealousy. Love between two individuals is, however, just a step towards the supreme love that the community feels for itself. Once a year, at the end of the summer, in a meadow that has been maintained for this purpose, the whole community gathers— men, women, children, embracing one another tightly to form a single body—and shares (here the narrative stalls because the narrator, who is only a guest, is not allowed to take part) the same ideals or beliefs or sensations in a tangible paroxysmal form.

More and more captivated by this society, the narrator learns their tactile language, with the help of lessons from the girl who is initiating him. But he comes up against barriers caused by his earlier upbringing. What he thinks in verbal he can translate into tactile and what people communicate to him in tactile he can reformulate to himself in verbal. As far as certain ordinary emotions such as love, fear or dissatisfaction are concerned, he manages to express and understand them directly. But the more advanced levels of the tactile language which, as far as his young tutor can explain it to him, seem to correspond to abstract entities or basic psychical states, remain beyond him. Because he is accustomed to verbal language he has a mental handicap which the people of this community, with their sensory handicap, are spared. Thus the more handicapped of the two is not the one we might think… In the end, his application to join the community is turned down. His partner, guilty of speaking a dual language, decides to talk to him henceforth only in tactile. Even if he were to gouge out his eyes and pierce his eardrums, it would still be too late: he could never attain the simplicity and pleni-tude of tactile communication that he would have had if it were original and exclusive. He leaves the community, carrying for ever in his heart an ineradicable nostalgia for it.

Whatever "scientific" reservations we may have about this "leg-endary" narrative—there is no mention of the sense of smell; hatred is split off from love and denied; a tactile language used by deaf-blind people could only be invented by those with hearing and sight who have thus acquired some mastery of the symbolic dimension, etc.— such objections are beside the point. The interest of science fiction lies in the fact that, rather like an experiment, it isolates one variable and draws the maximum logical and psychological consequences from it. The variable here is the idea that there is an original communication of skin to skin, that the skin is the first organ by which meanings are exchanged and that echopraxes and echolalia are only able to develop against an original background of echorhythmias, echothermias, and echotactilisms. Of course, Varley's novella represents a defensive phantasmatic construction, a romance of the origins of communica-tion, elaborated retrospectively in a counter-oedipal move, when the access to more developed semiotic systems has been cathected. In the meantime, this cathexis has been made both possible and necessary by the repression of primary tactile communications, set in motion by the taboo on touching.

What happens when this taboo has not been set up? What price is to be paid for transgressing it? Varley's novella seems to have something to say on both these questions. On the one hand, if the first taboo on touching, the one that forbids body-to-body contact, is not in place, then the oedipal prohibition, which organises both genital sexuality and the social order, is not set up either. On the other hand, the threat of phallic castration, which gives fleshly weight as well as the burden of anxiety to the thought of transgressing the incest taboo, has as its corollary a fear of sensory castration in the event of breaking the taboo on touching. The manifest content of Varley's novella states that the inhabitants escape the taboo on touching because they are deaf and blind. Its latent content must be understood in the opposite way: because they escape the taboo on touching, they are struck deaf and blind. Where the taboo on touching and the taboo on incest are not found, a state of permanent sexual fusion tends to occur in the individual and a state of permanent group delusion in the collectivity.

It is true nonetheless that repressed primary tactile communications are not destroyed (except in pathological cases); they are recorded and retained as the backcloth on which systems of intersensorial correspondences will be inscribed; they constitute a first psychical space into which other sensory and motor spaces can be slotted and an imaginary surface where the products of later operations of thought can be arrayed. To communicate at a distance through gestures and later through words, one not only needs to acquire specific codes but also to have preserved that original echotactile basis of communication and to be able to reawaken and reactivate it more or less frequently. Hegel's concept of *Aufhebung* is particularly useful to describe the status of these echotactile traces which are simultaneously denied, outgrown and preserved.

Just as the incest taboo, if it is introduced too early or too violently, may exceed its aim, which is to redirect sexual and amorous desire away from the family towards strangers and inhibit the impulse to carry out any genital heterosexual act with just any partner, so the primary taboo on touching may, if close contacts are prohibited too early or too harshly, not trigger a repression that is relatively easy to lift under certain socially codified circumstances—sex, play or sport, for example— but instead lead to a serious inhibition of physical closeness, which would create complications in one's sexual life, contact with children, the ability to defend oneself against physical attack, etc.

Conversely, in cases of serious problems of communication, linked to a significant handicap, whether mental (such as autism) or physical (such as inborn deaf-blindness), the semiotic function has to be exercised in its original form—body-to-body contact and echotactile exchanges. As we have seen above (pp. 120–122) this is used in the technique of the "pack".

Unlike the oedipal taboo, the taboo on touching does not demand total renunciation of a love-object, only the renunciation of echotactile communication as one's main way of communicating with other people. Such echotactile communication survives as the original semiotic source and is reactivated in empathy, creative work, allergies and love.

Access to intersensoriality and the creation of a common sense

Once the Ego has acquired its basic organisation as a Skin-ego, it can only acquire a new structure by breaking off the primacy of tactile experience and constituting itself as a space of intersensory inscription, as a *sensorium commune* (the "common sense" of the empiricist philosophers). This restructuring is not sufficiently explained by an impulse to integration on the part of the Ego (Luquet, 1962), nor by a desire to grow and adapt, correlative to the processes of maturation of the nervous system. In my view, we must postulate the effective intervention of a taboo on touching which precedes and announces the Oedipus complex, on the basis of three points—theoretical coherence, clinical evidence, and technical rigour.

Following a fairly thorough review of the psychoanalytic literature on the role of early bodily experiences in the genesis of cognitive disturbances in schizophrenics, Stanley Grand (1982), who works in New York, concludes that the dysfunction of thought in schizophrenia is indicative of a profound impairment in the organisation—or articulation—of the bodily Ego. This impairment is the consequence of an early failure to "articulate" the multiple sensory data (i.e., to constitute the multi-sensory space I have described above, with its various specific sense wrappings properly interleaved with each other) and to integrate them into the experiences of coenesthesia and balance that form the basis of the sense of orientation and the kernel of the experience of reality—in other words, an early deficiency in the first function of the Skin-ego, that of maintenance or "holding". Without an organised feeling of the cohesion and borders of the body, the clear distinction between inner and outer experience, between the Self and object-representations, cannot emerge. The core of the experience of oneself, of having a personal identity, fails to differentiate itself fully from the dual unity of the mother–child bond. Schizophrenics are incapable of benefiting fully from the self-corrective experiences provided by the feedback they receive when they act upon the external world, for this benefit can only be achieved by someone who experiences themselves as the initiator of their own actions. To have an Ego is, in fact, to have at one's disposal the power to initiate not only a single event but a series of events that unfold in chain- or loop-formations. Compensatory mechanisms may partially mitigate the integrative failure of the bodily Ego, especially in the area of sensory experiences related to warmth or the coenesthetic sense; these mechanisms support the cohesion of the psyche and prevent it from collapsing completely during regressive episodes.

Psychoanalysis is only possible if the taboo on touching is respected. Anything can be said, as long as the words are suited to the transferential situation and express thoughts appropriate to whatever the patient is suffering from. The analyst's words symbolise, replace, and recreate tactile contact without that contact actually being necessary, for the symbolic reality of the exchange is more effective than its physical reality.

PART III

PRINCIPAL CONFIGURATIONS

CHAPTER ELEVEN

The wrapping of sound

A t the same time as the boundaries and limits of the Ego are being established as a two-dimensional interface leaning anaclitically on tactile sensations, the Self is constituted by introjecting the world of sound—and taste and smell—as a pre-individual psychical cavity endowed with a rudimentary unity and identity. Associated, when a sound is emitted, with respiratory sensations that give a sense of volume emptying and filling, auditory sensations prepare the Self to form a structure that incorporates the third dimension of space (orientation, distance) and the dimension of time.

In the last few decades, the research of English-speaking psychoanalysts has introduced three major concepts. W. R. Bion (1962) has shown that if an infant's psyche is to develop to the point where the transition from non-thinking to "thinking" or from beta to alpha elements can take place, it must have had real experience of the ability of the mother's breast to "contain" in a delimited psychical space the sensations, affects and memory-traces that force themselves upon its emerging psyche. This containor-breast halts the aggressive-destructive back-projection of bits of the Self that have been expelled and scattered and allows them the possibility of representation, binding and introjection. Heinz Kohut (1971) has sought to differentiate between two opposing, alternative,

173

and complementary movements: in one, the Self is constituted by diffracting itself into objects with which it forms piecemeal narcissistic fusions ("Self-objects"); and in the other the Self accomplishes a single "grandiose" fusion with an ideal object. Finally, referring back to Lacan's concept of the mirror phase, in which the Ego creates itself as other on the model of the unified whole-body image of a reflection, D. W. Winnicott (1971) has described an earlier stage at which the mother's face and the responses of other people provide the child with its first mirror and it then creates its Self on the basis of these reflected images. However, like Lacan, Winnicott lays the emphasis on visual signals. I want to draw attention to the still earlier existence of a mirror of sound or an auditory-phonic skin, and its role in the psyche's acquisition of the ability to signify and later to symbolise.[1]

Case study: Marsyas

Here I report two significant sessions I had with a patient in psychoanalytic treatment; I am calling the patient Marsyas, in memory of the silenus flayed by Apollo.

> Marsyas had been in psychoanalysis for several years. At this time, I was seeing him in sessions of one hour, face to face, because he had begun to show a negative reaction towards couch-based treatment. Using this new arrangement, we resumed psychoanalytic work and there were a number of improvements in the patient's life, though he still found it hard to tolerate the interruptions caused by holidays.
>
> This was the first session following the short spring vacation. Marsyas described himself not as depressed but as feeling empty. When he returned to work, he felt as though he was far away from other people. To him I seemed equally far away. He had lost me. Then he observed that both the extended periods of depression he had experienced in the course of his treatment had occurred during the summer holidays, even though one of them was also the result of a professional failure that had hit him hard. At Easter, he

[1]See Guy Rosolato, "La voix" [The voice]. In: *Essais sur le symbolique* [*Essays on the Symbolic*] (1969, pp. 287–305).

had been able to go away himself for a long weekend. He had gone south and stayed in a comfortable hotel by a magnificent sea-shore, with a heated swimming-pool. He loved swimming and excursions, but this time things went wrong. He got on badly with the members of the small group he was travelling with, though they were friends and colleagues from work, both men and women, with whom he often spent time at the weekend. He felt neglected, abandoned, and rejected. His wife had had to stay at home with their child, who was recovering from an illness. He found walks tiring and things went from bad to worse when the group gathered around the pool: he felt short of breath, he had lost the rhythm of swimming, he tried too hard, in a clumsy, uncoordinated way, he was afraid of diving, feeling wet made the pool water unpleasant and, despite the sun, he shivered all the time; indeed, on two occasions, he slipped on the wet tiles and knocked his head quite painfully.

It crossed my mind that Marsyas came to our sessions not so much to be fed by me, as I had thought ever since we started our new arrangement, but so that I would carry him, warm him up, handle him and give him back, through exercise, the potential of his body and his thinking. For the first time, I spoke of his body as having volume in space, as being the source of sensations of movement, like the fear of falling, but Marsyas made no response beyond polite agreement. So I decided to ask him a direct question: not about how his mother had fed him but about how she had held him when he was small. He immediately brought up a story that he had already mentioned two or three times, which his mother was fond of telling him. Shortly after Marsyas was born, already very busy with her four other children—one older son and three daughters—she had been torn between looking after the new-born baby and attending to the youngest girl, just a year older, who had recently fallen seriously ill. She had put Marsyas in the charge of a maid who was more skilled at domestic work than at the care needed by a baby, but she made it a point of honour to breastfeed this little boy whose arrival had filled her with joy. She fed him generously but speedily and as soon as the feed was over and he was back in the hands of the servant, rushed to his sister, whose health remained so precarious for several weeks that there was even a short time when they feared for her life. Between these hasty visits, in which Marsyas gulped his feed down voraciously, he was both watched and neglected by the maid, who was old and unmarried, austere, principled, hard-working but acting out of duty rather than the wish to give or receive pleasure, and who had a sadomasochistic relationship with the mistress of the house. As far as Marsyas' body was concerned, she was only interested in training it prematurely and caring for it mechanically; she did not play with him. Marsyas was left to his own devices, in a passive and listless state. After a few months it became obvious that he was not reacting normally, and the maid said she thought he was hard of hearing or born retarded. The mother, horrified at this announcement, picked Marsyas up, shook him about, stimulated him and talked to him, and the baby gazed at her, smiled, babbled, and beamed, which reassured her that he was quite normal. She checked this in the same way several times over and decided soon after to replace the maid.

This account allowed me to draw several parallels, which I communicated in part to Marsyas as the treatment progressed. First, that he waited for his sessions with me in the same way as he longed for the breastfeeding visits of his mother, and thus the idea that I might be late or cancel a session made him as anxious as the fear that his mother would stop coming and he would waste away like the sister who was seemingly about to die.

The second parallel had already occurred to me at the beginning of that session and had now been confirmed: he had been fed adequately; what he wanted from me was what the maid did not give him—to be stimulated, to have his psyche exercised (there were times in which his inner life was so depleted that it seemed as though he had died psychically). Since I had been treating him face to face, we had more frequent dialogues, significant exchanges of looks and facial expressions or postural communications. By means of these exchanges, though at a distance, it was as though I was lifting him up, carrying him, getting him moving, even shaking him, making him react, gesture and speak; I told him this.

Thirdly, I now understood Marsyas' body image better. To his mother, he was a digestive canal that was hyper-cathected and eroticised at both ends (at the slightest emotion he was seized with a violent need to micturate and one of his fears was that he might urinate during sexual relations). The maid had not cathected his body in its fleshly totality, as volume or movement; this explained his terror of emptiness.

On these three issues, we had an active, lively, and warm verbal exchange. As he left, instead of his usual limp handshake, he grasped my fingers firmly. My counter-transference was dominated by a feeling of satisfaction at a job well done.

My disappointment at our next meeting was all the greater. Marsyas arrived in a state of depression and, to my great surprise, launched straight into a complaint about the negativity of our last session—which I, by contrast, had felt was enriching for him (as indeed it had been for my understanding of him, i.e., for me). I could not help feeling an inner sense of disappointment parallel to his, but of course I did not communicate this to him. I thought to myself: he takes one step forward, two steps back, and denies any progress he has made. It was clear to me that when he gained on one front he dreaded what he might lose on another; I told him this and reminded him of the law of all-or-nothing, which I had already pointed out as the principle governing his inner reactions. And I went into detail: at our last meeting, he had found the "bodily" contact that he had not had from his nanny; yet, as soon as this happened, he felt he had lost the other, more usual mode of contact between us, the brief, intense feeding he had got from his mother. My comments had an immediate effect: his psyche set to work again. He associated this alternating loss with his longstanding fear—which he had never before articulated so clearly—that psychoanalysis might take something from him—"I don't mean castration", he added spontaneously—depriving him of his mental capacities. The problem for Marsyas lay, in fact, in the deficiency of his narcissistic libido and the failure of his early environment to satisfy the needs of his Ego, as Winnicott distinguishes them from the needs of the body. But where did these Ego needs fit in to the scenario I have just outlined? Now that our psychoanalytic alliance was restored, we were able to take the work of analysis further and bring to light another dimension of his susceptibility to frustration (in other words, his narcissistic wound): if someone else gave him the thing he had not had from his mother, this did not count, for it was his mother who should have given it to him. In his head he was running a perpetual open-ended trial: his mother and the psychoanalyst must own up to the wrongs they had done him from the start! Marsyas was not psychotic because his mental functioning had in the main been sustained during his childhood: there had always been someone—his brother or one of his sisters, one of a series of maids or priests—who fulfilled this role, and here Marsyas mentioned a neighbour whom he had gone to see almost every day, from the time he could talk until he started school. He would chat away to her endlessly and quite freely, which he could never do with his mother, not only because she was too busy but also because she only let him express things that conformed to her moral code and her ideal of the perfect little boy. With me, Marsyas observed, it was sometimes like talking to the neighbour and sometimes like talking to his mother.

He had now settled back into his relationship with me. He said he felt I gave him a lot, he was happier in his life and he could not do without his sessions at any price. But a significant problem remained between us: often he did not understand what I was saying to him—the last time, this had been acute: he could not remember anything, he had simply not "heard" me, in the acoustic sense of the word. What was more, if he thought about his problems in the interval between sessions and had an interesting idea, he could not report it to me. He would suddenly be struck dumb, with nothing in his head.

At first I was taken aback by this resistance, and did not know how to deal with it. Then I made a connection and asked him a question: when he was little, how did his mother talk to him? He described a situation that he had not said a word about in all his many years of psychoanalysis, and which I summed up, when I was writing up the session that evening, with the term "negative bath of words".

On the one hand, his mother had a rough, harsh intonation, which corresponded to her sudden, frequent and unpredictable bouts of bad temper; thus, as a baby, Marsyas' relation to the melody of the mother's voice as a carrier of meaning was interrupted, disrupted, just as the intense and satisfying relationship with his mother during those feeds had been disrupted by the mechanical attentions of the maid. In this way, the two key infrastructures of meaning for an infant (the infra-linguistic meaning found in bodily care and physical play and the pre-linguistic meaning of listening to verbal sounds around it) were both affected by the same

disturbance. On the other hand, Marsyas' mother did not know
how to express what she felt or desired. This was, indeed, a source
of irritation or irony for those around her. It is probable that she
was also poor at guessing what her family were feeling or helping
them to put it into words. She had not been able to speak to her
youngest child in a language in which he could recognise himself.
Hence the impression Marsyas had that both his mother and I were
talking to him in a foreign language.

These two sessions taken together confirmed me in my opinion that
in the case of an early environment which fails to fulfil the needs of
the Ego, what the subject has lacked is the hetero-stimulation by a
good-enough environment of certain psychical functions, a hetero-
stimulation which would have enabled them eventually, by introjective
identification, to stimulate those functions themselves. In such cases,
therefore, the aim of psychoanalytic treatment is: (i) to provide this
hetero-stimulation by appropriate adjustments of the analytic setting
and by being determined to symbolise in place of the patient, whenever
the latter's mind goes blank; and (ii) to let the transference bring out
past flaws in the self and present uncertainties in the coherence and
boundaries of the Ego, so that both parties can work on them analyti-
cally (in fact, patients who are deprived but not neurotic will always
be profoundly dissatisfied with psychoanalysis and their psychoanalyst, but the symbiotic alliance that is established between the authentic
part of their Self and the analyst will allow them gradually to recognise,
through this dissatisfaction, that there are certain precise, specific, circumscribed, and identifiable flaws which are relatively surmountable
in new environmental conditions).

Hearing and phonation in infants

We must now review the established research on hearing and phona-
tion in infants.[2] It leads to the following conclusion: a baby is connected

---

[2]For a summary of the research, mainly in English but also in German and French, see
H. Herren, "La voix dans le développement psychosomatique de l'enfant" [The voice in the
psychosomatic development of children] (1971). I have borrowed substantially from this
article, and the works I cite in the following discussion are listed in Herren's bibliography.
See also Pierre Oléron, "L'acquisition du langage" [The acquisition of language] (1976).

to its parents by a truly audiophonic system of communications; the bucco-pharyngeal cavity, which produces the formants essential to all communication, is very quickly brought under the control of its embryonic mental life and at the same time plays an essential role in expressing emotions.

Apart from the specific noises made by coughing and by eating or digestion (which make the body itself into a resonant cavity, in which sounds are particularly disturbing because one cannot tell exactly where they are coming from), the most typical sound made by a baby immediately after birth is crying. Using a physical analysis of acoustic parameters, Peter H. Wolff (1963, 1966) was able to distinguish four structurally and functionally distinct cries in babies aged less than three weeks—a cry of hunger, a cry of anger (for instance, on being undressed), a cry of pain caused either viscerally or externally (for instance, at a blood sample taken from its heel) and a cry in response to frustration (for instance, if the teat it is sucking is taken away). Each of these four cries has its own specific temporal development, length of frequencies and spectrographic characteristics. The cry of hunger—though it is not necessarily linked to that physiological state—seems the basic one; it always follows the other three, which seem to be variants of it. All these cries are pure physiological reflexes.

In the mother—who in fact tries to distinguish between them very early in her baby's life—these different cries elicit specific responses which, with variations related to her experience and character, are directed to bringing the crying to an end. Indeed the most effective technique for quieting a baby is the mother's voice; by the end of the second week, her voice stops the crying better than any other sound or the visual presence of the human face. By the third week, at least in a normal family context, we find the "pseudo cry of distress, a way of seeking attention" (Wolff, 1963), which takes the form of wails ending in cries, whose structure is very different from the four basic cries. This is the first sound the baby makes intentionally—in other words, its first communication. At five weeks, the child can tell its mother's voice from all other voices, even though it cannot yet distinguish her face from other faces. Thus, before it is even a month old, an infant begins to be able to decode the expressive value of an adult's acoustic interventions. It is the earliest circular reaction that can be observed in a baby, well in advance of the responses of sight or psychomotricity—the spark and perhaps the prototype of the discriminations it will learn later on.

Between three and six months, a baby is constantly babbling. It plays with the sounds it makes. At first these are "clucking, clacking, and squawking" sounds (André Ombredane). Later, progressively, the baby practises differentiating, producing and consolidating, among the varied scale of phonemes, the sounds that make up what will become its mother-tongue. This is how it acquires what linguist André Martinet has called the second articulation of language (the articulation of the signifier to precise sounds or particular combinations of sounds). Some researchers believe that an infant spontaneously utters more or less all possible sounds and then narrows its range by adapting to the system around it; others are of the opposite opinion, that the sounds the baby makes at this stage are the product of imitation and it develops by progressive stages of enrichment. What is certain is that around three months, as a result of the maturing of the fovea, the visual-motor circular reaction begins: the baby's hand reaches for the bottle. But it also reaches towards the mother's voice! And while at this stage the child is capable of reproducing only those gestures it can see itself making (gestures of the extremities), its audiophonic imitations are much more varied: in its babbling, the baby imitates sounds it hears from other people as well as its own sounds; at three months, for example, contagious crying is found.

Two experiments are of interest here. It is difficult to know what a baby hears because there is no response that proves that it has heard anything. This methodological problem has been elegantly solved by Caffey (1967) and Moffitt (1968), who took electrocardiographic recordings of ten-week old infants: the babies were first accustomed to certain phonetic signals they were able to reproduce and then presented with signals that were either contracted in form or belonged to the phonetic repertoire of adults. The results confirmed that a new-born baby possesses a considerable wealth of perceptions, far superior to its ability to produce phonetic sounds, and this foreshadows the well-known fact, easily identifiable a few months later, that semantic comprehension precedes speech production.

Another solution to the problem was discovered by Butterfield (1968), who found that babies of a few days old suck more actively on a musical teat than an ordinary one. Measured by the intensity with which they suck, some babies show a preference for classical music or folk music or singing. After a few exercises of this kind, baby music-lovers, wide awake an hour before their feed (in other words, independently of the wish to eat), become capable of starting or stopping the recorded music connected to an empty bottle they have been given. These findings confirm Bowlby's theory that a primary attachment drive functions simultaneously with the sexual oral drive and independently of it. But they also append a corrective to that theory by suggesting that a child's mental capacities are exercised first upon acoustic (and I would be tempted to add: olfactory) material. This raises doubts about the views of Henri Wallon, whose authority is widely accepted in France and who argues that the differentiation of gestures and mimicry—in other words, of tonic and postural factors—is the basis of social communication and mental representation. It would appear that the baby's feedback loops with other people are formed much earlier than this and are audio-phonological in nature; that they relate first to crying and later to vocalisations (although there are patent functional and morphological similarities between these two); and that they constitute the first stage of learning semiotic behaviour. Put another way, the acquisition of pre-linguistic signification (cries and babbling sounds) precedes that of infra-linguistic signification (that of mimicry and gestures).

Of course, one thing coming after another does not mean that it derives structurally from it: vocal-motor and visual-motor coordinations each have their specificity and their relative autonomy, the former preparing the acquisition of the second articulation (which links signifiers to sounds) and the latter preparing the acquisition of the first articulation (which links signifiers to signifieds). One might even say that in order for the child to develop the linguistic function and, in the course of its second year, to begin to appropriate the code of the human mother-tongue, it must be able to tolerate the structural differences between vocal and gestural communication and to overcome these differences by setting up a more complex structure of symbolisation at a more abstract level. It is nonetheless true that the first problem which the developing intelligence has to deal with is how to differentiate organisationally between body noises, cries, and phonemes and that throughout the first year of life phonetic behaviours constitute an original factor in mental development.

One last example will illustrate this. Between eight and eleven months, the baby's vocal activity, imitation of forms heard and frequency of babbling slow down somewhat. This is the age at which the baby is afraid of strangers—both their faces and their voices—and it is also the age at which it is able, having acquired the opposition of thumb and forefinger around ten months, to copy another person's gestures without seeing itself doing so and, similarly, to get a mental image of objects or events outside its field of perception. But at the same time, and probably as a consequence, it is more inclined to analyse the phonetic behaviour of other people than its own.

Freud's thinking on sound

The idea of a "bath" of spoken words emanating from people in the baby's caring environment does not appear in Freud's work. On the other hand, in the "Project for a scientific psychology" (1950a) of 1895, he assigns a significant role to the baby's crying. At first, crying is the pure motor discharge of inner excitation, according to the reflex model which constitutes the first structure of the psychical apparatus. Later, it is understood by both the baby itself and those around it as a demand, the first means of communication between them, bringing about the transition to the second structure of the psychical apparatus in which the signal, the primary form of communication, occurs in a circular reaction. "In this way this path of discharge acquires a secondary function of the highest importance, that of *communication*" (1950a, p. 318; italics in original). The next level of complexity achieved by the psychical apparatus is, as we know, that of *desire*, which aims at a *mnesic image* of the object that will bring gratification. This is essentially a visual or motor image (no longer in the register of sound): it is the basis of the primary psychical process which aims at the hallucinatory fulfilment of a wish (an experience of self-gratification, by contrast to earlier experience, in which pleasure was always dependent on other people); and finally the association of mental images with instinctual activities constitutes the earliest form of symbolisation (beyond the level of the mere signal). This third structure of the psychical apparatus becomes more complex, in its turn, as verbal traces (or word-presentations) articulate with thing-presentations, which makes both the secondary psychical processes and thought possible. But it is interesting to note that Freud describes what I would call the zero level of this articulation, the articulation of sounds with perceptions: "In the first place, there are objects—perceptions—that make one *scream*,[3] because they arouse pain; [...]

---

[3]*Translator's note:* Anzieu uses the French "cri", which is normally translated in this context as "crying". In this section of the "Project", however, Strachey translates Freud's "Schrei/schreien" (the usual term for a cry, or a baby's crying) as "scream".

When otherwise, owing to pain, one has received no good indication of the quality of the object, the *information of one's own scream* serves to characterise the object [as hostile]" (1950a, p. 366; italics in original). It follows from this that one's first conscious memories are painful ones.

I can now set out my position by showing the limits of my agreements with Freud and where I believe his points need supplementing:[4]

a. The archaic sadistic Superego begins to change into a Superego regulating thought and behaviour at the point of the first articulation of language (the assimilation of the rules governing lexical usage, grammar and syntax).

b. Prior to this, the Ego has set itself up as a relatively autonomous agency, leaning anaclitically on the skin, at the point of achievement of two developments: the second articulation (limiting the flow of vocal utterances to the phonemes that make up the formants of the mother-tongue) and the extra-territorial status of the object.

c. Earlier still, the Self was formed as a wrapping of sound,[5] through the experience of the "bath of sounds" which accompanied breast-feeding. The bath of sounds prefigures the Skin-ego with its double surface, facing inwards and outwards, since this wrapping is made up of sounds emitted by both the baby and its environment. The combination of these sounds produces: (i) a common volume-space which permits bilateral exchanges (whereas breastfeeding and evacuation involve a one-way flow); (ii) the child's first (spatio-auditory) image of its body; and (iii) an actual bond of fused reality with the mother (without which the later imaginary fusion with her would not be possible).

Semiophony

Technological gadgetry and the inventiveness of myths and science fiction offer a further set of proofs.

---

[4]Freud's commentators have shown little interest in problems of hearing and the voice. The editors of the *Standard Edition* do not even feature the terms "voice", "sound" or "hearing" in the index. All they have are references to "screaming" and to "similarity of sound" as it relates to slips of the tongue or puns. A systematic study in French is Edith Lecourt, *Freud et le sonore: le tic-tac du désir* [*Freud and sound: the ticking of desire*] (L'Harmattan, 1992).
[5]Lecourt (1987) has studied the sound wrapping of words and music.

The idea of immersing children suffering from language problems in a bath of sounds before beginning any speech therapy has been put into practice in France under the name of "semiophony".[6] The child is enclosed in a spacious soundproofed booth equipped with a microphone and headset, a true "phantasy egg" in which it can withdraw narcissistically into itself and regress. In the first, purely passive phase, it plays freely (drawing, doing puzzles, etc.) while listening for half an hour to filtered music rich in high-pitched harmonics, and then for another half-hour it hears a filtered pre-recorded voice. In this way, it is subjected to a bath of sounds, reduced to rhythm, melody, and inflection. The second phase of the treatment relates to the second articulation: after listening to the filtered music, the child is asked to repeat aloud signifiers that have also been pre-recorded and passed through a soft filter that makes the voice perfectly audible and distinct and favours high-pitched harmonics; at the same time that it repeats the word, it hears itself in the headphones, discovers its own voice and experiences audio-phonitory feedback. In the next, more straightforward phase, the preliminary "musical bath" has disappeared along with the filtered sounds and the child has to repeat sentences organised into a story. If it makes mistakes in this repetition or adds in fanciful or crude variations, no one makes any comment, still less any reproach. The child may also go on drawing while it listens and speaks. After all, if one is to learn a code one must first play with it and be free to transgress it. "Thus, while believing it is conversing with another person, the child very quickly learns to converse with itself, with that other part of itself which it has failed to recognise and in fact projected on to others, thereby thwarting any possibility of real dialogue" (Beller, 1973, p. 64).

Beller takes a purely didactic viewpoint and thus excludes both the transference and interpretation, and indeed the importance of identifying and understanding the role of environmental deficiencies in the child's linguistic problems. The furthest he goes is to try and create a

---

[6]See Isi Beller, *La Sémiophonie* (1973). The author took his cue from the experiment of Birch and Lee (1955), which demonstrates that when patients suffering from expressive aphasia caused by permanent cortical inhibition were given binaural auditory stimulations of sixty decibels for sixty seconds each they experienced an immediate improvement in their verbal performance which lasted five to ten minutes. He also owes much to the conception of Tomatis' "electronic ear", which he adapts here.

healing machine that will work. But the intuition behind his thinking is fruitful.

> In the first, so-called passive phase of this therapy, during which external sounds are heavily filtered and thus made meaningless, the subject could be said to experience a pleasant feeling of strangeness. [...] This emotion induces a state of elation which is perceived as being within the person themselves, that is, in the representation they have of themselves. (ibid., p. 75)

The strangeness is not uncanny unless the environment fails to "contain" (in Bion's sense) the psychical experience of the subject.

The mirror of sound

Hearing the sounds of the other, when it wraps the Self in harmony—what other term can one use here than a musical one?—and when this hearing responds to the child's own sounds by echoing and further stimulating them, introduces it to the space of illusion. Winnicott (1951) lists babbling among the transitional phenomena, putting it on a par with other activities of this type. But a baby will only stimulate itself by making sounds while listening to them if it has been prepared by an environment that has immersed it early enough in a bath of sounds of the right quality and volume. Before the gaze and smile of the mother who feeds and cares for it reflect back to the child an image of itself that it can perceive visually and internalise in order to reinforce its Self and begin to develop its Ego, the bath of melody (the mother's voice, the songs she sings, the music she lets it hear) offers it a first mirror of sound, which it exploits first by cries—which the mother's voice reacts to with soothing noises—then by gurgles, and finally by playing with phonemic articulation.

The intermixing of the visual and sound mirrors in the constitution of narcissism is of course noted in Greek mythology. It is no coincidence that the legend of the nymph Echo is linked to that of Narcissus. Many nymphs and young women long for the young Narcissus but he is indifferent to them all. Echo duly falls in love with him but her love is not requited. In despair, she withdraws into solitude, loses her appetite and grows thin; soon all that remains of her fading body is a wailing voice that repeats the last syllables of whatever words she hears. At the same time, the girls scorned by Narcissus get their revenge through the goddess Nemesis: worn out from hunting on a very hot day, Narcissus leans down over a spring to slake his thirst, catches sight of his own beautiful face and falls in love with it. In parallel to the fate of Echo and her sound image, he too withdraws from the world, does nothing but gaze at his visual image and lets himself pine away. Even as he is crossing the river Styx to death, his eyes seek out a last view of his own features… This legend clearly marks the precedence of the sound mirror over the visual mirror, as well as the primarily feminine character of the voice and the link between the utterance of sounds and the demand for love. But it also provides the elements of an understanding of pathology: if the mirror, whether of sound or sight, only reflects back the subject's self—i.e., their demand, their distress (Echo) or their search for an ideal (Narcissus)—the result is a separation of the drives which frees up the death drives and gives them economic primacy over the life drives.

It is well known that the mother of a schizophrenic can often be spotted by the alienating effect her voice has on the clinician she has come to consult: her voice may be monotonous (lacking rhythm) or metallic (lacking melody) or harsh (with a predominance of low-pitched sounds, which makes the hearer mix up the sounds and feel invaded by them). Such a voice disrupts the constitution of the self: the bath of sounds no longer surrounds the person but becomes unpleasant (in terms of the Skin-ego, it can be described as "rough"), both punctured and puncturing. This is the case irrespective of what happens later when, as the child acquires the first articulation of language, the mother scrambles its logical thinking by double-bind commands and by contradicting its statements about itself (see Anzieu, 1975b). Only the conjunction of severe phonemic and semantic disturbances together produces schizophrenia; if they are both present but mild, the result is a narcissistic personality; if the first occurs without the second, there will be a predisposition to psychosomatic illness; and if the second occurs without the first, we find many problems of adaptation to school, intellectual or social life.

Characteristic defects of the pathogenic sound mirror are:

- its dissonance: it intervenes in ways that contradict what the baby is feeling, expecting or expressing;
- its abruptness: it is insufficient and excessive by turns and switches from one extreme to the other in an arbitrary manner that the baby

cannot understand; it inflicts multiple micro-traumas on the nascent protective shield (once, after a lecture I had given on the "sound wrapping of the Self", a member of the audience came up and spoke to me about problems he had in relation to "sounds invading his Self");

- its impersonality: the mirror of sounds fails to give the baby information either about what it is feeling or about what its mother is feeling about it. If for her the child is just a machine to be programmed, it will never feel assured of its Self. Often also, she talks to herself in front of the baby, either out loud or inwardly, but is not talking about it, and what the child learns from this bath of words or silence is that it does not matter to her. The sound mirror and, following it, the visual mirror will only contribute to the structuring of the Self and later the Ego if the mother expresses to the child something about herself and something about it, as well as something that refers to the early psychical qualities experienced by its growing Self.

The space of sound is the earliest psychical space: noises from outside which cause pain when they are loud or sudden, gurgles from inside the body that are disturbing because it is not clear where they are coming from, cries that arise automatically at birth and are later associated with hunger, anger or momentary loss of the object, but which are accompanied by an active motor image—all these noises make up something like what Iannis Xenakis must have meant to represent by the musical variations and light-show of laser-beams in his "polytope": a criss-cross of the signals of early psychical qualities, organised neither in time nor in space; or like what philosopher Michel Serres is attempting to describe when he speaks of the flux, scattering or primary cloud of disorder filled with flowing, burning signals of fog. Against this background of noises the melody of a more classical or popular music may arise—made up of sounds rich in harmonics, a real music, the human voice speaking or singing, with its inflexions or invariant quantities that so quickly come to characterise a particular individual. It is at this moment, in this state, that the baby senses a first harmony (presaging the unity that it will discover as its Self throughout the diversity of its sensations and experiences) and a first enchantment (the delusion of a space where there is no difference between the Self and its environment and where the Self may draw strength from the stimulation or calm of the environment with which it is conjoined). The space of sound—if we may be permitted to borrow a visual metaphor to describe it—is shaped like a cavern. It is a hollow space, like the breast or the bucco-pharyngeal cavity, a volume full of rustling, echoes and resonances. It is no accident that the concept of acoustic resonance has been used by scientists as the model for physical resonance in general, and by psychologists and psychoanalysts as the model for unconscious communication between individuals. The spaces successively inhabited by a child—visual, visuo-tactile, locomotor, and lastly graphic space—introduce it in turn to differences between what is "mine" and "not-mine", between the Self and its environment, differences within the Self and differences within the environment. Sami-Ali advanced our understanding of these phenomena in his book L'Espace Imaginaire [Imaginary Space] (1974). Early problems in the sound wrapping can handicap the development of this series of spaces.

Case study: Marsyas (Conclusion)

A few months after the two sessions outlined above, it became possible to see clearly how such a handicap worked in the case of this patient, as a result of the solid points of reference that those sessions had revealed, which I explicitly leaned on more than once (proof that these handicaps can be significantly alleviated by psychoanalysis, so long as one has enough time and motivation, the spatio-temporal set-up is right and one draws one's interpretations from a reliable theory).

> Despite having made undeniable progress in his inward and out-ward life, which he himself had to acknowledge, Marsyas went through another crisis—not so much a crisis of depressive anxiety this time as a crisis of scepticism: he felt he would never manage to change as much as he needed to, he was too different from other people, he felt discouraged and was convinced I believed he was incapable of completing his psychoanalysis and that we might as well agree to end the treatment. Marsyas could not differentiate clearly between what went on in his Self and what went on in his environment. He often felt invaded and disrupted by the emotions of his family; he tried hard to distance himself but his excessive self-criticism denied him any practical means of doing so; some-times he kept his feelings to himself and then complained that no one around him tried to understand him, other times he expressed them so sharply that people responded violently. Each time he

came to the same conclusion: it's up to me, Marsyas, to change, and I just can't. Within the transference I was able to interpret to him that he arranged his private and professional relationships exactly as he arranged his relationship with me, on the model of an inexorable discord between himself and other people, and I suggested a formula to describe this basic discord: the happiness of one is counterbalanced by the misfortune of the other.

Another of my patients, who had a similar background to Marsyas as far as his early childhood experiences and the defects of his Self and Ego were concerned, had reached exactly the opposite conclusion: he believed that it was up to his family and the psychoanalyst to change and that they just could not. The fundamental problem remains the same: being able to differentiate between the subject's own sensory and emotional experience and those of people around them fails to occur or occurs amiss when they have not successfully lived through an early experience in which people around them responded to their pleasure with pleasure, to their pain by soothing it, to their emptiness with fullness and to their fragmentation by harmonisation. Without needing to enclose the patient inside a semiophonic chamber, the psychoanalyst should talk about these things, in order to create an environment that resonates as much at the level of the voice as at the level of meaning.

In his research, carried out in parallel with my own and often in discussion with me, Roland Gori has developed the similar notions of "a sound mirror-image", "walls of sound", "the bodily anchoring of speech" and the "alienation of subjectivity in the code". I am indebted to him for drawing my attention to a science-fiction story by Gérard Klein, "La Vallée des échos" [The valley of echoes] (1966), which imagines the existence of "sound fossils".

> Some explorers on Mars are looking for traces of extinct life in the desert. One day they find themselves in a valley between jagged cliffs, which bears no resemblance to the rest of the eroded, sandy landscapes of the planet… and here they encounter the echo: "I heard a voice, or rather the murmur of a million voices. The uproar of a whole population speaking incredible, incomprehensible words […], this sound assailed our ears in repeated, swirling waves". […] In this valley of Echoes all the sounds of a vanished people are gathered; it is the only place in the universe where fossils

are not minerals but masses of sound. One of the explorers, eager to savour his discovery, moves forward cautiously and at once the voices softly fade away into a deathly silence, "for his body was a screen; he was too heavy, too material for these insubstantial voices to bear contact with him". (Gori, 1975, 1976)

This is a lovely metaphor for a material made of sound, alien to the living body, which maintains itself by a fruitless repetition compulsion of its own; it is both a prehistoric memory and the mortal threat of an audiophonic shroud fallen into tatters, which does not form a wrapping or retain in the Self either psychical life or meaning.

CHAPTER TWELVE

The thermal wrapping

The wrapping of warmth

An interesting phenomenon has often been observed in the practice of relaxation therapy. A patient arrives early and, finding themselves alone in the room, starts the first exercise. Quickly and pleasantly, they begin to feel warm all over their body. The therapist eventually arrives, and at once the patient stops feeling warm. The patient tells this to the therapist, who also happens to be a psychoanalyst, and the latter tries in vain, through dialogue, to elucidate and eliminate the cause of this loss of warmth. The psychotherapist then decides to remain silent and relax as well, leaving the patient to experience what Winnicott (1958) calls being alone in the presence of someone who respects one's solitude while protecting it by their proximity. Little by little, the patient then recovers that total sensation of warmth.

How are we to understand this observation? When a patient is alone in a room they are familiar with and comfortable in, they experience their Self as expanded and elated, which extends the boundaries of their bodily Ego to the dimensions of the room. The good feeling of having a Skin-ego that is growing ever larger and yet also belongs to them alone brings back the earliest experience of having a wrapping of warmth.

193

When the psychotherapist comes in, the spell is broken suddenly and traumatically, for the wrapping is both too big and too fragile (the barrier of warmth is a poor protective shield). With the warmth gone, the patient tries, with the help of the therapist, to find a new anaclisis to support their Skin-ego. This could be the archaic phantasy of a skin common to two partners. But instead of touching the patient's body, the therapist is talking, and the patient resists this regression. The patient only recovers that all-encompassing feeling of warmth once the terror of invasion has dissipated and their bodily Ego has shrunk back to dimensions closer to those of their own body. The discreetly protective presence of the therapist—analogous to the silently benevolent neutrality of a psychoanalyst—leaves the patient free to recover a Skin-ego by identifying with the confident Skin-ego of the therapist. Thus the patient avoids the triple risk of stealing another person's skin, having their own skin stolen by another person or being dressed in the poisoned gift of the other person's skin, which would stop them ever having a skin of their own. The wrapping of warmth extends outwards from the bodily Ego to the psychical Ego, and envelops the Self.

The wrapping of warmth (if it remains warm rather than hot) shows that the person is narcissistically secure and has a good enough cathexis in their attachment drive to be able to enter into relations of exchange with another person, as long as they have a mutual respect for each other's singularity and autonomy: everyday language illustrates this by speaking of such reciprocal relations as "warm". This wrapping marks out a peaceful territory, with border-posts at which travellers may come in and go out, only needing to show that they are carrying with them neither malevolent intentions nor weapons.

The wrapping of cold

The physical sensation of cold felt by the bodily Ego, linked to a "coldness"—in the moral sense—which the psychical Ego gives forth in response to other people's invitations to make contact, aims to create or recreate a protective wrapping that is more hermetically sealed, more closed in on itself, more narcissistically protective, a shield that keeps other people at arm's length. As I have noted, the Skin-ego consists of two layers more or less separate from each other, one facing towards exogenous stimuli, the other facing the excitations of the internal drives. There is a different outcome depending on whether the cold wrapping concerns only the outer layer, only the inner layer, or both, which may lead to catatonia.

I am going to focus on the case of the writer. The first phase of literary creation consists not only in regression to an unconscious sensation-emotion-image called up to supply the dominant theme or tone of the work but also in a phase of "gripping shock", which is represented metaphorically by a dive into cold water, a winter climb or an exhausting walk in the snow (*cf.* Mallarmé's swan trapped in the frozen surface of a lake) and accompanied by shivering and a physical illness with fever to restore body heat; it also brings a fatal sensation of losing one's bearings in the white-out of an icy fog and the "cooling-off" of relations of love and friendship.[1] The outer layer of the Skin-ego becomes a wrapping of cold, which suspends external relations by putting them on ice. The inner layer of the Skin-ego, thus sheltered and over-cathected, is in a maximum state of readiness to "grip hold" of instinctual representations that are normally repressed or even not yet symbolised, and whose elaboration will give the work its originality.

The opposition of hot and cold is one of the basic distinctions that the Skin-ego enables us to acquire; it plays a significant role in our adaption to physical reality, our oscillation between closeness and distance and our ability to think for ourselves. I recall here a case of paradoxical transference (which I reported in my article on this subject: Anzieu, 1975b), in which mood swings, a masochistic persistence in maintaining an unsatisfactory marital life and certain breakdowns in reasoning could be connected in the psychoanalytic work to an early disturbance in the hot-cold distinction.

Case study: Erronée

This was a woman for whom I can find no better pseudonym than Erronée [erroneous], given the frequency and dramatic intensity with which, all through her childhood and even as an adult, she had been told that what she felt was untrue. As a child, she was given her bath not together with her little brother, which would have been indecent, but immediately before him. So that the temperature

---

[1] I have given a more detailed account of this chilling shock in my book *Le Corps de l'Œuvre* [*The Body of the Creative Work*] (1981a, pp. 102–104).

would be right for the boy, Erronée's bath was scalding hot and she was plunged into it by force. If she complained that the water was too hot, her aunt—who looked after the children because both parents were working—called her a liar. If she cried out in discomfort, her mother, who was called in to give her opinion, said she was putting it on. When she got out of the bath, red as a lobster, staggering, and almost blacking out, her father, who in the meantime had been brought in as back-up, accused her of lacking physical stamina and strength of character. No one took her seriously until the day she actually collapsed in a faint. She was put through numerous similar situations, brought about by the jealousy of this abusive aunt, the distant indifference of her mother, overwhelmed by the pressures of her job, and by her father's sadism. One example will show the double bind at work here. Forced into scalding baths by her aunt and mother as a little girl, she was forbidden any baths by her father when she was older—because warm baths make the body and the character soft—and forced to take cold showers, summer and winter, in an unheated cellar in which the shower had been installed specially. Her father would come down and supervise, even after his daughter reached puberty.

On many occasions during her psychoanalytic sessions Erronée experienced the same difficulty in expressing her thoughts and feelings to me, in terror that I might deny their truth. On the couch she would suddenly get a sensation of icy cold; often she would groan or impulsively burst out sobbing. In several sessions she went into a state midway between hallucination and depersonalisation: reality was no longer reality, her perception of things became clouded, and the three dimensions of space went into freefall; she continued to exist but separated from her body, outside it. She understood this experience, once she had verbalised it in enough detail, as the revival of the situation in her childhood at bath-time, when her organism was at the point of losing consciousness.

I thought I could avoid a paradoxical transference with Erronée; but this time it was my turn to be wrong. She made a positive transference quite quickly and I was able to use it to unpick for her the paradoxical system her parents had placed her in, which she talked about endlessly. This positive therapeutic alliance produced good effects in her social and professional life and her relationship with her children. But she remained hypersensitive and fragile: the least little remark from one of her usual interlocutors would plunge her into that state of deep confusion in which she was no longer sure of her own sensations, thoughts or desires, in which the boundaries of her Ego were blurred. Suddenly she tipped over into a paradoxical transference, and from then on she identified her problems as belonging to her treatment with me, experiencing me as the person by whom she could not make herself understood and whose interpretations (which she attributed to me, distorting their sense) were directed at systematically negating her. Her treatment only began to progress again when

- I had fully accepted my position as the object of a paradoxical transference; and
- she had evidence that she could affect me emotionally but that I would remain firm in my convictions.

In denying that the child actually felt what she said she felt—"Your sensation of being too hot is untrue; this is what you say, but it is not true that you feel it; parents know better than children what a child is feeling; neither your body nor your truth belong to you"—the parents were no longer standing on the moral terrain of good and evil but had moved onto the logical terrain of confusing true and false, and the paradox they uttered forced the child to invert what was true and what was false. Hence the resulting problems in setting up the boundaries between the Ego and reality and in communicating her point of view to other people. This also brings about what Arnaud Lévy has described, in an unpublished communication, as a subversion of logic, perverting thought, in a new form of perverse pathology that can be added to the sexual perversions and moral perversion.

CHAPTER THIRTEEN

The olfactory wrapping

The secretion of aggression through the pores of the skin

Case study: Gethsemane

I have borrowed this pseudonym from the name of the Garden of Olives ("Gethsemane" in Aramaic) where, according to the third gospel—the only one that reports this detail—Jesus sweats blood the night before his arrest. His disciples have fallen asleep. He prays in vain to God his Father to spare him the ultimate test of being put to death. He suffers a profound "sorrow": "and being in an agony he prayed more earnestly: and his sweat was as it were great drops of blood falling down to the ground" (Luke XXII: 44).

Gethsemane was born in Italy. He was bilingual and chose to be analysed in French. After deciding against entering a seminary, he studied engineering and then law. He had rather conflictual relations with colleagues in the multinational firm where he worked and was generally "uncomfortable in his skin".

If I limit myself to the manifest content of the associations of ideas and affects raised in our sessions, I can say that, during the first three years of his treatment, Gethsemane expressed nothing but aggressive feelings: first against a middle-aged woman who taught science in a private school of good reputation which he had attended as a scholarship boy, being from a family of modest means (this woman threatened him with expulsion, which would have been a disaster); later against an authoritarian elderly lady whom he called his godmother, who lived with his parents until she died; and lastly against a younger brother who had replaced Gethsemane in his mother's love and care, and had been breastfed, unlike my patient, who had a bitter sense of injustice on account of this. Gethsemane went back over these three aspects of his past with considerable emotion. I followed his slow progress in externalising his aggression and his regression to ever more ancient hate-objects. I intervened by pointing out connections. I collected his enormous fund of resentment as though I were a receptacle for him to deposit it in. His work situation was improving. His relationship with the French woman he lived with was becoming more stable. They had had a child whom they wanted (but whom he never mentioned to me until it was born). But these effects were more psychotherapeutic than psychoanalytic. The more vindictive he was outside our sessions, the more he was submissive and full of good intentions inside them: he would invite my interpretations with deference and agree with them without reserve and without taking time to think. This, then, is what I took to be the reality of his analysis in the "here and now": a positive, idealising, dependent transference, but not a true transference neurosis. There was indeed another manifestation, which was omnipresent in the sense of its sensory power but which I did not know what to do with psychoanalytically: at certain moments, Gethsemane gave off a very strong smell, and it was all the more unpleasant because it was mixed with the perfume he poured on his hair, doubtless—I assumed—to counteract the effects of heavy perspiration. I attributed this idiosyncrasy of my patient either to his biological make-up or to his social background. That was my first counter-transferential resistance: thinking that the most noticeable material produced in the sessions could not have anything to do with psychoanalysis because it was neither verbalised nor had any apparent communicative value.

My second counter-transferential resistance was boredom. Gethsemane smelt worse and worse, while he went on dragging up the same old stories about his childhood tormentors. My mind was swamped and paralysed by both his talk and his smell. I could not think of a single new interpretation. At the same time I felt guilty about my failure to pay attention to him. I tried to justify this by telling myself that he was inducing in the transference a repetition of the childhood situation in which he had become a neglected, unloved son.

It was only through the intervention of a third party that my ability to think was reawakened. One day, an occasional patient, whom I happened to see immediately after Gethsemane, made as if to refuse to stay in my consulting-room. She launched into a tirade against the person who had been there before her and was poisoning the air of the room, asking ironically if this was one of the beneficial effects of psychoanalysis. That incident made me reflect on myself and I realised that indeed I had reached the point with Gethsemane where he was really... getting up my nose (in every sense of the term). Might it not be the transference neurosis that was both concealed and revealed by these foul-smelling emanations, a sneaky way of directing aggression towards me? Suddenly I found this analysis interesting again. But how was I to be able to talk to him about his odour without myself being aggressive or offensive? Neither my training nor my psychoanalytic reading had taught me anything about the olfactory forms of the transference, apart from the notion of the infant's bucco-nasal "primal cavity" described by Spitz (1965).

I came up with an intermediate, fairly general interpretation, which was the first I had made relating exclusively to the present, and I repeated it over a number of sessions in various different forms: "You speak to me more about your emotions than your sensations"; "It seems that you are trying to overwhelm me not only with your aggressive feelings but also with certain sense impressions". At this point Gethsemane spontaneously began to talk about a circum-stance from the past that he had never referred to before. His godmother had the reputation of being dirty. A countrywoman by birth, she rarely washed, apart from her face and hands. She let her dirty underwear pile up for several weeks before washing it, and my patient would secretly go into the bathroom, where it lay, to inhale its strong odour, for this gave him the reassuring, narcissistic feeling of being protected against all harm, even death. The under-lying phantasy was thus revealed to be that of a fusional contact with his godmother's protective, foul-smelling skin. At the same time, I learned that his mother prided herself on always being very clean and wearing plenty of eau de Cologne. In this way I could see—though I kept this observation to myself—that the two smells he filled my consulting-room with were a phantasmatic attempt to combine on his body the skin of his godmother and that of his mother. Did he not have a skin of his own, then? I asked him to go back over the dramatic circumstances of his birth, which he had often been told but had only reported to me briefly during our preliminary meetings. His mother's labour was not progressing well. On the basis of their Christian principles, the midwife and his godmother refused to intervene, saying that a woman must give birth in pain. When, after a long time, the doctor was called, he intimated to the father that he would have to choose between the mother's life and the child's, and then he made a final, desperate attempt at a forceps delivery, which succeeded. Gethsemane was born with skin torn away and bloody in many places and for several days it was touch and go whether he would live. It was said that his godmother saved his life by keeping him in bed beside her. All this got me thinking and encouraged me to intervene more directly.

Because he had been the first to mention a bad odour, I felt entitled to return to the subject. On days when he turned up perspiring particularly strongly, I underlined to him how important odours in general were to him. At the third or fourth such remark, for the first time in his analysis, he changed his style of speaking—up to then he had talked abundantly, continuously, and loudly, overwhelming me and scarcely leaving me the chance to get a word in—and now, in a low, broken voice, in a confiding rather than strident tone, as though making an aside, he said that he had felt very embarrassed on my account when he sweated during our sessions, and that this always happened when he felt emotional; he felt ashamed, each time he left, to shake my hand with a damp palm. Thus in the transference neurosis I represented the godmother—not only hated but also protective—with whom he had had a fusional relationship until he left Italy. This also showed me another counter-transferential resistance in myself: my Ego was unconsciously refusing to accept the role of a peasant-woman who was not only abusive and symbiotic but, on top of that, repulsive. If, deep down, I was connecting his symptom to the past both in order to understand him better and in order to defend myself better against it, Gethsemane was experiencing it in the present, but splitting (I only explained this mechanism to him later on) the emotions felt by his psychical Ego from the sensations felt by his bodily Ego. By fragmenting his experience in the here and now, he made it difficult for me to grasp it in its totality. Thus the psychoanalytic work I needed to do with him was to build up links of thought not only between the past and the present but first and foremost between the fragments of his present.

A few sessions later, Gethsemane announced that he was feeling the effects of an intense emotion. I reminded him of the link he had established between emotion and perspiration and asked him what emotion it was that brought about that effect of perspiration. He made the mental effort—which was quite new for him—of standing outside himself and letting his psychical Ego observe his bodily Ego and replied that when he felt frustrated he became aggressive. I immediately completed the interpretation by laying stress on the psychical container: "To save yourself from the pain of feeling that aggression, you sweat it out through your skin."

For about a year, we worked on bringing to light the characteristics of his Skin-ego. It was clear that the latter leaned anaclitically on the phantasy of a common skin between the little boy and his godmother, for this skin had saved his life and was still protecting him from death. Generally, the Skin-ego rests on a wrapping that is originally mainly tactile or acoustic. In the case of Gethsemane, the wrapping was essentially olfactory; the common skin combined specifically the smells of the genital and anal orifices with those of the secretions of the skin. A psycho-physiologist colleague whom I consulted told me that the sweat produced by the sudoriferous glands has no odour of its own but spreads the milky and odorous secretions of the apocrine glands which are produced by sexual excitation or emotional stress. I understood then that in the case of Gethsemane the thermic and hygrometric functions of sweat as a protective shield had become confused with the emotional signalling function of the odorous secretions.[1] Such an

---

[1] Psycho-physiologists have identified four types of olfactory signals: sexual desire, fear, anger, and a smell given off by people who know they are about to die. I was not able to distinguish these four smells in Gethsemane, either because my sense of smell is

olfactory wrapping creates an undifferentiated totality combining the skin with the erogenous zones. It also unites opposing instinctual characteristics: the contact with his godmother's body was at the same time narcissistically reassuring and libidinally attractive and, on the other hand, invasive, overpowering, and irritating. The same ambivalence—this time on the part of a daughter towards her father—is described in the folktale "Donkey skin", which I reread and found enlightening in relation to my patient. In the story, the essentially olfactory Skin-ego is a wrapping that is neither continuous nor solid. It is riddled with holes, corresponding to the pores of the skin and without sphincter control; these holes allow the excess of inner aggression to seep out through an automatic process of discharge that has no place for the interventions of thought; in other words, it is a sieve Skin-ego. Moreover, this wrapping of smells is shapeless, loose, and porous: it does not permit the sensory differentiations that form the basis for the activity of thinking. Through this discharge at the level of the bodily Ego and this lack of differentiation at the level of the psychical Ego, Gethsemane's conscious Ego remained untouched by any suspicion of complicity with his aggressive drives. For him, aggression was an idea and he could talk interminably about it; but he remained ignorant of the nature of the bodily and psychical wrapping that failed to contain his aggressive impulse. One result was the following paradox: he was conscious of what was operating deep down (the drive) but unconscious of what was going on at the surface (having a psychical container that was full of holes). The bad smell he gave off during our sessions had a directly aggressive character but was also meant to seduce, in a completely non-symbolic way: he was provoking, enticing, and defiling me. But because this was "involuntary", it spared him, on the one hand, from making the effort to think and, on the other, from feeling too guilty about it.

> In the subsequent course of his analysis, Gethsemane's pungent perspiration diminished. It only reappeared during trying times in his life which I could thus interpret as repetitions of certain

---

particularly repressed or because the overall fusional communication between him and his godmother did not allow him to differentiate between them. It is possible that a psychoanalyst's intuition and empathy are largely based on the sense of smell, but this is difficult to establish.

old traumas which he would recall with a considerable effort of attention, recollection, and judgment. Indeed he had to learn how to exercise the secondary psychical processes, a practice he had been spared hitherto by the automatic discharge activity of his drives and which the gradual construction of his Skin-ego as a more supple and solid container now made possible. He also had to learn how to bear feelings of guilt and deadly hatred, first towards his mother and later his father, even though it caused him intense anxiety which expressed itself in the form of cardiac pains. Bit by bit he thus overcame the split between the psychical Ego and the bodily Ego that had held up the analytic process at the start of his treatment.

Some very brief observations on patients who attacked the continuity of their own skin by squeezing their pimples or blackheads are reported by Freud and Bion; according to them, this is the manifestation of an archaic castration complex threatening the integrity of the skin in general rather than specifically that of the genital organs. Gethsemane's olfactory wrapping, with its many holes, was different from this. It represented first of all a fundamental defect in the container. In the second place, it served to reinforce the castration complex, as the rest of his treatment was to make clear.

> The detailed understanding of his olfactory Skin-ego took Gethsemane and me several weeks of active work. I had become very attentive once again in our sessions. Gethsemane perspired less often and less strongly. When it was about to happen to him, or when it did, he would say so and we would look together into the emotion that was causing it.

As for me, I reflected on the counter-transference I had experienced and I believe these were its main components:

a. a personal resistance, due to medical treatment on my nose in childhood, which had blunted my sensitivity to smell and caused me to decathect it;
b. an epistemological resistance, due to the lack of any psychoanalytic theory of the olfactory sense that I might have been able to lean on;
c. resistance against a form of transference that sought to enclose me in an olfactory wrapping common to my patient and myself, just as he

had been enclosed in an olfactory wrapping common to himself and his godmother.

How did I get myself out of this counter-transference? First by recognising that this was what it was; then by creating the fragment of psychoanalytic theory I needed—the concept of a continuous, invasive, porous, secreting, ambivalent olfactory wrapping, as a particular case of the notion of the Skin-ego which I had already invented in response to similar problems of counter-transference that I had encountered in dealing with so-called borderline cases.

> The following year, Gethsemane drove to Italy to spend the summer holidays with his family of origin. All the way there he was in a panic, obsessed by the fear of causing a fatal accident to himself or his wife and son. On the way home, he suffered the same torments—though they diminished once he had crossed the border and he ultimately felt satisfied to have triumphed over his ordeal.
>
> An association seemed obvious to me. He had often spoken about an accident his pregnant mother had had when he was around eighteen months old. She was walking down a stone staircase from the apartment to the street, with Gethsemane in her arms, and she slipped. She had the choice of letting go of the child, with the risk that he might fall head-first on the stone surface and be killed, or making herself fall on her back, so as to cushion his fall with her body, but then the risk was that she might hurt herself badly and bring on a miscarriage. In a flash she chose the second option. Gethsemane survived but with the feeling (reinforced by his mother's repeatedly telling the story) that his survival was pure chance. His mother did indeed have a miscarriage and she limped for the rest of her life. Only some years later did she give birth to another boy, Gethsemane's hated rival. His anxiety on the road— that he would kill either himself or his wife and child—reproduced his mother's dilemma on the staircase: either she would kill the child she had or she would injure herself and kill her unborn baby. Gethsemane felt guilty for having survived; he had taken his life from someone else; the other person should have lived in his place. Later, when his little brother was born and he felt jealous of him, this reactivated the dilemma, now overladen with an unbearable

intensity. This time it was in his power to kill the other and actually he had to kill him in phantasy if he wanted to survive. Long ago Gethsemane had escaped from this cruel situation by choosing to go away with his godmother for long holidays in the country. A dilemma like this is at the root of what Jean Bergeret (1984) has researched under the term "basic violence".

Far from calming his anxiety, the association I had given Gethsemane reawakened it. He was appalled to find himself in a situation in which he could only live at the expense of someone else and that other person could only live at his expense. His response made me thoroughly uncomfortable. I no longer knew how or what to interpret. I was afraid he would start sweating and smelling again. Suddenly, that association made everything clear to me. I asked him if he had perspired during the holiday. He was surprised: indeed, he had not perspired all summer. He only realised this now I mentioned it. It was all the more strange, he added, because all through the motorway journeys the sun had been blazing down. I was then able to convey to him the reason, as I saw it. Before the summer break, we had shed light on the way he unconsciously excreted his aggression through the surface of his skin. So now he could no longer use that method of getting rid of his aggressive impulses, but they had not gone away. On the contrary, they were now causing anxiety to his conscious mind, which had to confront them rather than resort to the safety-valve of an automatic physical discharge. This was why he was afraid of not being able to contain them, since he had not yet learned how to do this by the exercise of his mind. But, I added, wouldn't his mind be better at it than his skin, which just lets them ooze out? Instead of discharging the quantitative excess of aggression that was hampering him, he could now "think" the aggression qualitatively, by recognising what portion of it was his own and separating that portion off from the elements that belonged to his mother or godmother or younger brother. This long intervention of mine brought Gethsemane immediate relief. The material that emerged straight after showed that he could practise this activity of thinking his thoughts best by leaning on the image of his father: of all the family members, his father was in fact the best at tolerating his son's defiance and outbursts of temper.

This transfer of the task of managing aggression from his skin to his Ego enabled me to gain a fuller understanding of exactly how the Skin-ego is generated by both anaclisis and transformation. In the face of his aggressive drives, Gethsemane's Ego was so tightly merged with his skin that it acted as a pure Body-ego, without any intervention from the Pcpt.-Cs system. When, as a result of our psychoanalytic work, his Ego was separated from his skin, Gethsemane became able to use his skin as an anaclitic support for the function of a psychical container, which is itself the precondition for the functioning of the Pcpt.-Cs system. But this separation of the Ego in its capacity to be conscious, retain, defer, understand—and at the same time tolerate the anxiety created by the presence of aggressive representations—could only be achieved after a change in the principle of mental functioning had been brought about, giving up the principle of automatic discharge of instinctual tensions and instead linking the instinctual motive to psychical images and linking affects to representations.

> With the aid of my interpretations, Gethsemane became aware of the split between his psychical Ego and his bodily Ego: what happened at the level of his skin or more generally in his body had previously escaped his notice and he had to make a sustained effort of attention to perceive it. He was determined to make this effort, but it was going to take some learning (this reflects Freud's view that the secondary psychical processes—the processes of thought—begin with attention). This was the precondition for him to be able to start representing his aggression to himself and reflecting on it instead of sweating it out.
>
> After that there was a period in which Gethsemane thought hard about his transference. Little by little he discovered a negative transference not just to the analyst but to the analysis: he said he expected no good to come of it: the feelings he was letting out towards his parents were dangerous; in fact he had suspected from the beginning that the analysis would do him harm. I gave him the following interpretation: he was thinking unconsciously that the analysis would cause his death. This interpretation triggered considerable emotional agitation in him, but it no longer needed to flow out through either perspiration, tears or cardiac symptoms. The malaise was now entirely in his thoughts. For several weeks, Gethsemane experienced this intense fear that analysis might be

fatal to him. Then he admitted, following comments from me, that it was a phantasy, and he was able to retrace its origin. His parents were very hostile to psychological ideas. "Some things are better left unsaid", they would repeat. They had not taken kindly to Gethsemane's decision to go into analysis: "No good will come of it". Ever since, Gethsemane's analysis had been unconsciously overshadowed by the imaginary fulfilment of this threat: he would discover truths that would harm or even kill him.

It is clear how the link between the external and internal origins of his transference neurosis had come about. The internal origin was his act of turning back upon himself the death-wish towards his mother and the other children she might be carrying inside her. The external origin—i.e., the anti-psychological talk of his parents—had provided the manifest text (the equivalent of the day's residues for the construction of a nocturnal dream) which enabled the latent thought to be expressed. Until that articulation specific to a patient's personal history is identified and undone, the transference neurosis does its work in silence and the analysis cannot make any decisive progress. Thus Gethsemane's analytic treatment had remained completely mired in a negative therapeutic reaction.

At this point I understood one of the peculiarities of my counter-transference. The thought that psychoanalysis could be harmful in general and that it could kill Gethsemane in particular was such a blow to my own identity and my ideal of what an analyst should be that I rejected it for weeks before I could accept that it was one of my patient's guiding phantasies.

A few months later, Gethsemane's analysis concentrated—at the cost of great anxiety and powerful guilt-feelings, alternating with occasional outbreaks of foul-smelling sweat—on the sexual phantasies he had developed at puberty. In these phantasies, he was no longer trying, as he had been when younger, to imagine what went on in bed between his mother and father. He conceded to his father the right to possess his wife. Instead, he now imagined being initiated sexually by his godmother, in a sort of implicit pact with his father: I let you have my mother but, in exchange, you let me do what I like with my godmother (this woman was originally his father's godmother, but everyone in the family called her

"Godmother"). He had made some rudimentary attempts to fulfil this phantasy. When he woke up from a bad dream and could not get back to sleep, Gethsemane would go to his godmother's bed and spend the rest of the night beside her, trying a few tentative fumbles. But he was prevented from going any further by another phantasy, which had been revealed by a recently reported dream: the female genital seemed to him dangerous, like a greedy, devouring mouth. It was he himself who, as an adolescent, pronounced the incest taboo, and after that he never went to his godmother's bed again, regretting the fact that his father had not imposed that prohibition more firmly.

Thus, by invading me with his odour, Gethsemane was not only saying to me "Look out, you're in danger from my aggression"; he was wrapping me in the same aroma of sexual seduction that he associated with his godmother's underwear and which he gave off himself when he joined her in bed. I realised that a counter-transference is never complete, and that by closing my nose and my intelligence to this all too concrete sensory signal I was resisting letting my conscious mind be penetrated by the image—which I found repellent—of a young boy trying to snuggle up to me in a bath of dubious odours and force me into the role of a lascivious old maid, until I understood that this was the secondary eroticisation of contact with the primal support-object, the original guarantor of the ability to stay alive.

I am indebted to Gethsemane not only for having helped me discover the specifics of the olfactory Skin-ego but also for having taught me this lesson about the protean character of the counter-transference and its infinite wiles.

CHAPTER FOURTEEN

Confusion of qualities of taste

*The love of bitterness and confusion between the
digestive and respiratory tracts*

Case study: Rodolphe

Rodolphe, who had the imposing bearing of an archduke and a
mind in constant dread of a mortal threat, was in his second analysis with me. The first analysis had focused chiefly on his oedipal
problems. He now brought me his narcissistic flaws, some of which
took the form of psychosomatic symptoms. Nausea and vomiting
could be associated with his paradoxical relation to his parents:
they told him bitter-tasting things would do him good and he was
forced to eat them to the point of triggering the organism's reflex
response; wine, blood, and vomit were poorly differentiated; and
he was warned that sweet things were bad for him. Thus in his
early life Rodolphe had experienced a repeated failure of the taste
qualities that are natural to the organism (see p. 62). As a result,
he suffered from confusion in both thinking and communication.
Scenes in his dreams often took place in a fog. At work, he sometimes muddled up questions he was asked: he generated fog or put

up a smokescreen, to drown out problems. In addition, he smoked a lot. It seemed that smoking was a way of screening out the paradoxical demands of his parents, particularly during mealtimes, which took place in the kitchen, filled with the fug of steam rising from boiling laundry or simmering saucepans.

In one session Rodolphe reported a quarrel at work that could be connected to the transference. In the previous session, in fact, he had recounted a dream and produced a whole host of associations, without leaving me a second to think, let alone intervene. My interpretation was that he had tried to cloud my vision by putting up a barrier of fog between us. He added that this was a way of quarrelling with me,[1] but instead of taking it on board consciously, he had acted it out the next day in the quarrel with his colleague. The session went on. He felt less befugged, more sure of himself and better able to think. Yet before coming to the session, he had had to smoke a cigarette. He described his dilemma thus: either he would think and that would put him in a state of extreme anxiety; or he would do something that gave him pleasure (smoking a cigarette, taking a tranquilliser) and that would stop him thinking. This is what happened in his first analysis.

My interpretation was that there was no smoke without fire and that smoking (with the respiratory and digestive problems he complained of, especially a painful burning sensation in his lungs) was his way of consigning something to the fire so as to save the rest. To keep everything going he had chosen to sacrifice one organ, to manage a mortal danger by localising it in a particular part of the body.

A few sessions later, Rodolphe returned to that symptom of smoking and connected it to his food-related symptoms. He described in detail how he smoked: he would fill his lungs with smoke and hold it in, unable to breathe. That was one mode; the other was that he could not hold onto food and expelled it when breathing out. This caused him to vomit with hiccups. His description of how he vomited was so realistic and vivid that I had to

---

[1] *Translator's note*: the words for "fog" [*brouillard*], "cloud my vision" [*me brouiller la vue*] and "quarrel" [*se brouiller*] are etymologically linked and Anzieu is developing this untranslatable pun in his presentation of Rodolphe.

struggle against a rising nausea. I made an effort to associate the symptom he had induced in me with the circumstances in which it occurred in him: his father would get up from the table to vomit or urinate in the sink; at the same time, the television was blaring and the kitchen smells surrounded Rodolphe with a repulsive wrapping, reinforced by the frequent bouts of yelling directed against him. I interpreted that he identified with his father vomiting and was trying to draw me in to the same contagion he had suffered.

We spoke about a plate of spaghetti in tomato sauce that Rodolphe had eaten with pleasure recently but which had given him indigestion; it reminded him of a mistake he had made as a child: he thought his father was vomiting blood, when actually it was tomato sauce. I pointed out the excessive acidity of tomatoes and the way that the form of spaghetti emphasises the uncertainty of the borders between self and other.

Rodolphe went back over the first session I have reported here. He filled up the space of our sessions with so much material that I could neither catch my thoughts nor "get a word in", even though he thirsted for my words. He was filling himself with air and disgorging food.

I suggested that he was confusing the respiratory tract with the digestive tract and spelled out his body image—flattened out, with one tract passing through it that had to be filled to bursting with air or smoke, in order to acquire thickness, volume, to move from two-dimensionality to three-dimensionality.

Rodolphe made the following associations: as a child he used to swallow air when he was eating, as indeed he still did now on occasions, and his parents had warned him of the dire problems of aerophagy. He emphasised how erotic it was to feel smoke in his lungs: to his intelligence, the burning sensation he felt indicated the threat of a lung disease (and the fact that he should stop smoking), but to his senses it was a good feeling: "It made [him] feel warm inside".

I interpreted, on the one hand, the displacement of the pleasure of absorption from the stomach (where it brought no satisfaction) to the lungs (where he could control it and produce it in himself) and, on the other hand, the paradox that made him feel something was good when it was bad for his organism; and lastly, I suggested a connection between those two points: when his mother fed him copiously but badly, the image of the mother that he was absorbing with the food she gave him did not make him "feel warm enough inside".

Rodolphe added that his father also had something to do with it and he knew why he felt nauseous: his father used to make him eat spinach, though he was repelled by the bitter taste, saying it was good for him because it contained iron and would make him strong.

I said: something your body spontaneously identified as nasty— the bitter taste of that food—was presented to you as nice. This explains your tendency to get pleasure in a way that runs counter to natural conditions. To children, sweet things are good and bitter things are bad. Things that taste salty are in between: at first they find them unpleasant, but later they come to like them, at least up to a point. Rodolphe replied that for him the basic difference among flavours was between sweet and salty; he hated it when they were combined in cooking. By contrast, he still enjoyed many bitter-tasting foods even though he now knew they were bad for him: this was what caused his bouts of vomiting, indigestion or nausea, which could occur on public transport, when invited to friends' houses, or even during our sessions.

In the next few sessions, Rodolphe came back to the theme of fog. Not only was his digestion fogged up but he also felt that he had a core of fog inside him which he called his mad core. This turned out to be connected to a phantasy of the primal scene: when describing a dream, Rodolphe recalled the memory—or screen-memory?—of a frequent scene in which his father, who was ageing and jealous—was keeping an eye on his young wife, whom he suspected of flirting through the window with a neighbour. Rodolphe was there, witnessing the scene, wanting to defend his mother. His father would spy through the opaque glass of the kitchen door or through the curtain of smoke or steam that arose when his mother was cooking or ironing. The father was going mad, he had picked up a kitchen knife, or at least this is how Rodolphe glimpsed him through the fog of his dream, a fog that made a screen in both senses—it formed a barrier and it created a surface for projection. I pointed out the connection between two senses of "brouiller" that he had relived one after the other in the transference: he was clouding my sight [il me brouillait la vue] and he was quarrelling with me [il se brouillait avec moi]. This combination worked through the elaboration of an oedipal phantasy: his father could "see" his wife's infidelity through the fog—as well as Rodolphe's own incestuous desires when in imagination he took his mother's side against his father—and Rodolphe in turn "saw", through the fog, how his father was making threats of death against both her (in the manifest content) and him (in the latent content).

After that, several sessions were devoted to the analysis of this "mad" core of Rodolphe's—mad in the sense that it combined, muddled together and fogged up a problem of narcissism with an oedipal problem, each of which has its own "logic" or "madness".

In Rodolphe's later childhood, the paradoxes of taste and breathing to which he had been subjected in his early years were supplemented by semantic paradoxes that he kept hearing in his head without yet being aware where they came from (this confirms Freud's hypothesis that the Superego has an acoustic origin). These acoustic paradoxes, entangled with the gustatory and respiratory ones, added to the fogginess of his logical thinking and extended the confusion from primary, perceptive thought into secondary, verbal thought. Rodolphe's double narcissistic hypercathexis—of logical thought and of the image he presented to others as a man given to disputation and discussion—had emerged in adolescence, with varying success, to paper over the cracks of a narcissistic insecurity and an uncertainty regarding the borders between the Ego and the Superego, on the one hand, and the psychical and bodily Egos, on the other.

When, between these stages, he had had to deal with the oedipal problematic (Rodolphe had faced and, to a great extent, resolved it with the help of his first analysis), the flaws in his narcissism, represented by the fog, had distorted and obscured this confrontation. Perceiving in his parents an excessive violence of the drives (both sexual and aggressive) had handicapped his ability to recognise and deploy the power of his own drives. Lacking a Skin-ego good enough at containing to allow him to appropriate them, all he had to protect himself against them was a wrapping of fog. Hence his terror of the instinctual urges which he interpreted as the threat of madness. Instead of admitting retrospectively his own incestuous and parricidal desires towards his mother and father, Rodolphe saw in the fog (in other words, in his poorly defined Self) his mother's sexual madness and his father's murderous madness—i.e., other people's drives instead of his own.

This fragment of Rodolphe's treatment leads me to make three comments:

a. Analysis is always the analysis of the Oedipus complex, but it is not only that. The oedipal problematic is always tangled up with, clouded by a narcissistic problematic. Sooner or later it has to be disentangled from it. This varies from one case to another; it may be achieved by the work of interpretation alternating flexibly between the two (when the essential post-oedipal identifications are in place) or in separate phases (when the narcissistic problems have been and still are major ones). In the latter case, one has to take the time to regress the patient to those problems, investigate them and work them through, before the patient can move on by themselves from a mirror transference (in the case of narcissistic personalities) or an idealising transference (in borderline cases) to an oedipal transference. Some psychoanalysts, who insist dogmatically on bringing everything back to oedipal problems, are basically putting the cart before the horse. If they interpret their patient's narcissistic transference as a resistance to confronting the Oedipus complex (it is this too, and that must be interpreted, but only at the right moment), they are actually projecting onto the patient their own resistance to working on what Rosolato (1978) has called the narcissistic axis of depression. The turning-point in Rodolphe's second treatment came when, with the aid of my topographic (as well as economic and genetic) interpretations, he became conscious of the particular configuration of his Skin-ego: a wrapping of fog, a squeezed, flattened internal space, and a lack of distinction between the digestive and respiratory tracts.

b. Rodolphe had had good skin-to-skin contact and meaningful tactile exchanges with his mother and he had acquired the base structure of his Skin-ego. What was lacking in him was a result of the tactile wrapping failing to interweave with the gustatory wrapping and later the wrapping of sound. One of the main effects of his second analysis was to create a better interweaving of these wrappings.

c. Like the great majority of phantasies, Oedipal scenarios are visual. To move on from the narcissistic problematic to the oedipal one is to progress from the level of touch, taste, smell, and breathing to that of sight (hearing belongs, in two different forms, to both levels): this development cannot happen without what I called earlier the double taboo on touching.

CHAPTER FIFTEEN

The second muscular skin

Esther Bick's discovery

In a short article of 1968, as a result of the systematic observation of infants, a methodology which she devised and perfected, the English psychoanalyst Esther Bick, who was a disciple of Klein and Bion, developed the hypothesis of a "second muscular skin". She shows that in their most primitive form, parts of the psyche are not yet differentiated from parts of the body and are felt to lack a "binding force" that would hold them together. They need to be kept together passively by the skin functioning as a peripheral boundary. The internal function of containing parts of the Self derives from the introjection of an external object capable of containing parts of the body. This containing object is normally constituted during breastfeeding, through the dual, simultaneous experience the baby has of the mother's nipple contained in its mouth and its own skin contained by the skin of the mother holding its body and by her warmth, voice and familiar odour. The containing object is concretely experienced as a skin. If the containing function is introjected, the baby is able to acquire the notion that its Self has an inside and accede to the splitting of the Self and the object, each contained in its own skin. If the mother does not fulfil the containing function adequately, or if it is damaged by the baby's phantasmatic destructive attacks, the latter will not be able to introject it: in place of a normal introjection, there will be a continual pathological projective identification which causes confusions of identity. States of non-integration persist. The baby searches frantically for an object—a light, a voice, a smell, etc.—which would maintain a unifying attention to the parts of its body and allow it thus to have, at least momentarily, the experience of the parts of its Self being held together. The poor functioning of the "first skin" may lead the baby to form a "second skin", a prosthetic substitute or muscular *ersatz*, which replaces the normal dependency on the containing object with a pseudo-independence.

This "second skin" has echoes of the muscular character armour beloved of Wilhelm Reich. As for Bick's "first skin", it corresponds to my own concept of the Skin-ego. I first formulated it in 1974, after her, but I only became acquainted with her article after mine was published, thus proving the correctness of the same fact described simultaneously by two researchers working independently. I summarise here some of the observations reported by Bick.

Case study: Alice

Alice was the firstborn child of an immature and awkward young mother, who stimulated the baby's vitality in an indiscriminate way but who gradually, over the first three months, managed to exercise the containing function of the first skin; this effectively reduced her daughter's unintegrated states, with their accompanying trembling, sneezing, and uncoordinated movements. At the end of the first trimester, the mother moved to a new house which was not yet finished. This disruption reduced her "holding" ability and led to a withdrawal from the baby. She forced Alice too early into muscular control (making her drink by herself from a feeding-cup, leaving her in a bouncer) and pseudo-independence (coldly refusing to react to her crying by day or night). She resumed her original attitude of hyper-stimulation, encouraging and admiring Alice's hyper-activity and aggression, nicknaming her "the boxer", from her habit of pummelling people in the face. Instead of her mother providing her with a true containing skin, Alice found a substitute container in her own musculature.

Case study: Mary

Mary was a little schizophrenic; her analysis, which began at the age of three and a half, revealed a severe intolerance of separation, connected to disturbances in her infancy: the birth had been difficult, she was lazy at the breast, she got eczema at four months and scratched herself raw, clung to her mother, could not bear waiting for feeds and was generally backward in her development. She would arrive at sessions hunched, grotesque, and her joints stiff, looking like a "sack of potatoes", as she later expressed it. The sack was in constant danger of spilling its contents—this was both a projective identification with the mother as an object that did not help her contain the parts of herself and a representation of her own skin as perpetually being pierced with holes. Mary did finally become relatively independent: she acquired the ability to hold herself up straight by taking advantage of her second muscular skin, which had been both strengthened and made more supple by the treatment.

Referring to a neurotic adult patient, Bick describes two alternating and complementary versions of the second muscular skin. The analysand describes himself as being in one of two states—either a "hippopotamus" (this is the second skin viewed from the outside: aggressive, tyrannical, scathing, and egocentric) or a "sack of apples" (apples have a thin, fragile skin and are commonly associated with the breast; the sack represents the inside of the Self, protected and hidden by the second skin, which contains bruised psychical parts, the result of an early period of feeding difficulties; in this state, the patient was vulnerable, anxious, demanding attention and praise, dreading disaster and collapse).

Esther Bick's very dense and sometimes elliptical observations lead me to a number of additional comments:

a. The second muscular skin becomes abnormally overdeveloped when it is brought in to compensate for a serious deficiency of the Skin-ego, to shore up the flaws, fissures, and holes of the first containing skin. But everyone needs a second muscular skin, as the active protective shield that reinforces the passive protective shield which is the outer layer of a normally constituted Skin-ego. This is often the role played by sports or clothing. Patients may protect themselves against psychoanalytic regression or the exposure of the bruised and/or poorly connected parts of their Self by going to the gym just before or after their analytic session or by keeping their coat on or wrapping themselves in a blanket when they lie down on the couch.

b. The specific instinctual cathexis of the musculature and thus of the second skin is that of aggression (whereas the primary tactile Skin-ego is cathected with the drive for attachment, clinging or self-preservation): attack is an effective mode of defence, for it means one takes the initiative, keeps oneself safe by holding danger at bay.

c. The abnormality typical of the second muscular skin is a confusion between the protective-shield wrapping and the wrapping which is the surface for inscription; hence the problems of communication and thought. The explanation seems to me to be as follows. If the stimuli coming from a hypertonic mother and/or the early environment have been too intense, incoherent or abrupt, the psychical apparatus needs to protect itself against them quantitatively rather than filter them qualitatively. If the exogenous stimuli were too weak because they came from a mother who was depressed and withdrawn, then there is almost nothing to filter and seeking out stimuli becomes a priority. In both cases, the second skin serves a useful purpose, to strengthen either external protection or internal activation.

Two short stories by Robert Sheckley

The phenomenon of the second muscular skin, as a protective prosthesis replacing a Skin-ego that has not developed well enough to fulfil its function of establishing contacts, filtering exchanges and registering communications, is illustrated by a science-fiction story by Robert Sheckley, entitled "Early model" (1956).[1] The protagonist, Bentley, is an astronaut sent by the earth authorities to make friendly contact with the inhabitants of planet Tels IV. It is clearly a satire on American commercial politics and technology: this friendly contact covers an ulterior motive, to sign advantageous financial contracts with the natives and to test the protective equipment Bentley has brought with him.

---

[1] This story first appeared in the American magazine *Galaxy*. I am grateful to Roland Gori for having drawn my attention to it; see Roland Gori and Marcel Thaon (1975).

Professor Sliggert has perfected the "Proteck", a machine designed to protect space explorers from all possible dangers: at the slightest alarm, it automatically sets up an impenetrable force-field around whoever is carrying it on his back and makes him invulnerable. But it is unwieldy and heavy (forty kilos) and when Bentley disembarks it gives him a strange bulky look, rather like the appearance observed by Esther Bick in the children who looked like a hippopotamus or a sack of apples. Actually Sheckley compares his hero once to a fortress, once to a man carrying a monkey on his back, once to "a very old elephant wearing tight shoes". The Telians are naturally frank and warm-hearted, but when they first meet this character who looks ill at ease and misshapen, with a get-up that makes him hard to identify, they are wary. The Proteck picks up this suspicion and becomes activated. It automatically repels all the approaches and attempts at greeting that the Telians make any-way, coming forward with outstretched hands, holding out their holy spears and food to eat. The Proteck suspects possible dangers hidden behind these unfamiliar gifts. It tightens its protective grip on Bentley, who can henceforth have no physical contact of any kind with the natives; and the latter, more and more mystified at the strange behav-iour of this earth astronaut, conclude that he must be the devil. They organise an exorcism and surround the Proteck with a wall of flame; perpetually activated by the fire, it draws the force-field ever more tightly around its wearer. Bentley is trapped in a sphere that no longer lets through either light or oxygen. Blinded, half-asphyxiated, he strug-gles on. Still in radio contact with the professor through a microphone implanted in his ear—the material equivalent of the acoustic Superego described by Freud—he pleads to be released from the Proteck, but in vain. The voice in his ear insists that he must continue his mission for the good of science, without modifying anything in the terms of the experiment; there can be no question, it says, of "trusting people [...] with a billion dollars worth of equipment on your back". In a supreme effort (and in the interests of a happy ending) Bentley manages to hack through the straps binding him to the Proteck and break free of it. He can now accept the friendship of the Telians, understanding that their hostility was directed not at the man but at the machine-demon that was conjoined to his body without actually being him; they grant him this friendship as soon as they see him perform a first act of humanity—as he shakes off the Proteck he steps to one side to avoid treading on a small animal.

The theme of the false skin had already appeared in an earlier short story by Sheckley, "Hunting problem" (1955). Some extra-terrestrials go hunting, swearing that they will bring back the hide of an Earthling for their chief. They spot one on an asteroid, capture and flay him, and return in triumph. But the victim is safe and sound because they have only stripped him of his space-suit. Going back to "Early model", we could list the following underlying themes, which are significant in the case of patients equipped with that false skin in place of an underdeveloped Skin-ego: a phantasy of invulnerability; the automatised behaviour of a man-machine; a bearing that is half-human half-animal; the protective withdrawal into a hermetically-sealed shell; a distrust of what other people tell us is good but which may be bad; a splitting of the bodily and psychical Egos; a "bath of words" that does not add up to an acoustic wrapping of understanding but proves to be nothing more than the repetitious voice of a Superego implanted in their ear; the weak level of communications given out, in both a quali-tative and a quantitative sense; and the difficulty other people have in communicating with them.

Case study: Gérard

Gérard was a social worker, aged about thirty. The turning-point of his analysis with me was an anxiety dream in which he was being carried off by a torrent and only just managed to grab hold of the arch of a bridge. Up to then, he had complained—with justification—that I either said nothing, which left him flounder-ing, or made interpretations that were too vague or general to be of use to him. Gérard himself associated the torrent with his mother's breast, which was generous, over-abundant, and excessive during breastfeeding. I followed this up by reminding him that once he was older and weaned, this mother, who had over-fed the desires of his mouth (drowning him in oral pleasure and the outflow of greed that she had overstimulated in him) no longer gave him enough to satisfy the needs of the skin: she talked to him about himself in terms that were too vague and general—just as he experienced in the transference/counter-transference with me—and always bought him clothes in sizes too big, for fear he would grow out of them. Thus neither his bodily Ego nor his psychical Ego were con-tained in a way that fitted properly. Soon after, Gérard recalled that as an adolescent he had begun to buy trousers in a size too small, to counterbalance the outsized garments (and thus the outsized containing skin) that his mother had provided. His father, who was a practical but taciturn man, had taught him how to handle inanimate materials but not how to communicate with living beings; in the early part of his analysis he had transferred to me this image of a father gifted with technical skills but silent, until the dream of the torrent tipped the transference over towards the maternal register. The more he spent time in sessions exploring that register the more he felt the need of intensive physical exercises outside the sessions, to develop his breathing (threatened by over-greedy suckling) and pull in his belt of muscles (instead of being held in by clothes that were too tight). Eventually he was training lying on his back, lifting ever heavier dumb-bells. I wondered for a long time what he was trying to tell me by this, in relation to his position on my couch—my difficulty being increased by my personal lack of taste for this kind of physical feat. Gérard ended up associating it with the earliest frightening memory he still had from his childhood; he had mentioned it before, but in a way that was too vague and general for us to draw any meaning from it. Lying in his cot, he had taken an interminable time to fall asleep, because he could see an apple on the sideboard in front of him, which he wanted someone to give him without having to ask for it. His mother did not stir, not understanding why he was crying, but leaving him to cry himself to sleep. This is a fine example of how the taboo on touching can remain too confused and the mother's containing function too imprecise for the child's psyche, secure in its Skin-ego, to be able to give up its dependency on tactile communication easily and effectively, replacing it with linguistic exchange as a form of mutual comprehension. Body-building with dumb-bells was a way of building up the strength of his arms so that he could take the apple for himself; this was the unconscious scenario that underlay the development of the second muscular skin, localised in a single part of his body.

Rightly or wrongly, I did not choose to interpret the part of his dream in which he clung to the arch. I did not want an excess of interpretation to make my words into a torrent, nor to deprive Gérard too soon of the support of the arch that he had transferred on to me. It is possible that this discretion on my part tacitly encouraged him to build up his second muscular skin. It is generally the case that the anxiety of not being able to grasp the object of attachment (or the containing skin-breast) is more severe when, by contrast, the libidinal drive is intensely satisfied in the object-relation to the mouth-breast. I felt that my interpretative work on other aspects, which was coherent and substantial, should be enough to restore Gérard's ability to introject a containing skin-breast. As far as one can judge the results of any analysis, this seems to have been achieved later by a spontaneous mutation of the Ego, similar to that described above in the case of Sébastienne. (see pp. 144–148)

CHAPTER SIXTEEN

The wrapping of suffering

Psychoanalysis and pain[1]

In this chapter I am looking at physical pain for two reasons. The first was highlighted by Freud in the "Project for a scientific psychology" (1950a [1895]). As each of us knows, any intense and prolonged pain causes disruption to the psychical apparatus, threatens the integration of the psyche in the body and affects both the capacity to desire and the activity of thought. Pain is not the opposite or inverse of pleasure; the relationship between them is asymmetrical. Satisfaction is an "experience"; suffering is a "trial". Pleasure means a release from tension, the restoration of economic balance. Pain forces its way through the network of contact barriers, destroys the facilitations that channel the circulation of excitations, short-circuits the relays that transform quantity into quality, suspends differentiation, reduces the differences in level between psychical sub-systems and tends to spread out in all directions. Pleasure denotes an economic process which leaves the Ego both intact in

---

[1] There is very little material on pain in psychoanalytic theory. Apart from the studies cited in this chapter, other works of note are by Jean-Bertrand Pontalis (1977) and Joyce McDougall (1978), in each of which a chapter is devoted to the subject.

its functions and expanded in its boundaries through fusion with the object: I feel pleasure and I feel it even more when I give you pleasure. Pain causes topographical disturbance and, in a circular reaction, the awareness that certain fundamental, structuring distinctions are being obliterated—the distinction between the psychical and bodily Egos, the distinction between the Id, the Ego, and the Superego—makes one's state more painful still. Pain cannot be shared, except when it is eroticised in a sadomasochistic relationship. Everyone faces it alone. It takes up all the space available and I no longer exist as an "I"—pain is. Pleasure is the experience of the complementarity of differences, an experience governed by the principle of constancy, which aims to maintain a stable level of energy by oscillating around that level. Pain is the ordeal of dedifferentiation: it mobilises the Nirvana principle, with its goal of reducing tension (and differences) to zero: better to die than to go on suffering. Giving oneself up to pleasure implies the security of a narcissistic wrapping, the prior acquisition of a Skin-ego. But pain, if one fails to tend to it and/or eroticise it, threatens to destroy the very structure of the Skin-ego, i.e., the gap between its inner and outer surfaces, as well as the difference between its function as protective shield and its function of registering signifying traces.

The second reason for my interest is that, apart from the case of mentally ill mothers or mothers who are repeating the genealogical fate of children dying from generation to generation,[2] the signs of an infant's physical distress are what a mother perceives most commonly and most accurately, even if she is inattentive or ineffective at noticing and interpreting other perceptible signals. Not only does she take the initiative in providing the appropriate practical care—putting the baby to bed, calling the doctor, giving pain relief or binding wounds—but she picks up the baby when it is screaming, crying or gasping, clasps it to her body, warms it, rocks it, talks to it, smiles, reassures it; in a word, she satisfies its need for attachment, protection, and clinging and maximises the skin functions of holding and containing, so that the child can reintroject her adequately as a supporting object, restore its Skin-ego, strengthen

---

[2]See Odile Bourgignon's research on families in which several children have died in *Mort des enfants et structures familiales* [*Family structures and the death of children*] (1984). On the theme of transgenerational transmission, see the collective volume edited by René Kaës, *Transmission de la vie psychique entre générations* [*The transmission of psychical life between generations*], Dunod, 1993.

its protective shield, tolerate the pain, which has been reduced to a bearable level, and maintain the hope of getting better. What can be shared is not the pain but the defence against it: this can be seen in the example of pain in cases of third-degree burns. If, through indifference, ignorance or depression, the mother does not generally communicate with her child, pain might be the trump card the child plays in order to get her attention, be wrapped in her care and in other signs of her love. It is the same with patients who lie down on our couches and reel off a litany of hypochondriacal complaints or suddenly feel acutely a whole series of bodily aches and pains. As we shall also see, at the extreme there are those who inflict a real wrapping of suffering on themselves as a way of recreating the function of containing skin which the mother or other carers have not provided: I suffer therefore I am. In this case, as Piera Aulagnier (1979) observes, it is through suffering that the body acquires its status as a real object.

Cases of third-degree burns

People with third-degree burns have suffered severe damage to their skin; if more than a seventh of the skin's surface has been destroyed, there is a high risk of death; if this persists for three weeks to a month, the failure of the immunological system may lead to septicaemia. With recent advances in treatment, badly injured burns victims may survive, but every burn takes a complex and unpredictable course and may have nasty surprises in store. Treatment is painful, hard both to give and to receive. Once every two days—once a day at particularly sensitive stages or in the most skilled burns units—the injured person is plunged naked into a bath of highly chlorinated water, in which their wounds are disinfected. The bath causes a state of shock, especially if it is carried out under a local anaesthetic, which may turn out to be necessary. The nurses tear off damaged shreds of skin so that the skin can heal overall; in doing this they are unconsciously reproducing the events of the Greek myth of Marsyas. Every time they come into the over-heated treatment rooms, even if they have just gone out for a few minutes, they have to undress and change into sterile uniforms under which they are themselves normally more or less naked. The patient's regression to the defenceless nudity of a new-born baby, exposed to the attacks of the outside world and the possible violence of grownups, is difficult to bear, not only for the burns victims but also for the nurses;

one defence mechanism they use is to exchange erotic remarks among themselves, while another is to refuse to identify with the patients, who are deprived of more or less all possibilities of experiencing pleasure.

Burns offer the equivalent to an experimental situation in which certain functions of the skin are suspended or damaged, so that it is possible to observe the corresponding repercussions on certain psychical functions. Deprived of its anaclitic support on the body, the Skin-ego presents a number of weaknesses, but these may in part be remedied by psychical means.

One of my doctoral students, Emmanuelle Moutin, succeeded in getting a temporary secondment as a clinical psychologist in a burns unit. What is there for a psychologist to do, people objected, when these problems and treatments are purely physical? She was systematically undermined by the medical and nursing staff, who directed at her all their latent aggression against the patients, reacting in a persecutory way to seeing the work of their unit observed by an outsider. By contrast, she was given total freedom in her psychological contacts with the patients. She was able to conduct sustained, long, and occasionally repeated interviews with several victims of third-degree burns and assist some who were dying. The one prohibition imposed on her related to contact with the staff: she was not to "disrupt" them in their work: thus "psychical" care had to take second place to the priority of physical care. This prohibition was difficult to obey, since the dramatic tensions that affected the patients and threatened to endanger the success of their treatment always arose in the course of the physical care, because of an inappropriate psychological relation between the doctor or nurse and the patient.

Here is the first of two case studies which Emmanuelle Moutin was kind enough to place at my disposal.

Case study: Armand

"One day I went into the room of a patient with whom I had a consistent, good relationship. This man, who was in the prime of life, was a prisoner who had attempted autolysis by fire. He was partially burned; his life was no longer in danger but he was going through a period of considerable pain. When I saw him, he could do nothing but complain of the violent physical suffering that gave him almost no respite. He called the nurse and begged her to give him an extra dose of painkillers, as the last one had worn off. As this patient did not complain without good reason, she agreed, but she was called away to an emergency and came back only half an hour later. During this time I stayed with him and we had a spontaneous, warm conversation about his past life and some personal problems that meant a lot to him. When at last the nurse came back with the analgesics, he refused them, saying, with a big smile: 'It's all right, I'm not in pain any more'. He was as surprised as anyone. We continued our conversation, and afterwards he fell asleep peacefully without the help of drugs."

Having a young woman sitting beside him, who was not interested in his body but purely in his psychical needs, the lively and lengthy dialogue that developed between them, the reestablishment of an ability to communicate with another person (and thus with himself) enabled this patient to rebuild a Skin-ego that was able to allow his skin, despite his physical injuries, to exercise its functions of protecting against external attack and containing painful affects. The Skin-ego had lost its biological dependency on the skin. Instead, through talking, and through the conversation with himself and the symbolisations that grew out of it, it had found another anaclisis, a socio-cultural one (remember, the Skin-ego works through multiple anaclitic supports). The skin of words harks back to the bath of speech in which a baby is immersed by people talking to it or by it crooning to them. Then, when the child develops the ability to think verbally, the skin of words provides a symbolic equivalent of the softness, suppleness, and relevance of contact by taking the place of the faculty of touch which has become impossible, forbidden or painful.

A skin of words that can soothe the pain of a patient suffering from third-degree burns may be created in anyone, independent of their age or sex. Here is another case-study of Emmanuelle Moutin's, this time concerning a young woman.

Case study: Paulette

"I was present during the bath of an adolescent girl, who was not badly injured but very sensitive. The bath was painful but was administered in a soothing atmosphere. There were just three of us in the room: the patient, the nurse, and me. The attitude of the nurse, who was energetic but reassuring and affectionate, would normally have helped the treatment along. As I was anxious not to disturb her work and she was someone I trusted and admired, I took little part. Yet Paulette was reacting badly, and this nervous behaviour increased her pain. Suddenly she shouted at me, almost aggressively: 'Can't you see I'm in pain? Say something, anything—I beg you, just talk, talk!' I knew already by experience how a bath of words could help stop the pain. Signalling discreetly to the nurse not to speak, I set about encouraging the girl to talk about herself, directing her towards comforting topics like her family, people or places she knew, essentially her sources of emotional support. This intervention came a little late and so was only partially successful, but it allowed the bath to proceed without problems and almost without pain."

A burns unit can only function psychologically if collective defence mechanisms are set up against the phantasy of flayed skin which the situation inevitably arouses in everyone's mind. There is, indeed, only a slim margin between tearing shreds of dead skin off someone for their own good and flaying them alive out of sheer cruelty. The sexualised hyper-cathexis of relations among the carers is meant to help the staff hold the line between phantasy and reality, a dangerous reality because it is too similar to the phantasy. As for the patients, it is through listening to their stories, through a living dialogue with them, that the distinction can be secured between the phantasy of a flaying inflicted with the intention of being cruel and the representation of a therapeutic removal of skin. The phantasy that they are being deliberately made to suffer adds psychical suffering to their physical pain, which is already considerable, and the result is all the more unbearable because the function of psychical container of affects can no longer lean anaclitically on the containing function of an intact skin. Nonetheless, the skin of words that is woven in the interaction between the burns victim and an understanding interlocutor can symbolically restore a containing psychical skin, which is able to mitigate the pain of an attack on the real skin.

From the body in abeyance to the body of suffering[3]

The two main characteristics of the masochistic wrapping have been described by Micheline Enriquez,[4] from whom I borrow the term "body of suffering":

a. The failure of identification: if a baby has not experienced enough identificatory pleasure in early exchanges with its mother, the affect which keeps its psyche alive is an "experience of suffering": its body can best be described as a body "of suffering".

b. The insufficiency of the common skin: "No subject can live without the cathexis of a minimum of reference-points confirmed and valorised by another person in a common language. They may survive, at best, in a vegetative state, *remaining in abeyance*. The subject will not be able to cathect themselves and will be like a house awaiting its owner". Their body is a body "in abeyance, incapable of experiencing pleasure or creating representations, without affect, disused, uninhabited, whose meaning for another person (most often their mother or mother substitute) will remain always […] more than enigmatic to them". Hence the endless vacillation in their identificatory processes and their recourse to weird initiatory procedures, some of which involve bodily pain (Enriquez, 1984, p. 179).

The *body in abeyance* can be found in the treatment of some borderline cases. Their body invades the whole of space, it has no owner; it is up to the analyst, if possible, to give life to it and give it back to the patient. Analysing such a patient reveals that they had a mother who took care of them because it was required of her rather than out of pleasure. Their body is affectless, disused, reduced to a mechanical functioning that goes nowhere, giving no satisfaction. Other people are purveyors of

---

[3] *Translator's note*: Anzieu's term here, "en souffrance", means "pending" or "in abeyance" (e.g., an outstanding debt, a payment in arrears, or an item awaiting delivery). The French play on words—see also the next note—is unfortunately lost in translation.

[4] Micheline Enriquez, "Du corps en souffrance au corps de souffrance" [From the body in abeyance to the body of suffering], in *Aux carrefours de la haine* [*At the crossroads of hatred*], Part II, Chapter Four (1984).

power and abuse, never of pleasure. The patient is nothing but a body of need, and that need is abused. The result: the body functions in a way that they cannot appropriate as theirs: as a possible object of knowledge or intense pleasure; the distinction between what is mine and what comes from others has not been acquired; there is nothing but a lament, not even accusations levelled at a cause, culprit or persecutor; afraid of confronting an insurmountable conflict of identification, the patient is incapable of any activity of representing or phantasising desires or pleasures that they could call their own.

At the same time, they are desperate for the least sign of recognition from another person and will use any means to find it, to the point of resorting to violence or slavery: hence the perverse masochistic scenarios of their sexual life. The marks of violence inflicted on their body bring them not only guaranteed pleasure but also a feeling of having reappropriated themselves; they can gain mastery over their own body only by disguising this mastery behind the pose of a victim apparently deprived of all means of defence. Secondary masochism allows them to restore affect to their body through the experience of a direct suffering which gives orgasmic pleasure to both them and a partner; in other words, by cathecting their painful body through object libido. But the underlying primary masochism remains: accidents, serious illnesses, emergency surgical operations have disabling and painful after-effects and leave visible scars. The patient eagerly appropriates the pain and scars and makes them into a narcissistic badge of honour. Here the cathexis of the painful body consists of narcissistic libido.

To understand how the body in abeyance changes into the *body of suffering*, according to Micheline Enriquez, we must bear in mind that a body whose affection and identity are failing is subject not to laws (the laws of desire and pleasure) but to the arbitrary power of another person. This body in abeyance carries two potentialities:

- a paradoxical "persecutory potentiality" (see Piera Aulagnier): in order to feel alive, the subject needs to cathect a person who is a persecutory object, needs their presence and the direct link with them; but at the same time, the subject attributes to this person both the wish and the ability to kill them;
- an extreme ability to act out, represent and incarnate suffering. This incarnation is an ordeal, a sacrifice, a Passion. But it is also the chance to live that experience in one's own name.

Case study: Fanchon

I am summarising here the long study of this case published by Micheline Enriquez.

Fanchon was abandoned at birth and raised by adoptive parents; she was subjected to the repeated account of a grandiose, disturbing "family romance" about her origins and to the exclusive, passionate bodily care her adoptive mother gave her: the ideal body must always be clean, hence the rituals of washing and purification which leave little room for pleasure—nor, I would add, for the security of at last having her own, clean skin.[5] This closed maternal space (which is akin, in my view, to what Meltzer calls "the Claustrum") did not create any openings for phantasy, other than the route of the romance of origins. Fanchon's body and identity thus remained in abeyance, but this did not cause her suffering: she was spared by her passivity and inertia from the conflicts and anxieties of death or separation, apart from a few episodes of violent anger. Puberty tipped her over into psychosis, and she began to present painful symptoms which changed her into a subject of extreme suffering and shattered the comfortably distant relationship she had had with her mother: an eating disorder which caused variations in weight, making her unrecognisable but also bringing her oral pleasure and a rudimentary sense of control over her body; the mutilation of one breast; and auditory hallucinations, in which she heard herself called a "slut", "dragged out of the gutter" etc.

Then—like Marsyas—she found herself embodying a myth of rebirth. She gave herself a new forename (I would associate this with the action of an artist giving body to a code around which they could organise their artwork; creating the work in this way is like recreating themselves by autogenesis). Fanchon perfected a ritual of washing every object or piece of underwear that had been in sullying contact with her skin, in order to wipe away the pollution of her origin and her natural mother's original sin. She washed and

---

[5] *Translator's note*: Here Anzieu repeats the adjective *propre*—sa peau propre et sa propre peau—and thus exploits its double meaning: "clean" and "of one's own".

scrubbed her skin till it bled, and she ruined her hair by rubbing it
with lotions and shampoos and tearing it out.

At the age of sixteen or seventeen, she was saved by creating a ritual of
representational writing. Every morning, in her struggle against madness and suicide, she would wake up, take a piece of paper and write
down, alternately, set phrases describing concrete facts about the current
state of her bodily functions (food intake, cleanliness, etc.) and phrases
of her own, in the tone of a personal diary, containing judgments, interpretations, and meanings. "Yet the latter [the personal diary] could only
be achieved because of the skeletal structure of the immutable body of
the text which brought order to space and time, outlining a boundary
between Self and non-Self". Thus a place for representational activity
and thought was marked out, "by the creation of written signs gathered
around a textual body" (I continue my association: the body of the text
often gives the creative artist a substitute for their own body, which has
failed them). These "phrases" were an antidote she could use against
her persecutory voices (to be more precise: these statements about the
body asserted the existence of a Skin-ego and confirmed its continuity,
stability and consistency: this bodily Skin-ego, limited to primary sen-
soriality, provided the background for a psychical Ego to emerge as a
subject saying "I" and implementing mental functions: it must inhabit a
body with continuity if it is to find itself and recognise its own identity).

As for her extreme rituals of bodily purification, I would add
(i) a quantitative remark: their excessive destructiveness repeated
inversely—i.e., undid or counterbalanced—the excessive passionate
care she had received from her mother; and (ii) a qualitative remark:
Fanchon was the bearer of a skin that belonged not to her but to another
woman, the ideal skin that was wanted, granted and imposed by her
second mother; she had to scrub and rub at it until it was completely
gone, for this tunic was the poisoned gift of an abusive adoptive mother
and it held her in its alienating grip. In its place Fanchon might put a
skin of suffering, ugliness, and ignominy, a common skin with her first
mother which alone could lay the foundation for a Skin-ego of her own.

> During the face-to-face analysis reported by Micheline Enriquez
> there was a dramatisation of the girl's psychotic episode, repeated
> in the transference: in one night Fanchon pulled out half her
> hair and developed a skin condition that brought her face out in

purulent spots. Scratching these spots left her with disfiguring marks, and her voices returned, saying: "She is so deeply wicked that you can see it on her face. She has leprosy [...]; they are coming to take her away, put her in isolation and lock her up... Fanchon is not really human; she's a monster; she must be destroyed."

The psychoanalyst, aghast at this turn of events, was nevertheless set on the right track by Fanchon herself: she was expiating the sin of her first mother, who must have been hateful, despicable, and worthless, an inhuman monster, hidden behind the tale told by her adoptive parents, who claimed she was a superior person. Instead of waiting for her like a fairytale mother—beautiful, brilliant, intelligent, returning one day to carry Fanchon off back to her home—Fanchon could bring this first mother to life, invent a history for her in many believable versions and imagine her suffering from conceiving the child, giving birth to her and giving her up.

As this new first mother gradually took shape, Fanchon herself did too: she found a good hairdresser who rearranged her hair and recommended an attractive wig and at the same time a discreet and kindly dermatologist dressed her wounds without fuss. For a whole year she applied herself assiduously to painful psychoanalytic work. Having recovered her human face, she went abroad the following summer to visit childhood friends. She came home having literally made her skin over, as "the skin of her face had peeled completely and been replaced by a fresh skin smooth as a baby's". She decided that she had finished expiating her first mother's fall and that now she could form her own judgment of her and begin to mourn her. She felt she was "normal" again.

According to Micheline Enriquez, the analytic work with Fanchon centred on three themes: (i) giving up the crazy sexual theory suggested initially by what her adoptive parents had told her and arriving at more ordinary phantasies of origin; (ii) learning to resist the incursions of her mother's voice, discordant in both sense and sound, denying her feelings and desires, failing to name affects or to create what I call the acoustic wrapping of the Self; and (iii) building a Skin-ego, at first through derisory attempts at controlling the body and its contents (activities of emptying and filling the body—anorexia, bulimia, constipation, and diarrhoea, i.e., developing what I call the Skin-ego as a bag, a containing skin) and then through registering her suffering upon her bodily wrapping (here the Skin-ego acquires the function I have described as the surface upon which sense qualities are inscribed).

This suffering, exposed to the eye and inviting other people's fascination and horror, allowed Fanchon to extricate herself from her mother's grip, to create an untouchable wrapping and acquire a fundamental feeling of security in her own skin. After this the latter could become the object of an auto-erotic cathexis and experience the pleasures of touch. She started going to the pool and enjoyed swimming; she bought herself new clothes and would take them out of a big shopping bag to show her analyst; before sitting down, she would touch the armchair and other objects in the consulting-room; she smelled the flowers and made comments to the analyst about her clothes or perfume; she wept: "I love feeling warm, salty tears rolling down my face ..." (all this shows that the Skin-ego is indeed set up by means of tactile anaclisis). This Skin-ego allowed Fanchon to give and receive sensory information (made easier by the face-to-face setting) on the basis of two things, the activity of understanding and the experience of satisfaction.

Changing the body in abeyance to the body of suffering, Micheline Enriquez concludes, is the "price that must be paid in order to *be* for other people and to *have* things for oneself"; it is the first identificatory position, within a polarity of inclusion and exclusion, which lays down the conditions for later identifications (specular, narcissistic and oedipal). In my case study of Zénobie (see pp. 243–250), I shall show how the film of dreams may become a way out of the wrapping of suffering.

CHAPTER SEVENTEEN

The film of dreams

Dream and its film

In the primary meaning of the term, a "film" is a fine membrane that covers and protects certain parts of a plant or animal organism; by extension, the word refers to an equally fine layer of solid matter on the surface of a liquid or the outer face of another solid. In its secondary meaning, the "film" used in photography is a thin strip supporting the sensitive layer which will receive impressions. Dream is a "film" in both these senses. It is a protective shield that envelops the psyche of the sleeper, protecting them against the latent activity of the day's residues (the unsatisfied desires of the previous day, merged with the unsatisfied desires of childhood) and the stimuli of what Jean Guillaumin (1979) has called the "night's residues"—sensations of light, sound, warmth, touch, coenesthesia, organic needs, etc., that impinge during sleep. This protective shield is a fine membrane that puts external stimuli and internal instinctual impulses on an equal level, flattening out their differences (unlike the Skin-ego it is not an interface that separates inside from outside). It is a fragile membrane, apt to break or dissipate— leading to an anxious awakening—and an ephemeral membrane, which lasts only as long as the dream does—even though one might imagine its presence would reassure the sleeper so much that, having unconsciously introjected it, they could curl up inside it, regress to a state of primary narcissism in which bliss, the end of all tensions and death were all mixed up together and sink into a deep dreamless sleep (see André Green, 1984).

On the other hand, a dream is an impressionable film: it registers mental images which are for the most part visual, occasionally with added sound or subtitles, sometimes more like photographic stills, but most often animated like cinematic films, or rather—to use a better, contemporary comparison—like a video-clip. This is certainly the activation of one of the Skin-ego's functions—that of the sensitive surface which registers traces and inscriptions. Or if not the Skin-ego, then at least one can say that the image of the dematerialised, flattened-out body provides the dream backcloth on which projected figures appear, symbolising or personifying psychical forces or agencies in conflict with one another. The film may be of poor quality, the reel may get stuck or let in light, making the dream disappear. If all goes well, when one wakes up one can develop the film, view it, re-edit it or even project it in the form of a story told to someone else.

In order for a dream to occur there must be a Skin-ego (babies and psychotics do not dream, strictly speaking, for they have not acquired a secure sense of the difference between sleep and waking life or between reality and hallucination). Conversely, one of the functions of dreaming is to repair the Skin-ego, not only because it runs the risk of coming undone during sleep but above all because it has been, to one degree or another, riddled with holes by incursions from the day before. In my opinion, this vital function of the dream, restoring the psychical wrapping day by day, explains why everyone—or more or less everyone—dreams every night, or more or less every night. Though this is necessarily omitted in Freud's first theory of the psyche, it is implicit in his second theory, as I shall endeavour to explain.

Freud's theory of dreams revisited

Between 1895 and 1899, under the influence of his passionate friendship with Fliess and elated by his discovery of psychoanalysis, Freud interpreted night dreams as imaginary wish-fulfilments. He described the psychical work a dream does on the three levels which, for him at that time, made up the psychical apparatus. An unconscious activity associates instinctual impulses with thing-presentations and affects and thus makes them representable. A preconscious activity takes these representative and emotional presentations and articulates them on the one hand with word-presentations and on the other with defence mechanisms, enabling them to develop into symbolic figurative representations and compromise formations. Lastly, the perception-consciousness system, which transfers its functioning during sleep from the progressive pole of motor discharge to the regressive pole of perception, hallucinates these figurative representations with a sensory and affective vividness that lends them a delusory reality. The dream-work succeeds when it overcomes the successive obstacles of two censorships, first the one between the unconscious and the preconscious and then the one between the preconscious and the conscious. There are two ways in which it can fail. If the second censorship is not fooled by the disguise of the forbidden desire, then the dreamer wakes in a state of anxiety; if the unconscious representations short-circuit a detour through the preconscious and pass straight into the conscious, the result is night-terrors, or nightmares.

When Freud developed his second concept of the psychical apparatus, he did not take the time to revisit the whole theory of dreams in the light of it but contented himself with revising a few aspects. These, however, led the way to a more complete systematisation.

Dreams realise the desires of the Id, understood as including the whole gamut of instinctual desires that Freud had just added: sexual, auto-erotic, aggressive, and self-destructive. They realise them in accordance with the pleasure principle—which governs the psychical functioning of the Id and requires the immediate and unconditional satisfaction of instinctual demands—and also with the tendency of the repressed to return. Dreams realise the demands of the Superego: for, while some dreams seem more like wish-fulfilments, others are the fulfilment of a threat. Dreams realise the desire of the Ego, which is to sleep, and they do this in the service of two masters, creating imaginary satisfactions for the Id and the Superego at the same time. Dreams also realise the desire of what some of Freud's successors have called the ideal Ego: to restore the primitive fusion between the Ego and the object and rediscover the blissful state of organic intra-uterine symbiosis between infant and mother. Whereas when it is awake the psychical apparatus obeys the reality principle, maintains the boundaries between Self and non-Self and between the body and the psyche, accepts limitations on what it can do and asserts its claim to individual autonomy, when it is dreaming, by contrast, it lays claims to omnipotence and expresses its aspiration to infinite powers. In one of his short stories, in which he describes the "City of the immortals", Borges shows the latter as spending all their time dreaming. Indeed, to dream is to deny one's mortality. If we did not have this night-time belief in the immortality of at least one part of ourselves, would life by day be tolerable?

In the post-traumatic dreams studied by Freud (1920g) in the introduction to his second psychical topography, the dreamer repeatedly relives the conditions immediately prior to the accident. These are anxiety dreams but they always stop just short of representing the accident itself, as though it could be retrospectively suspended, avoided at the last moment. Compared to the dreams described above, these dreams fulfil four new functions:

- to repair the narcissistic wound caused by having undergone a trauma;
- to restore the psychical wrapping torn by the incursion of that trauma;
- to regain control retroactively of the circumstances that triggered it; and
- to re-establish the functioning of the pleasure principle in the psychical apparatus, which the trauma had caused to regress to the repetition compulsion.

It occurs to me to wonder whether these characteristics of dreams associated with traumatic neurosis actually are a special case. Or rather—this is what I believe, at least—given that trauma acts as a magnifying glass, are we not actually looking at a general phenomenon that lies at the root of all dreams? The drive, as a form of urge independent of its aim or object, irrupts repeatedly into the psychical wrapping during both sleeping and waking hours, causing micro-traumas whose qualitative variation and quantitative accumulation, once they exceed a certain threshold, constitute what Masud Khan (1983) has called a cumulative trauma. This means that the psychical apparatus must find a way, on the one hand, to discharge the overload and on the other to restore the integrity of the psychical wrapping.

Of the range of possible ways of doing this, the two most immediate, often found in tandem, are to create a wrapping of anxiety and a film of dreams. When the trauma occurred, the psychical apparatus was shocked by the surge of external stimuli that broke through its protective shield, not simply because they were too strong but also— Freud (1920g) emphasises this point—because of its unpreparedness: it was not expecting anything like this. Pain is the sign of this shocking incursion. For an experience to be traumatic, there must be a difference of level between internal and external energies. Certainly, with some shocks, whatever attitude the subject takes towards them, the organic disruption and the rupture of the Skin-ego they cause are irreparable. But in general, the pain is less severe if the incursion did not come as a surprise and if someone is quickly found who can treat the injured person by talking to them and tending them and thus supplement or replace their Skin-ego—treat them, in other words, as the victim of a narcissistic injury as much as a physical one. In *Beyond the Pleasure Principle* (1920g), Freud describes this defence against trauma as a way of mobilising equivalent counter-cathexes of energy, aiming to make the cathexis of internal energy *equal to* the quantity of external energy created by the surge of stimuli. This operation entails a number of consequences: the first three are economic, and these are the ones Freud particularly focuses on. The fourth is topological and topographical: Freud only gives a vague sense of this one and I shall develop it here.

a. These counter-cathexes cause a corresponding impoverishment of the other activities of the psyche, particularly sexual and/or intellectual life.

b. If a physical trauma causes a long-term lesion, there is less danger of a traumatic neurosis, for the lesion creates a narcissistic hypercathexis of the affected organ, which binds the excess excitation.

c. The greater the level of cathexis and the extent of bound (i.e., quiescent) energy in a system the stronger its capacity for binding and thus withstanding trauma. This leads to the constitution of what I call a wrapping of anxiety, the protective shield's last line of defence: by hypercathecting its receptive systems, anxiety prepares the psyche to anticipate the possible sudden occurrence of a trauma and to mobilise as near as possible the equivalent internal energy to counteract the external stimulus.

d. Viewed topographically now, the pain of the incursion remains but it is surrounded and sealed off by a permanent counter-cathexis, so it subsists as an unconscious psychical suffering, localised like a kind of cyst on the periphery of the Self—similar to the "crypt" described by Nicolas Abraham (1978) or indeed to Winnicott's notion of the "hidden Self".

The wrapping of anxiety (the first defence, which works through affect) prepares the way for the film of dreams (the second defence, which works through representation). The holes in the Skin-ego, whether produced by one major trauma or an accumulation of micro-traumas derived from the residues of the previous day or from stimuli during sleep, are transformed by the work of representation into theatrical locations in which the scenarios of the dream are played out. The holes are thus stopped up with a film of images that are essentially visual. The original Skin-ego is a tactile wrapping backed by acoustic and gustato-olfactory wrappings. The muscular and visual wrappings come later. The film of dreams is a way of trying to replace the failing tactile wrapping by a visual wrapping that is finer, more fragile but also more sensitive: the function of protective shield is minimally restored, but the function of registering traces and changing them into signs is increased. Every night, to escape from the sexual appetites of her suitors, Penelope undid the tapestry she had woven that day; dreaming goes in the opposite direction: it weaves up again by night whatever elements of the Skin-ego have been undone the day before by the impact of exogenous and endogenous stimuli.

My concept of the film of dreams ties in with an observation by Sami-Ali (1969) about a patient suffering from urticaria; noticing that she alternated between periods when she had episodes of urticaria but did not dream and periods when she had dreams but no urticaria, Sami-Ali made the assumption that dreams serve to cover up a displeasing body image. I would summarise his intuition as follows: the delusory skin of the dream masks a raw, inflamed Skin-ego.

These points also lead me to reconsider the relation between the latent and manifest contents of a dream. As Nicolas Abraham (1978) and Annie Anzieu (1974) have noted in two different ways, the psychical apparatus is a structure of interleaved layers. In fact, in order for there to be contents, there must be a container, and what is a container at one level may become a content at another. The latent content of a dream aims to contain instinctual impulses by associating them with unconscious thing-presentations; the manifest content aims to be a visual container of the latent container. Recounting a dream on waking aims to be a verbal container of the manifest content. The interpretation a psychoanalyst might make of a patient's dream narrative does two things: it both undoes the interleaving, as one peels off the skins of an onion, and restores the conscious Ego, stripped of its layers, in its function as containor of the representative and affective representations of instinctual impulses and traumatic incursions.

Case study: Zénobie

This patient was the eldest of her siblings and bore the scars of the loss of her position as only child; I have given her the pseudonym Zénobie after the brilliant queen of ancient Palmyra who was dethroned by the Romans.

> Her first analysis, with a colleague, seems to have focused on her oedipal feelings, which took the form of hysteria, on the resulting complications in her sexual life, and on her frigidity, which had diminished but not disappeared altogether. She came to consult me first because of a more or less constant state of anxiety which she was no longer able to repress since her first analysis, and second because of this persistent frigidity which she was trying both to cure and to deny by throwing herself into ever more complicated relationships.

> The first few weeks of her second analysis were dominated by an intense love-transference or, to be more precise, by her transferring into the treatment the seductive manoeuvres she habitually used with older men. I recognised—though I did not say this to her—the underlying hysterical ruse behind this over-obvious seduction: to keep the interest and attention of a possible partner by offering him sexual gratification, while in reality trying to obtain from him the satisfaction of Ego needs that her family had ignored when she was young. Little by little I showed Zénobie that her hysterical defence-mechanisms were protecting her—ineffectually—against flaws in her basic narcissistic security, flaws connected to a terror of losing her mother's love and to many ways in which her early psychical needs had been frustrated. Zénobie was still scarred by the near-traumatic contrast she felt between these frustrations and the generosity and pleasure with which her mother had satisfied her bodily needs until the birth of her rival, a brother.

The seductive transference disappeared as soon as Zénobie became certain that the psychoanalyst was willing to care for the needs of her Ego without demanding a bonus of erotic pleasure in return. At the same time, the quality of her anxiety changed: her depressive anxiety, linked to the experience or threat of losing her mother's love, gave way to a persecutory anxiety which was more ancient and more powerful.

When she returned from a summer holiday abroad, she told me she had enjoyed living in a flat that was larger, brighter and in a nicer area than her Paris home. Though I did not say this to her, all these details seemed to me to reflect the development of her body image and Skin-ego: she was feeling more at ease "in her skin" and was very keen to say so, but this rudimentary Skin-ego gave her neither an adequate protective shield nor a filter that could help her understand where the excitations came from or what they were like. In fact, the dream-apartment by day became a real nightmare after dark. Not only did she not have dreams but she could not get to sleep: she was convinced that burglars might break in. This anxiety persisted after she came back to Paris, and she had still not got back to normal sleep.

I interpreted her fear of being burgled as having two aspects: on the one hand the idea of an incursion coming from the outside— a stranger breaking in to the intimate parts of her body (fear of rape), but also the idea of being violated by the psychoanalyst entering the intimate parts of her psyche—and on the other the idea of an incursion coming from the inside, from her own drives, which she would not admit to, especially a violent resentment of frustrations imposed upon her, both long ago and in the present. I explained that the intensity of her anxiety was due to the combination and confusion of these external and internal incursions, as well as the confusion between sexual and psychical penetration. This inter- pretation was meant to consolidate her Skin-ego as an interface between external and internal stimuli and as a set of interleaved wrappings differentiating the psychical and bodily Egos within the same Self. The effect was immediate and fairly long-lasting: she was able to sleep again. But the anxiety she had experienced all her life tended to reappear in the analysis.

The next few sessions were marked by a mirroring transference. Zénobie kept asking me to do the talking, to say what I thought, tell her about my life, so that I would echo what she said, or express what I thought of what she had said. These insistent and endless demands put my counter-transference to the test, causing me almost physical strain, as they prevented me from thinking freely. I could neither keep silent, because she took this as a violent rejection and it might have damaged the Skin-ego she was just beginning to form, nor could I enter into her hysterical game of inverting the situation so that I became the patient and she the analyst. By trial and error I developed a two-pronged interpretative strategy. On the one hand, I clarified or reiterated an interpretation I had already given her, which responded partially to what she was asking of me and would show her my thinking as an analyst and how what she said found an echo in me. On the other, I tried to elucidate the meaning of her demand: sometimes I would explain that checking to see there was this corresponding echo in me showed her need to receive an image of herself from another person so that she could create an image of her own; sometimes that certain questions—knowing what her mother was thinking or what her life with her husband was like, what relationship she had with a male cousin who was said to be her lover or why she had had more children—had remained both painful and unanswered; and sometimes that by subjecting me to a barrage of questions she was reproducing (in order to master it) a situation she had experienced as a young child, in which she had been subjected to a barrage of stimuli that were too intense or too premature for her to be able to incorporate them into her thinking.

Sustained analytic work allowed her to get some distance from her persecutory position. With me she recovered the security of the primary link to the good maternal breast and body, a security that was then destroyed by the disappointments of a series of births from inside that body.

Her summer holidays passed off without difficulties and with-out any disruptive actings-out. But when we started up again, she fell into a major regression. In the forty-five minutes of the session she went through a massive experience of emotional distress. She relived the whole agony of being abandoned by her mother. The details of this suffering which she had been able to recover and put into words clearly showed how far her Skin-ego had developed: she had achieved the wrapping that could contain her psychical states and the doubling of the conscious Ego that enabled her to observe herself and symbolise the parts of her that were ill. She brought out three kinds of detail, which I grouped together each time in my interpretation. First of all, I explained that she had suffered at being abandoned by her mother, being dethroned from the position of only child: we already knew this theoretically but she needed to recover the feelings of intense suffering which she had both experienced and repudiated at the time. Second I proposed a hypothesis which had suggested itself to me during the recent period of mirroring transference: even during the time she was an only child, the communication between her and her mother had not been strong: Zénobie's mother had given her plenty of food and cuddles but she had not considered the baby's inner feelings enough. In response to this, Zénobie told me that her mother would shout at the least little thing (which I associated with her fear of loud noises breaking in on her); she had been unable to distinguish for sure, in her own feelings, what came from her mother and what came from herself: loud noises expressed someone's fury but she did not know whose. Thirdly, I suggested that this failure to take her primary sensations, affects, and phantasies into account had no doubt been reinforced by her father, and from this point on my patient was able to evoke explicitly the latter's jealous, violent character.

That session was one of extreme and prolonged emotional intensity. Zénobie sobbed and seemed on the brink of collapse. I warned her in advance when the session would finish so that she could prepare herself inwardly for the ending. I assured her that I was taking on her suffering and that she was going through, perhaps for the first time, an emotion so powerful that she had never before allowed herself to feel it and had sealed it, removed it and enclosed it in a sort of cyst at the periphery of herself. She stopped crying but was walking unsteadily as she left. This suffering, which she had at last made her own, had created a wrapping for her Ego that strengthened her sense of the unity and continuity of her Self.

The following week, Zénobie had reverted to her usual defence mechanisms: she said that she never again wanted to go through such a painful experience in her analysis. Then she mentioned the fact that she had been dreaming a lot, constantly, every night since she came home from holiday. She had not intended to tell me about this. In the next session, she announced that she had decided to tell me about her dreams, but as there were too many of them she had grouped them into three categories: the "beauty-queen" dreams, the dreams of spheres—I have forgotten the third category, as I did not have the chance to write it all down at the time, being overwhelmed by the profusion of material. Session after session she reported her dreams, both in detail and in bulk. I was drowning in it—or rather, giving up the attempt to retain, understand or interpret it, I let myself be carried by the flood.

In the first category of dreams she was, or she saw, a very beautiful girl whom some men were about to strip naked in order to examine her beauty. As for the second category, the "sphere" dreams, she interpreted them herself, relating them to the breast or testicles. She picked up this point and added: the sphere is a breast-testicle-head. She recalled the everyday expression "to lose your marbles", meaning "to go off your head".[1]

Zénobie's dreams helped her weave a psychical skin to replace her weak protective shield. She began to reconstitute her Skin-ego from the moment I interpreted her auditory persecution, stressing the confusion between the noises coming from outside and the noise in her head caused by her inner rage—split, fragmented, and projected. She went on to recount all her dreams one after the other, without stopping over any particular one or giving me enough time or information to make interpretations. It was as if she was hovering above everything—or, to be more exact, I felt as if her dreams were hovering above her and surrounding her with a bower of images. The wrapping of suffering was being replaced by a film of dreams that made her Skin-ego more firm and consistent. Moreover, her psychical apparatus was able to symbolise this restored activity of symbolisation through the metaphor of the sphere, which combined a number of representations: that of a psychical wrapping becoming complete and unified; that of the head—in other words (to borrow Bion's term), a machine for thinking one's own thoughts; that of the all-powerful maternal breast, inside which Zénobie had gone on living, in a regressive phantasy; and that of the male reproductive

---

[1] *Translator's note:* The French term used by Zénobie for this category of dreams is *"les boules"* (lit. "balls", but not in the English slang sense of testicles). The expression she/ Anzieu refers to is *"perdre la boule"*.

organs, which she had felt the painful lack of when she was displaced by her brother's birth from her position as privileged love-object of the mother. This metaphor brought together the two dimensions of her psychopathology, narcissistic and object-related, prefiguring the intersecting interpretations I was to give her over the following weeks, which alternated between focusing on her set of sexual, pregenital and oedipal phantasies and on the flaws and the hypercathexes (for example, the seductiveness) of her narcissistic wrapping. In fact for a subject to acquire a sexual identity, two conditions must be fulfilled. One is a necessary condition: they must have a skin of their own to contain it, in which they can indeed feel that they are a subject; the other is a sufficient condition in relation to their polymorphous-perverse and oedipal phantasies: they must have experienced erogenous zones and intense pleasures on that skin.

At last, a few sessions later, Zénobie produced a dream we could actually work on. She was coming out of her house; the pavement had collapsed. You could see the foundations of the building. Her brother turned up, with his whole family. She was lying on a mattress. Everyone was looking at her quietly. But she felt outraged, wanting to scream aloud. She was being forced to go through a horrible ordeal: she had to make love with her brother in front of everybody. She woke up exhausted.

Her associations led her back to a recent dream of bestiality which had upset her very much, recalling the disgusting nature of the sexuality she had experienced as a child and during her first heterosexual experiences in adolescence, which had also felt like a revolting ordeal. "My parents making love: they looked like animals... (a pause). What really scares me is that my trust in you will be called into question."

Me: "That's the pavement crumbling under you, the threatened foundations. You expect me to help you contain the excessive sexual excitation that you've been carrying inside you since you were a child, which the analysis has made you more and more aware of". This was the first time the word sexuality had been spoken aloud in her treatment, and it had been spoken by me.

She went into more detail. All through her childhood and adolescence she had been in a perpetual state of unpleasant, confused stimulation that she could not manage to shake off.

Me: "That was sexual stimulation, but you couldn't identify it as such because no one around you had explained anything about this to you. You also couldn't find exactly what parts of your body the stimuli were coming from because you didn't have a clear enough idea of your female anatomy". She seemed reassured as she left.

At the next session, she referred back to the profuse dream-material she had flooded me with: it had poured out of her, she said, and she was afraid it would overwhelm my ability to control her.

Me: "You're putting me in the same position of being over-whelmed by the flood of your dreams as you are by your sexual excitation."

Zénobie could now formulate the question she has been holding back since the beginning of the session: what did I think of her dreams?

I said I was willing to answer the question about her dreams right away because her family had not answered her questions about sexuality long ago, and since then she had had an uncontrollable need to ask people what they were feeling and also what they thought she was feeling. But I made it clear that I was not going to judge either her dreams or her actions. I was not going to express a view, for example, about whether incest or bestiality was good or bad. I went on to give her two interpretations. The first aimed to distinguish between the object of attachment and the object of seduction. In the dog that was clasping her in the earlier dream, she had experienced an object she could communicate with at a vital, primal and essential level, through touch, feeling the softness of its fur, the warmth of its body, and the caress of its licking. These sensations of well-being in which she let herself be wrapped made her feel so good in her skin that she felt a properly sexual, feminine, but disturbing desire—the desire to be penetrated. In the later dream, with her brother, the sexuality was bestial in a different sense, for he was violent, she had hated him when he was first born and now he could get his revenge by possessing her; and it would be a monstrous incest, like animals. He was the fearsome lover she had imagined as a little girl, who would carry out her sexual initiation.

Second, I stressed the interference, which she found embarrassing, between the sexual, bodily need that she had not yet completely fulfilled and the psychological need to be understood.

> She offered herself as the victim of a man's violent sexual desire in the belief that it was the only way to get his attention and to obtain, at the price of the pleasure she would give him, the satisfaction of her own Ego's needs; yet this satisfaction was sometimes hypothetical and sometimes insatiable (here I am referring to the two kinds of experiences she had had, in turn, in the course of her sexual life). This explained the seductiveness she exhibited in her relationships with men, which was a game that ensnared her just as much as them; I remind her of the first few months of her analysis, which were taken up with replaying and undoing that game.

The psychoanalytic work we began during that series of sessions went on for several months. It triggered some important changes, in successive fits and starts (which was consistent with this patient's way of moving forward in a rhythm of breaks and sudden restructurings) in both her sexual life and her work. It was only much later that we were able to analyse Zénobie's direct leap from orality to genitality, short-circuiting the stage of anality.

The wrapping of excitation, the hysterical basis of all neuroses

The sequence detailed above illustrates the necessity of acquiring a Skin-ego and the concomitant feelings of unity and continuity in the Self not just in order to accede to sexual identity and enter into the oedipal problematic but, even before that, to identify the location of erogenous excitation accurately, to set limits on it while at the same time enabling it to find routes of satisfactory discharge, and to free sexual desire from its role of counter-cathexis against premature frustrations of the psychical Ego and the attachment drive.

This case also serves to illustrate the sequence *wrapping of suffering—film of dreams—skin of words*, which is needed to create a Skin-ego that will be able to contain, filter, and symbolise, in patients who have suffered from early failures in the satisfaction of Ego needs and thus present major narcissistic flaws. Zénobie's unconscious aggression against men could be linked to the successive frustrations she had suffered at the hands of her mother, then her father and finally her siblings. As her Skin-ego developed into a continuous, flexible, firm interface, her drives, both sexual and aggressive, became a force based in specific bodily zones that she could direct towards better chosen objects and with aims that would bring both physical and psychical pleasures.

If it is to be recognised—i.e., represented—a drive must be contained in a three-dimensional psychical space, be located at certain points on the surface of the body, and stand out as a figure against the ground of the Skin-ego's backcloth. It is because the drive is delimited and circumscribed that the full force of its pressure is felt, a force that can find its aim and object and can reach a clear and vivid satisfaction.

Zénobie exhibited many aspects of the hysterical personality. Her treatment revealed the "wrapping of excitation", to borrow Annie Anzieu's term (1987). Unable to create her psychical wrapping on the basis of sensory signals from her mother (strikingly, there was a serious discordance between the warmth of her mother's touch and the harsh sounds she made), Zénobie tried to find a substitute Skin-ego in a permanent wrapping of excitation, cathected in a broad, diffuse way by the aggressive as well as the sexual drives. This kind of wrapping results from introjecting a loving mother who stimulates the baby during breastfeeding and bodily care. It surrounded Zénobie's Self with a belt of excitations which perpetuated, in her psychical functioning, the dual presence of a mother who was attentive to her bodily needs and a state of continuous instinctual stimulation which allowed Zénobie to feel she had a permanent existence. But the mother who stimulated her body was doubly disappointing, for she was not good at responding to her child's psychical needs and would suddenly call a halt to the physical excitation she had provoked, when she felt it had gone on too long or been too pleasant or too ambiguous or too much trouble; she would suddenly get irritated at what she had caused and punish the child, who was filled with guilt. At the same time, this sequence of excitation and disappointment was played out at the level of the drive, which was over-activated without ever reaching a fully satisfying discharge.

In Annie Anzieu's view, such a psychical wrapping of physical excitation is not only typical of the Skin-ego in hysteria but forms the hysterical bedrock of any neurosis. Instead of exchanging signs constituted by early sense communications, which are the foundation for the possibility of mutual understanding, the mother and child only exchange stimulations, in an escalating process that always ends badly. The mother is disappointed that the child does not bring her the pleasure she expected; the child is doubly disappointed, both because it has disappointed its mother and because it carries inside it the burden of an unsatisfied excitation.

I would add that this hysterical wrapping perverts the third function of the Skin-ego by inverting it: instead of taking refuge narcissistically in the wrapping of a protective shield, the hysteric gets satisfaction from living inside a *wrapping of excitation* which is both erogenous and aggressive, to the point where they suffer themselves, accusing other people, resenting them and trying to drag them into the repetitious circle of this game of excitation leading to a disappointment which in turn provokes more need for excitation. In his article "Grudge and the hysteric" (1974), Masud Khan gives a good analysis of this dialectic.

The neurophysiology of sleep and the diversity of dream material

Electroencephalography has revealed a number of levels of sleep, each with a specific corresponding type of dream.

1. As we fall asleep, we experience hypnagogic images which are midway between those of waking life and those of dreams. This is the phase in which we move from rest, with the muscles relaxing, to slow-wave sleep. Respiratory and cardiac rhythms slow down, the body's temperature and tension drop and metabolic activity slacks off. The individual falling asleep becomes insulated from sensory excitations, which allows them to decathect the protective shield. The sensory wrappings that belong to the various sense organs coexist in a weakened form but are no longer interleaved. This breaks down the figure/ground structure and three-dimensionality is lost. The psychical wrapping falls away. By contrast to dreams proper, these "aesthetic" (in the sense of the opposite of "anaesthetic") images have no storyline. They represent states rather than actions, appear one after another without any link, kaleidoscopically— grimacing figures, a horse-race, a house fallen into ruins, clouds in the sky, etc. These images express the distortion of the body image and its surrounding space that results from one's position lying flat in bed, one's withdrawal of interest from sensory-muscular excitations and the separation of one's bodily and psychical Egos. Paul Federn carried out a systematic study of these images in himself.

Bertram Lewin refers to the "blank screen" (1946) of dreams: the dream is reduced to its container, it has not yet acquired a content. Lewin sees this as standing for the breast emptied by feeding, a flattened-out surface that forms the backcloth on which the future action of real nocturnal dreams will later be projected: this fragment of whitish fog represents the sensation—part visual, part tactile—of the texture of the mother's skin as she breastfeeds, and seeing it brings a feeling of contentment, fullness, and repletion. Isakover describes another phenomenon, of similar origin but with a nightmarish flavour: a hypnagogic sensation of having sand or rubber in one's mouth; Robbe-Grillet gives an example of this at the beginning of his first novel, Un Régicide [A Regicide]. Isakover explains this illusion in terms of the mother's nipple, still in the baby's mouth when it drops off, having drunk its fill, but no longer libidinally cathected, so that it is experienced as something grainy or rubbery.

Falling asleep calls into question the psychical framework of the waking state, the three-dimensional body schema with its internal symmetry, the familiar body image. The tactile and visual images we produce while we fall asleep are not organised in relation to each other but arise in series. The main themes are: the flattening out of the body, reduced from a volume to a plane; the uncertainty of bodily limits (swollen or shrunk); the distortion of faces, grinning or threatening (i.e., representations of the imago in its raw state); plane surfaces twisting or losing their hardness (as in the nightmare of a little boy seeing the sheets on his bed turn into a shapeless mass of hollows and bumps); the sudden unexplained displacement of objects which tear and rip space and threaten to run through the dreamer's body; sensations of uncanniness in general.

2. "Slow sleep" is characterised by slow, regular breathing; the body is almost completely immobile (but not paralysed: the sleeper may snore or turn over) and by the slow, regular activity of the brain, which no longer passes on orders or movements. The sleeper loses contact with their surroundings. Their sense organs no longer send messages of information or stimulation to the brain. There is no longer a psychical wrapping acting either as a surface to receive and filter excitations or as a backcloth on which meanings may be inscribed. Consensuality is dismantled. The activity of dreaming

is no longer possible. Slow, deep sleep is dreamless; it fulfils the Nirvana principle.

3. By contrast, the progressive arrival at this sleep is accompanied by intense dreaming. In fact, the small amount of psychological consciousness that remains is disturbed by the gradual dual loss of sense and motor functions. Losing motor control may be expressed by a total relaxation of the sphincter (enuresis) or by an automatic motor protest (somnambulism). The sleeper mumbles, speaks or cries out. This is the phase during which night terrors may occur. Two kinds of anxiety are mobilised and thus furnish the terrifying content of the dreams: the neurotic fear of castration or the psychotic fear of annihilation (always connected, respectively, to muscular "castration" or to the "annihilation" of the psychical wrapping that grounds the subject). Once, when I was writing a lecture on dreams I had a typical nightmare, two nights before the event: I dreamt that members of the audience raised violent objections to my lecture and I "cut them short" (as you might say!) by shouting at them, loudly and clearly: "I'm going to cut off your balls". My wife reported these words to me the next morning—they had woken her up, yet I had no recollection of them. One of my patients, who had been affected by accounts of war and torture, had the following dream, which recurred for a long time: a glass pane was smashed (symbolising the shattering of the protective shield) and she was masturbating with the shards of glass, wrecking her vagina and destroying all possibility of genital pleasure.

4. It is only to paradoxical sleep—the last type of sleep (chronologically)—that Freud's original statement on dreaming is applicable: "A dream is the imaginary fulfilment of a wish", to which we must add: organised into a storyline. To summarise: the hypnagogic images are specific representations of the abandonment (or loss) of the psychical containers of the waking state. The dreams we experience when entering into deep, slow sleep are a representation of threats to destroy the body and the psyche, terrifying psychical contents no longer contained by an adequate psychical framework; they unfold in two phases: the first represents the destruction of the bodily and/ or psychical wrapping, and the second represents a fundamental anxiety that arises or "breaks through".

Paradoxical sleep, unlike the preceding type, is active. At first the sleeper's body remains immobile but their face and fingers begin to tense gently: they stop snoring and their breath becomes irregular—very fast, then slow—and they may even stop breathing for a few seconds. Under their eyelids, the corneas bulge and sink by rapid turns. If you gently raise their eyelids, they actually seem to be following some moving object with their gaze. Blood flows to the brain and their body temperature rises, although the main body muscles are still paralysed: the arms, legs, and trunk remain immobile. Penile erections occur in adult men—and in new-born boys. One theory has it that paradoxical sleep is not true sleep but a phase in which the subject is awake yet paralysed and subject to hallucinations. The dreams of this phase are commonplace ones, typically cathecting the surface of inscription, with their content organised into a storyline, representing wish-fulfilments, particularly sexual, pregenital, and genital ones (see Freud). The disjointed nature of the dream is concerned with a confused relationship of part to whole (whereas the hypnagogic images are concerned with the confusion of the relationship of figure to ground).

Paradoxical sleep takes place in a series, each lasting ten to twenty minutes, one and a half hours apart. It is peculiar to mammals and other species that have prolonged sleep. It is paradoxical in the sense that it maintains a level of wakefulness while still allowing the subject to go on sleeping. It combines aspects of the waking state (movement of the fingers, eyes, and facial features, which accounts for the tactile and visual images, accelerated cardiac rhythm and erections) with aspects of sleep (muscular relaxation, which makes cathexis of the protective shield unnecessary).

Each of these varieties—three types of dream and dreamless sleep—follows one of the four principles of psychical functioning: the decathexis of the reality principle (hypnagogic images at the point of falling asleep); repetition compulsion (nightmares when entering the phase of slow sleep); the Nirvana principle (slow dreamless sleep); and the pleasure principle (paradoxical sleep). In other words, they follow the psychical principle that is most suitable to deal with the type of neurophysiological material that occurs at each stage of sleep.

This distinction between three types of dream has the advantage of bringing some order into the variety of post-Freudian psychoanalytic theories on the meaning of dreams. We can apply to hypnagogic images the psychosomatic theory of Christophe Dejours, who argues that dream is the "attempt to express mentally a change in the body's state" experienced during sleep. The nightmares that precede the entry into slow-wave sleep illustrate Angél Garma's Kleinian theory that dreams are the "intensely relived instances of the sleeper's experiences of horror or panic, traumatic instances arising from anxious contents that the Ego cannot shake off and which therefore it believes to be real". These contents represent death drives that once overwhelmed the fragile psyche of the infant, are now revived by the regression of the sleeping state and which find a resonance in the trauma of birth. The dreams of paradoxical sleep require sub-division. One of them, the programme dream, has been studied by Jean Guillaumin, in his discussion of Freud's originating dream of Irma's injection in the light of Michel Jouvet's neurophysiological theory: in Guillaumin's view, dream serves to recharge the genetic programme that activates the functioning of the drives. Lastly, Claude Debru's neurophysiological theory that paradoxical sleep and dreaming are the guardians of psychical individuation maps on to the function of individuation that I attribute to the Skin-ego.[2]

The eight functions of the Skin-ego seek fulfilment in dreams, in particular because they are threatened with failure as a result of the weakness of the waking ego and the topological regression due to sleep. Here are some examples.

Dreams of falling (for example, from the top of a cliff) express attacks against the function of maintenance or holding. Dreams of worms that come swarming out of the skin express attacks against the function of containing. Dreams of meetings where everyone is talking at once and no one is listening to the dreamer express attacks against individuality. Multi-sensory dreams (in which the visual material is intersected by elements of sound, smell, taste or touch) express attacks against consensuality.

---

[2] See Christophe Dejours, *Le Corps entre biologie et psychanalyse* [*The body between biology and psychoanalysis*] (1988); Angél Garma, *Le Rêve: traumatisme et hallucination* [*Dream: trauma and hallucination*] (1970, Paris: PUF, 1981); Jean Guillaumin, *Le Rêve et le Moi* [*Dream and the Ego*] (1979); Claude Debru, *Neurophilosophie du rêve* [*A Neurophilosophy of dreams*] (1990).

CHAPTER EIGHTEEN

Summaries and further observations

Origins of the notions of psychical wrapping and psychical skin

Freud's use of the term wrapping

The concept of "a wrapping" and its verbal derivatives "to wrap/ envelop" or "wrapping/enveloping" first appear in Freud's writing in 1920, when he was reworking his thinking on psychical topography (adding the Id-Ego-Superego model to the earlier model of conscious-preconscious-unconscious), psychical economy (adding the principles of repetition compulsion and Nirvana to the pleasure and reality principles) and the duality of the drives (integrating the opposition of object libido and narcissistic libido into the more general opposition of the life and death drives).

But, as is frequently the case with Freud, overwhelmed by the richness and multiplicity of a crowd of new ideas glimpsed intuitively but as yet obscurely, he seized on and exploited the three theoretical amendments outlined above and left the concept of wrapping lying fallow. He did not return to it in any later text. The word survives as a metaphor (the Ego is configured as an all-encompassing sac) and a metonym (the Ego is the surface of the psychical apparatus and the projection of the surface of the body on the surface of the psyche). The fact that the surface of the body is called the skin is left implicit by Freud and it is not expressed explicitly until half a century later in the work of Esther Bick (the "psychical skin", 1968) and eight years after Bick by Didier Anzieu (the "Skin-ego", 1974). As for the notion of wrapping, between 1975 and 1986 I attempted to give the status of a concept to what had hitherto only been a term of imagery.

Here are the passages in which Freud uses the term wrapping (with my emphases in italic). In the first, from *Beyond the Pleasure Principle* (1920g), he uses the metaphor of a wrapping, i.e., an interface which is a closed surface (on the model of a sphere):

> What consciousness yields consists essentially of perceptions of excitations coming from the external world and of feelings of pleasure and unpleasure which can only arise from within the mental apparatus; it is therefore possible to assign to the system *Pcpt.-Cs.* a position in space. It must lie on the borderline between outside and inside; it must be turned towards the external world and must *envelop* [*umhüllen*] the other psychical systems. (1920g, p. 24)

And, two lines further on:

> [...] we have merely adopted the views on localisation held by cerebral anatomy, which locates the "seat" of consciousness in the cerebral cortex—the outermost, *enveloping* [*umhüllende*] layer of the central organ. (ibid.)

Later he brings in comparisons, explicitly to a vesicle and a shell and implicitly to a crust:

> Let us picture a living organism in its most simplified possible form as an undifferentiated vesicle of a substance that is susceptible to stimulation. Then the surface turned towards the external world will from its very situation be differentiated and will serve as an organ for receiving stimuli. Indeed embryology, in its capacity as a recapitulation of developmental history, actually shows us that the central nervous system originates from the ectoderm; the grey matter of the cortex remains a derivative of the primitive superficial

layer of the organism and may have inherited some of its essential properties. It would be easy to suppose, then, that as a result of the ceaseless impact of external stimuli on the surface of the vesicle, its substance to a certain depth may have become permanently modified, so that excitatory processes run a different course in it from what they run in the deeper layers. A crust would thus be formed which would at last been so thoroughly "baked through" by stimulation that it would present the most favourable possible conditions for the reception of stimuli and become incapable of any further modification. (ibid., p. 26)

"Wrapping" and "membrane" are thus considered by Freud as synonyms: the "protective shield against stimuli" [*Reizschutz*] is the "outermost surface [which] becomes to some degree inorganic and thenceforward functions as a special envelope or membrane [*Hülle oder Membran*] resistant to stimuli" (ibid., p. 27).

In *The Ego and the Id* (1923b), Freud adds the comparison to the homunculus:

The ego is first and foremost a bodily ego; it is not merely a surface entity but is itself the projection of a surface. If we wish to find an anatomical analogy for it we can best identify it with the "cortical homunculus" of the anatomists, which stands on its head in the cortex, sticks up its heels, faces backwards and, as we know, has its speech-area on the left-hand side. (ibid., p. 26)

Esther Bick's concept of the psychical skin

In her short article of 1968, Esther Bick sets out the concept of the psychical skin, though she does not formulate it fully. Here I have chosen to use the six-point summary proposed by Albert Ciccone and Marc Lhopital in *Naissance à la vie psychique* [*The birth into psychical life*] (1991):

First premise: the parts of the personality, which are experienced in their most primitive form as having no binding force between them, are held together by the introduction of an external object felt to be capable of fulfilling that function.

Second premise: the introjection of the optimal object, the mother (breast), which is identified with this containing object-function, gives rise to the phantasy of inner and outer spaces.

Third premise: the introjected containing object is experienced as a skin. It has the function of a "psychical skin".

Fourth premise: the introjection of a containing external object, which gives the skin its boundary function, is a precondition for the implementation of the processes of splitting and idealisation of the self and the object.

Fifth premise: if the containing functions are not introjected, projective identification continues undiminished with all the confusions of identity that follow from it.

Sixth premise: the disturbances of introjection that result either from the inadequacy of the real object or from phantasmatic attacks against it lead to the development of a "second skin" formation.

Didier Anzieu's concept of psychical wrapping

The topographical model of the psychical apparatus was drafted by Freud in *Beyond the Pleasure Principle* (1920g) and picked up again, finetuned and represented in the form of a diagram in *The Ego and the Id* (1923b), "Note upon the 'mystic writing pad'" (1925a [1924]) and the thirty-first of the *New Introductory Lectures on Psychoanalysis* (1933a); as I have conceived and developed it following Freud, this model is asymmetrical and multi-layered. The psychical wrapping consists of two layers which differ in structure and function. The outer layer, at the periphery, which is hardened and more tough, is turned towards the outside world. It forms a screen against stimulations from that world, mainly physical and chemical ones. It is the protective shield. The inner layer, which is thinner, more flexible, and more sensitive, has a receptive function. It perceives clues, signals, and signs, and registers their traces. It is both a film and an interface: a delicate film with two faces, one turned towards the external world, the other turned towards the internal world—and thus an interface separating these two worlds and relating them to each other. In combination, the protective shield and the film form a membrane. The structure of the film is symmetrical, while that of the protective shield is asymmetrical: there is just one protective shield, facing the outside, and no protective shield facing inwards; this is why confronting the excitation of the drives is more difficult than confronting exogenous stimuli. We must think of the protective shield's functioning in terms of force, and of that of the film in terms of sense. These two layers of the membrane can be considered as two wrappings, more or less differentiated and articulated according to the person and the circumstances—the wrapping of excitation and the wrapping of communication or meaning.

Psychical functioning depends on several factors. One factor is economic: it is concerned with the relative quantities of cathexis of the wrapping of excitation and the wrapping of meaning. Another is topographical, comparing the configuration and location of the two wrappings. A third is dynamic: it concerns the nature of the representations representing the drives, on the one hand, and the mental and bodily framework inside which those drives are handled, on the other. Lastly, we should take account of a particular factor that is specific either to a sense-field (the visual wrapping is organised differently from the auditory wrapping and, at a more elementary level, the light-darkness wrapping is organised differently from the chromatic wrapping) or to the psychopathological process involved (the paradoxical wrapping of a hysteric is structured differently from the Moebius-strip wrapping typical of borderline cases).

The opposition/complementarity of the two general categories of wrappings—that of excitation and that of meaning—underlies the fundamental rule of psychoanalytic activity. It operates on the basis of that opposition. This is an example of how the correspondence and complementarity principles on which Niels Bohr based quantum theory can be transferred into psychology.

The protective shield is provided by the psychoanalytic setting. The analyst's consulting-room provides a safe space for the patient against overwhelming sensations (of sight, sound, smell, etc.). The regular timetable and adequate length of sessions mitigate the discontinuities created by variations of physical and organic rhythms.

Two watchwords of psychoanalysis, which are often presented as two sides of the same fundamental rule, correspond to the interfacing film. For the patient, the two rules are indeed complementary and the psychoanalyst has a correlative rule for each. The first, the rule of non-omission, is the demand that the patient must think in free association and verbalise these thoughts; the corollary is the analyst's attitude of evenly suspended attention. The second, the "rule of abstinence", requires the patient to limit themselves to verbal relations with their analyst; this includes the taboo on touching and sets social relations off limits, along with sexual and aggressive acts; the corollary here is the psychoanalyst's attitude of benevolent neutrality—neutral because analysts must abstain from satisfying the patient's transferential desires, and benevolence because they must try to understand these desires rather than condemn or reject them.

Why this particular analytic framework? My answer is that such a framework could only have been invented by Freud and confirmed by those who followed him because it is homologous to the topographical structure of the psychical apparatus. In fact, each of the two rules has its corresponding psychical wrapping. The interleaving of the two within a single fundamental rule reflects the original interleaving of the wrappings that form the psyche, making it into an apparatus for thinking thoughts, containing affects, and transforming the economy of the drives.

The two surfaces of the psyche's sensitive film—the surface receptive to stimuli and the surface that registers traces and signs—are in fact implemented, respectively, by the rule of abstinence and the rule of free association. Abstaining from any acts other than semiotic or symbolic ones protects both partners from external excitation and channels it into the transference. The psychoanalytic setting minimises exogenous stimuli and maximises the attention given to internal excitation, which is the precondition for understanding it.

The rule of free association too has nothing to do with excitation but produces meaningful material that can be communicated: memories, dreams, incidents from daily life, thoughts that are ambiguous, paradoxical or absurd, and also affects.

A child's psychical apparatus acquires an Ego—which remains a bodily pre-Ego or, as I prefer to call it, a Skin-ego—at the point of initiation of this topographical structure of the dual wrapping, one receiving excitations, the other receiving meanings (signals, clues, simulacra, and linguistic signifiers).

The original lack of differentiation between the two layers of the psychical wrapping produces what Donald Meltzer calls "aesthetic experience"; and the fascinating and disturbing intensity of that primordial experience arises from the inseparability of sensation and emotion.

A geometrical model

In geometry, surface area is derived from the idea of limits, the boundary of a body or a volume. A *closed* surface is understood as the wrapping of a volume whose prototype is constituted by a spherical surface. This type of surface divides space into two portions, the inside and the outside, which may thus follow the same regime or two different ones. It accounts for representations of the psychical apparatus as a "bubble" (see the case study of Nathalie) or a "sphere" (Zénobie), both signs that an autonomous, three-dimensional Skin-ego has been set up.

If the surface is *open*—like a burst balloon—it can get progressively flatter until it is more or less a plane; thus the notion of depth really makes no sense for a person whose psychical space remains two-dimensional. A plane surface also divides space into two, but the two parts cannot be distinguished from one another. If the body image is flattened out this may cause an imaginary confusion between the digestive canal and the windpipe, and consequent somatic problems (see the case of Rodolphe).

Catherine Chabert has used the plane surface as a topographical metaphor for psychotic space: it is a boundary that separates *ad infinitum* (the impermeability of the Unconscious in relation to the Preconscious-Conscious system), yet does not allow any differentiation between the two spaces it defines, which leads to confusion (mixing up inside and outside, the inner world with the outer world, crushing the second topography). In psychosis differentiation is thus impeded by the actions of levelling out and flattening down that govern the relationship between reality and phantasy, inside and outside, subject and object, telescoping them in a way that denies thickness, relief, and the third dimension. According to Chabert again, in cases of schizophrenia and long-term psychosis, the Rorschach test shows a flat image which never really uncovers the depths of the psyche: the other side of the mirror remains shut away in the shadows of its objects. In *Alice in Wonderland* and *Through the Looking Glass*, Lewis Carroll describes well how his heroine discovers surfaces.

Some points about the theory of psychical wrappings (their constitution, development, and changes of form)

- To Freud's distinction between thing-presentations and word-presentations we need to add representations of changes of form (Gibello) and representations of containers (Bion). These are either a particular kind of thing-presentation and word-presentation (comparable to what Rosolato calls signifiers of demarcation and what I call formal signifiers) or they belong to a common root from which thing- and word-presentations are differentiated.

- Basic narcissistic security consists in acquiring the faculty of holding (leaning against a solid vertical load-bearing axis), containing (creating a bounded horizontal plane which ensures that the mind dwells in the body, the body dwells in space and the Self is inhabited by the Ego) and consensuality (introjecting a unifying external object from which arise sensations of many kinds that the child can feel and connect to each other).
- The growing autonomy of the psychical apparatus is based on the phantasy of a skin common to the mother and the child, on the subdivision of this skin into a surface of excitation and a surface of meaning and on the construction of an apparatus for thinking thoughts (containing them, representing them, symbolising them, and conceptualising them).
- The self-referential self-regulation of the psyche results from the mutual construction of the Ego and the object, achieved jointly by the Ego and the object, in which both the Self and the Ego depend on the object in order to appear as relatively autonomous and interdependent agencies—the Ego arising as the wrapping of the Self. It should be noted that this empowerment depends on the ability of the primal object to contain the baby's instinctual impulses and its total experience of emotion-phantasy-sensation-action. Later it depends on the ability of the baby's psyche to introject the container-content relation that the object thus carries out for it and to develop its (psychological) consciousness as a container capable of containing (and then differentiating) the contents of thought.
- A certain level of consciousness of the senses and rhythm exists from birth. It begins to take shape in the foetus but is absent in the embryo. The presence and growth of psychological consciousness accompanies and/or stimulates the evolution of a self-regulating system into a self-referential one. Sensory consciousness prepares the ground for the wrapping of space; rhythmic consciousness prepares the ground for the wrapping of time.
- It may also be the case that consciousness is coextensive with life. In more concrete terms, this means that, so far as the psyche is concerned, being equipped with a consciousness means experiencing, both at the same time, the feeling of *having* a consciousness that enwraps things and *being* that consciousness wrapped around me; it means being conscious simultaneously of being oneself and being present in the world; in addition, it means being conscious that my primal object is

conscious of being present in the world, to themselves and to me; and thus that they can and/or wish to enwrap me. Before consciousness represents itself as an individuated wrapping, it is experienced as "reciprocal inclusion" (Sami-Ali), like a single wrapping for two— my mother (or her substitute) surrounds me and I surround her at the same time.

- Any violent experiences undergone by the foetus, through its mother's body, may affect its consciousness, which is still unformed but already active, and leave traces that will negatively affect its later psychical functioning, even though they are unrepresentable. This is one aspect of inter-generational transmission. More generally, any trauma experienced before a double-layered psychical wrapping has been formed will be registered in the body, not in the psyche. To elaborate it psychically in the course of psychoanalytic treatment requires not so much a labour of interpretation as one of construction.

- The first global image of the psyche is not formless but based on an embrace of body to body, which keeps the Skin-ego maintained. The two bodies of mother and child cling to one another as though each were filling a gap or a distortion in space created by the other: thus they are nested, back against front. If one of them moves, the other cannot leave the freed-up space empty and tries to restore contact (as in the gravity model of economics)—this is confirmed in the psychoanalysis of twins. As Jack Doron (1987) has shown, this is the beginning of the relationship of synchronisation/echopraxis between the baby and those around it; it is also the geometric form of René Thom's first type of catastrophe, the fold. The fold and the gesture establish a precarious balance within a random functioning, marked by the chaos of perceptions and a total sum of movements that are unconnected to each other. The fold is a means of defence against inertia, repetition, and dismantling.

- The second type of "catastrophe", in Thom's sense, the cusp, organises the psyche—which at this stage is a paradoxical form without form, having neither a boundary nor a centre—through a rhythm that comes from the outside, the vibration of the landscape, of mother nature, just as a piece of seaweed, carried by the water, shows the rhythm of the swell (see Jack Doron, citing Kenneth White). To Edward T. Hall, this rhythm is "the dance of life". The discontinuous change thus produced establishes the Skin-ego as a closed wrapping.

- The third type of "catastrophe", the butterfly, brings about two possible changes. One is a smooth change leading towards tearing or collapse; the other is a discontinuous change, in which the wrapping is turned inside out like a glove. The psyche is a pouch, a site of oscillation between chaos and creative "supercooling"; this site functions characteristically as an all-or-nothing, a battle between destroying itself and becoming submerged in things or people. Turning inside out shatters the accustomed relationship between perception and objects and allows a new idea to take shape through a kind of supercooling. Turning inside out gives the closed psychical sphere an opening to the outside world (Jack Doron, 1987).

- As a psychical agency, the Ego is contiguous on two sides, with the Id and the Superego. It is the agent of both secondary psychical processes (generally conscious) and defence mechanisms (generally unconscious). This agent constitutes the solid core of the Ego which results from the introjection of the primal object: in addition, the Ego has the configuration of a wrapping, which separates and connects the inside world and the outside world: that is the perception-consciousness system. I have listed the functions performed by this wrapping, stopping provisionally at eight: maintaining/holding, containing, the shield against stimuli, individuation, intersensoriality, support of sexuality, libidinal recharging, and the registration of traces.

- Once it is constituted, the Agent-ego tends to be represented in a normal or neurotic individual as the centre of the psychical apparatus. The nearer one gets to borderline cases or the psychoses the more the core of the Ego tends to be situated at the periphery, i.e., on the wrapping itself or even in an extraterritorial position. In such cases the Ego does not inhabit the psyche. Split off, it stands outside the psyche like a double and observes it from the outside: the subject—who is not a true subject—watches themselves living, lives the life of an automaton, mechanically, discontinuously, buffeted by unpredictable surges of the drives.

- Between the Core-ego and the Wrapping-ego there is a psychical space which could be described as the "flesh" of the Ego, by analogy with the body, in which the flesh lies between the skin and the skeleton. This Flesh-ego may be more or less large and more or less flexible. If it becomes hardened it may serve to substitute for a weak wrapping—this is Esther Bick's muscular second skin.

In another psychopathology, the psychical flesh is replaced by a terrifying empty space—for example, in psychosomatic illnesses, white psychoses etc.

- Studies of the capabilities not just of new-born babies but of foetuses, looking at how to deal with functional disturbances in the latter, have shown that

  o the mother's womb, once it has placed the foetus in the right position, proceeds to massage its back and spinal column, thus preparing the Skin-ego of the future baby to carry out its primal function of holding (support or backing);

  o the foetus's five sense organs receive stimuli derived from the mother, and this prepares the future Skin-ego to carry out its function of consensuality.

Problems of the psychical wrappings

Key problems of the relationship between the two psychical wrappings

The first pathology, which relates to psychical containers, is characterised by *a failure to differentiate between excitation and communication* which persists in the growing child and the adult to a massive, generalised and well-nigh permanent extent. This is the wrapping of the hysteric, whose painful and paradoxical structure has been described by Annie Anzieu in her contribution to a collective volume, *Les Enveloppes psychiques* [*Psychical Wrappings*], which I shall summarise briefly below.

Hysterics try to create a shield against excitations by surrounding their body and psyche with a wrapping of excitation, which is a paradoxical structure: this wrapping of excitation is never discharged and thus changes into a wrapping of anxiety. In childhood, they received too many stimuli but were not given enough explanations of their states of mind or psychical contents. Later on, they reproduce this excess of excitation by inflicting it on other people or on their own body. For example, when she reaches adolescence or adulthood, a female hysteric driven by her genital desires will put the hyper-stimulated and hyper-stimulating surface of her body on display. She offers it to be looked at, rarely to be touched. From her earliest sessions with Freud, Frau Emmy von N. shouted at him: "Don't touch me!" Genital sexual excitation is nothing but a bait offered up to attract and retain the partner, in order to obtain from him the psychical communication she did not get from her primal objects in childhood and the suspension of this excitation, in the throes of creating an economic overload in her psyche. But what happens most often, of course, is that her partner, disappointed in his sexual expectations, withdraws from this psychical exchange which he was not prepared for and more or less violently demands the promised sexual satisfaction. All this just increases the hysteric's resentment, her wrapping of anxiety and the search for excitation which she confuses with communication.

A second pathology has to do with *the relation between the container and the content*: Bion speaks of the importance of the psychical container and this container-content relation. A close study of Bion's writings in the light of clinical experience led René Kaës to distinguish between the functions of container [*fonction contenante*] and containor [*fonction conteneur*]. This is a fundamental distinction, since—here I am adding to René Kaës's point—the function of container pertains to the protective shield while the function of containor pertains to the surface of inscription.

The container proper, which is stable and immutable—generally, the mother plays this role—is a passive receptacle in which the baby's sensations-images-emotions can be deposited, to be neutralised without being destroyed. By contrast, the containor corresponds to the active aspect, to what Bion calls "maternal reverie", projective identification, carrying out the alpha function, which gives the child back a developed and transformed representation of its sensations-images-emotions, thus made representable, tolerable, and capable of being used to compose thoughts.

Two forms of anxiety correspond to a deficiency in the containing function of the Skin-ego. One is the fear of an instinctual excitation that is diffuse, perpetual, scattered, without location or identity and impossible to calm; as a psychical topography it is represented as a kernel without a shell; individuals suffering from this anxiety search for a substitute shell in the physical pain they inflict on themselves—an example of this is the wrapping of suffering described by Micheline Enriquez—or in psychical distress: here we think of Annie Anzieu's description of the hysteric. The second form of anxiety is the fear that the continuity of the wrapping may be full of holes that will cause their entire insides to leak away, emptying them not just of their drives but of everything that can make up a subject's narcissistic strength—the fear of a narcissistic haemorrhage through these holes.

Clinical experience shows that in certain patients the two functions of container and containor have not been performed by the same person and for this reason the action of those two functions is compromised, even though each one taken separately works well, because they have failed to be properly interleaved or articulated together. For example, the role of container was taken by the mother but that of containor was taken by the grandmother or a nanny or an aunt or the neighbours. Or again, the grandmother was the container, and the mother was neither container nor containor but her communications with the child were essentially governed by an extremely strict superego, so that the container function was overdeveloped while the containor function was underdeveloped.

Thirdly, there may be a *pathology in the gap* between the two surfaces of excitation and communication. This pathology, as I hinted just now, is manifested by the lack or ineffectiveness of the transitional space and thus by the lack or ineffectiveness of its consequence, which is the act of phantasising—for phantasising is one way to articulate the two surfaces together, so long as a certain gap is maintained.

In this pathology of the missing gap, the two wrappings are differentiated but joined to each other, without the free play that is necessary for phantasmatic experience. Thus they form a single wrapping, with a layered structure, configured as a sac; in many psychosomatic cases psychical life is reduced to taking place essentially inside this sac and exchanges with other people are limited to communications without emotion or imagination. Often in such cases we find that the original relationship with the mother or her substitute was coloured by indifference, whether that was due to depression or marital problems with the father, or to any other cause—this is what André Green calls "the dead mother". I prefer to stress the concept of an "indifferent mother", for this term is more than simply a pun: it shows that an indifferent mother is a mother who prevents differentiation from taking place, who stops the principle of differentiation from working.

Let us now consider the fourth pathology. In the last-mentioned, "psychosomatic" pathology, communication was subordinate to the protective shield; in the one I am about to describe, excitation is subordinate to communication, in fact it is its servant. My example here is not from the clinic but from that social clinic we find in Greek mythology—the theme of the poisoned tunic, the deadly lining that sticks to the natural skin, imprisons it, eats away at it and sets it on fire. Medea is the opposite of the hysteric. What the hysteric presented to her partner as a form of excitation was meant to be understood as a demand for communication and understanding. Medea, who special-ises in the crime of passion and who had once been a sorceress, works in the opposite way. As a wedding present she sends her rival Creusa a dress and jewels but as soon as Creusa puts them on her body bursts into flames. Thus Medea presents as a message—a communication—something that would turn out to set off an intense, destructive excita-tion. This theme of the poisoned gift—often in the form of the difference between a kind word and a cruel act—seems to me, among other things, typical of what one might call *the wrapping of perversity.*

Specific problems of the protective shield and the surface of inscription

I shall now discuss the more specific problems of the protective shield, on the one hand, and the surface of inscription, on the other.

Specific problems of the protective shield

Here I shall simply refer to Frances Tustin. In primary autism both wrappings are absent: this is the amoeboid ego. In secondary autism, the protective shield is there while the surface of inscription is still miss-ing. But the protective shield is present in a rigid, impermeable form: this is the crustacean or carapace ego. There is no surface of inscription: instead there is raw flesh without any skin, and communication with other people is cut off either by a barrier of motor agitation—i.e., maximum excitation—or by withdrawal, i.e., by no excitation at all.

These deformities of the protective shield can be observed not only in autistic people but also in those who are normal or normally neu-rotic, if they have retained traces of these old configurations.

Specific problems of the surface of inscription

Of the two major kinds of problem that may affect the surface of inscrip-tion, the first involves the fear—related to the Superego—of one's body and Ego being covered by indelible marks of ignominy: these range from blushes or eczema to symbolic wounds or the famous infernal machine of Kafka's "In der Strafkolonie" [In the penal colony], which carves into the whole surface of the condemned man's body (in gothic script, so that it causes more pain) the article of the legal code that he has transgressed, and which he learns only at the very last moment, when the inscription is complete and he dies. This means that he receives the explanation and the punishment at the same time.

The other anxiety is the opposite—the fear that the inscriptions will disappear under the weight of their excess, or that one will lose the ability to retain traces. The example of the little girl Éléonore, with her head like a sieve, whom I presented on pp. 71–72, corresponds precisely to this loss of the capacity to fix traces: the particular holes in her Skin-ego corresponded to the absence of certain Ego functions.

A few words now on the *structure of allergies*, in which there is a problem of the surface of inscription that shows up in the form of an *inversion of the signals* of safety and danger. I have already noted how familiar things, instead of being reassuring and protective, are seen as bad and thus shunned; contact is desired but as soon as it is achieved it causes pain; and strangeness—that uncanny of which Freud speaks[1]— is revealed, by contrast, to be attractive. This explains the paradoxical response of allergy-sufferers, and perhaps also drug-addicts, who avoid what could do them good and are fascinated by what does them harm. The fact that the structure of allergies often takes the form of an alterna-tion between asthma and eczema helps to describe the topographical configuration of the Skin-ego that is at work here. The aim is to com-pensate for the failure of the Skin-ego as a sac to act either as a container or as a containor. The two allergic conditions correspond to two pos-sible modes of approaching the surface area of this sphere—from the inside and from the outside. Asthma can be seen as an attempt to feel the containing wrapping *from the inside*: patients fill themselves up with air to the point where they can feel the borders of their body from below and assure themselves of the increased limits of their Ego. But in order to retain the sensation of the inflated Sac-self, they hold their breath

---

[1]*Translator's note*: in French, "das Unheimliche" [the uncanny] is translated as *inquiétante étrangeté*, which literally means "disturbing strangeness".

in, at the risk of obstructing the flow of respiratory exchange with the environment, and suffocating.

Eczema is an attempt to feel the bodily surface area of the Self *from the outside*, with the skin's painful lacerations, rough feel, humiliating appearance and at the same time a wrapping of warmth and diffuse erogenous excitations.

The continuity or discontinuity of the two wrappings in borderline states

We return now to the relations between the two main wrappings of excitation and communication, in order to discuss a new pathological configuration in which these two wrappings, partly differentiated, are not superimposed and interleaved but juxtaposed end to end, continuous with one another. Thus there is just a single wrapping, in one piece, closed in upon itself and twisted like a Moebius strip; owing to this structure, it presents here the protective shield and there the surface of inscription.

This psychical topography seems to me typical of *borderline states*. To summarise briefly the effects on the organisation and functioning of the psyche, the subject has problems distinguishing between what comes from inside and what comes from outside and problems distinguishing between container and content.

The aetiology of this Moebius strip-like peculiarity seems to me to go back to the infant's early contradictory relations with those who look after it—a mother (or her substitute) who switches abruptly between excitation and communication and who, in each of these two activities, switches abruptly between too much stimulation and a sudden halt to stimulation and between no communication at all and suddenly overloading the child with communication.

The construction of the psychical wrapping

Formal signifiers

A psychical wrapping is a particular type of representation; it does not derive, like others, from the fate of the drives but from the play of positioning in space and from the degrees and types of constitution of a psychical territory. Freud intuited this when he wrote, in the notes published just before his death under the title "Findings, ideas, problems" (1941f [1938]), "Psyche is extended; knows nothing about it".[2] Let us take the example of a patient who has a bulimic episode. The classic interpretation focuses on the substitution of a physical need for the desire to be loved and understood by the mother (this interpretation falls within the register of the drives) and/or on the power struggle with the mother (this interpretation refers to object-relations). Experience shows that both these interpretations are inadequate unless they are supplemented by a topological analysis: the mother occupies the child's psychical space and in order to take back some of that space, the patient must grow larger.

Another example: Marie was terrified of seeing her complete image in a mirror or projected in a video recording of herself. Here is a first interpretation, based on the drives: she was seeing herself with a death's head, which expressed her deadly hatred of her mother, who would meet her when she came home from school with a cold, antagonistic face: it reduced her fear, but did not get rid of it altogether. Several months later, after the psychoanalytic process had progressed, I suggested to Marie that we should revisit that symptom and this time she suggested a topological explanation for it: she knew she was in front of the mirror and yet she could see herself behind it—how could she be both here and over there at the same time? This caused her a sharp terror of depersonalisation. The formal signifier at work here was: my body is being split in two. What I mean by "formal signifier" is a way of representing configurations of the body and objects in space, as well as their movements.

Such formal signifiers occur at the join between

- the conscious and the preconscious, which they serve to differentiate;
- thing-presentations and word-presentations; they represent wrappings and are constitutive of the subject in his or her relationship with the environment as outside/inside space;

---

[2] *Translator's note:* This enigmatic note—"Psyche ist ausgedehnt, weiss nichts davon"—was published at the end of the volume of posthumous works of the *Gesammelte Werke* in 1941. I have followed Strachey's translation here (1941f [1938] p. 300; GW XVII [1941], p. 152) but it should be noted that "weiss" is ambiguous, as it can mean either first or third person. Anzieu's French explicitly gives the third person: "Psyché est étendue, mais elle ne le sait pas"; in *Corpus* (2006, p. 22), Jean-Luc Nancy gives the somewhat closer, but still unambiguously third-person translation "La psyché est étendue: n'en sait rien".

- the Ego and the Self, serving to establish their boundaries and the fluctuations of those boundaries.

Here are a number of statements I propose to make about them:

- psychical wrappings are derived from the phantasy of the common skin between mother and child and from its transformations;
- the patient recognises them immediately when we describe or name them; this can revitalise the process of free association and making connections;
- they are cathected particularly by the attachment drive and the self-destructive drive;
- they can be developed by the analyst inducing metaphors which help the thinking Ego to lean anaclitically on the body and on bodily sensations and images;
- they are threatened by an archaic terror of space being torn open by an object changing its position, carrying with it the bit of space it occupied: because an object is contained by its position, the content is experienced as destroying its container;
- working psychoanalytically on formal signifiers contributes to creating the Ego and making sense of its flaws in relation to distortions of the analytic setting and what Christian Guérin has termed the transference of the containor.

Here is an example of a formal signifier in the case of a patient who had gone through an autistic period in her life. Nathalie wrote to me, asking for a meeting with a view to undertaking a third analysis with me; the two others had each succeeded up to a point in getting her out of that phase, but she felt they had not completed the job and that my work on the Skin-ego might well be able to help her.

I replied offering her a date to meet and discuss this. The night after she received my letter, she dreamt that she was in my consulting-room and I gave her a large cloth or scarf of blue silk; she reported this dream during our preliminary interview and that decided me to start a face-to-face psychoanalytic psychotherapy with her, focusing on her psychical wrappings. We actually interpreted the dream together. She pointed out that the scarf was a covering for the body and I suggested that the word "silk" stood for "the Self" and the blue colour was a metaphor for the ideal Self she was seeking in the treatment, which she hoped would give her a "coating".[3]

Our first few sessions were taken up with the inventory of the many, diverse, and intense anxieties she suffered from. Then she produced the distressing image she had of herself: a piece of seaweed floating half-submerged and sinking down. This formal signifier expressed the inconsistency of her Self, regression to a plant-like state (when she did not have to go to work, she would spend her time lying down, reading and listening to music) and fear of collapse. But in my interpretation I also offered some positive aspects: seaweed captures solar energy and moves around within the water, which recall two activities she had said were vital in her life, sunbathing and swimming.

After several weeks of work on her anxieties and on that formal signifier, she reported a daydream in which she had had the vision of a cedar with a thick trunk (which she could lean on securely) with broad branches parallel to the ground (the horizontality of the branches tempered the verticality of the trunk). Her Ego was straightening up, standing firm on its roots. But the metaphor remained tied to the plant world: her Ego was not yet differentiated enough to give her the benefit of instinctual forces she might have had available in a state of stasis.

Stages in the construction of the psychical wrapping and the Ego

The Wrapping-ego is constructed in correlation with the primal object, by a process one could describe as an interactive spiral. The autonomy of the Ego, which is never complete or definitive, goes through successive stages which I suggest—without claiming to be exhaustive—are the following:

The uterine wrapping: this corresponds to the emergence of consciousness and the rudimentary form of the perception-consciousness system. At this stage, scraps of consciousness appear in the foetus. As the foetus's anatomical container, the mother's womb provides the rudiments of a psychical container. This undifferentiated anatomical-psychical

---

[3]*Translator's note:* In French the words *la soie* [silk] and *le Soi* [the Self] have the same sound; and the term translated here as "coating" is *nappée*, a term from cookery for a topping, coating or covering, which derives from *nappe* [a large cloth].

container is the original container. The womb is experienced as the sac that holds together fragments of consciousness. The mother's body, especially her belly, acts as the protective shield. A field of sensitivity common to the foetus and its mother begins to develop. This explains the nostalgic wish to return to the mother's womb, in which one would not only be held, nourished, kept warm, in a state of perpetual well-being, but also be vaguely conscious of this well-being—the condition for being able to enjoy it. The existence of this uterine wrapping is well known to traditional therapists in so-called primitive societies (see Claude Lévi-Strauss, writing of the symbolic effectiveness of the shaman, referred to in Tobie Nathan's work on the psychotherapy of immigrants). When a mother knits her baby's layette this is a substitute for the uterine wrapping and a way of supporting the maternal "reverie" (see Michel Soulé, 1978).

The wrapping of mothering: this name was invented by Brazelton: it describes the care given to an infant by its mother and others, which creates a wrapping or "envelope" of sensations and gestures that is more active and unifying than the uterine wrapping. Winnicott links it to early maternal care, which anticipates and fulfils the baby's needs—a merging of the psyches and bodies of mother and child, mainly through smells and tastes, in a dyadic unit; if this unit is interrupted, the child experiences what is called "primal" distress. This merging may obstruct the independent development of the Self and the Ego.

The habitat wrapping: this term, created by Didier Houzel, describes the baby's acquisition of the distinction between bodily needs and psychical needs, and the types of communication that pertain to each (the unity of a psychical Self and a bodily Self which are differentiated and integrated, together with the two contrasting experiences of moments of non-integration and moments in which the psyche is felt to reside in the body).

The narcissistic wrapping: goes with the distinction between parts which are mine and parts which are not mine (an overall narcissistic self which forms a whole simply through the juxtaposition of the parts, each part having the same structure as the whole)—*cf.* "fractal" objects in mathematics or physics.

The imaginary individualising wrapping: this ensures the formation of the Ego within the Self and the formation of a sense of individuality based on what the visual and auditory mirror of the face and gestures of the mother and other carers reflect back to the child and on the echoes that come from the bath of words (the experience of inverse symmetry on both the vertical and horizontal planes).

The transitional wrapping: is paradoxical. It simultaneously ensures the separation and the union of the skins of the mother and the child. It alleviates the phantasy of tearing and gives the child a feeling of trust in its own existence and in the existence of an outside world that can be mastered (the experience of the transitional space). This wrapping is reversible: the surrounding world enwraps me and I can enwrap the world.

The "tutelary" wrapping: correlates to the acquisition of a sense of continuity of the self (*cf.* the Winnicottian experience of being alone in the presence of a familiar person who respects and protects my solitude). Later on, this wrapping, introjecting such a person, guarantees the symbolic presence of a reassuring and tolerant "guardian angel" at the heart of the psychical apparatus.

The singing skin

The following story can be considered as an Arabic variant on the Greek myth of Marsyas.[4]

A man had two daughters, both young and pretty. One day his wife fell ill. From the ceiling she hung a small purse called an "amana"—the precious depository that people give their loved ones when they are going away for a long time—and, after making her husband promise that he would not remarry until their daughters were tall enough to reach it, she died.

The widower had a neighbour, a widow who was still deliciously attractive and who wished to remarry. Every day she would cross the terraces and visit the two girls in their father's house. She washed them, deloused them, combed their hair and looked after their laundry. Thus the orphans found in her something of the maternal affection they had lost.

One day, the elder girl asked her father why he did not marry this woman, who was so kind and loved them so much. The father refused, invoking the promise he had made to his late wife.

[4]I am indebted to Mme Leila Cherkaoui-Benjeloun, a psychologist in Casablanca, for introducing this story to me.

The neighbour was very angry at this but did not show it; on the contrary, she became more eager and helpful than ever. One morning, however, she resorted to a trick to achieve her ends. She lifted the younger of the two little girls onto her shoulders, and the child was thus able to catch hold of the amana.

That evening, the child triumphantly showed her father the little purse that she had unhooked from the ceiling.

"See, father", she said, "we are big enough now: you can get married".

Defeated, the father agreed, and the wedding took place.

For a time, the new wife, who was cunning, went on behaving in a kind and devoted way. But one day, when she felt she had gained enough power over her husband, she warned him:

"It's time to choose, husband: your daughters or me!"

But she had spoken too soon. Her husband was not yet as subjugated as she thought: he refused to part from his daughters and compelled his wife to stay in the house.

"All three of you shall stay here. That's an order!" When he spoke like this, there was no point in protesting.

The wife said nothing more but she changed her attitude. Her kindness vanished and she started treating the two girls badly, jostling and shoving them, overburdening them with work and sometimes even beating them when their father was away. When he was at home, by contrast, she resumed the role of tender, loving mother. The two children did not dare complain, knowing what would be said.

Days passed… nights passed… for a long time they went on in this way…

One day there was a shortage of work in the land and the father had to take to the road to try and find work to feed his family.

The woman, left alone with the two little girls, gave free rein to her nastiness. She gave them not a moment's respite, making them do all the housework, sending them out to draw water at the well and fetch wood for the fire, and all she gave them to eat was the bran-swill she fed to the hens. The children grew more unhappy and wretched by the day. Soon the stepmother could no longer bear to have them around and vowed to be rid of them. One night, while they were sleeping, she slit their throats. She buried the elder one underneath the house and, in her cruelty, decided to take revenge on the younger one who, being more lively and intelligent, was less easy to dominate than her sister. She stripped her of her skin and used it to wedge the axis of the door, which was loose in its hole. But in the evening, when she wanted to close the door, the axis, as it turned, was grinding on the skin, which began to sing:

> "Hday, hday, ya mart bâ... Hday, hday, ya mart bâ
> Ana aala ourikat l'hanna... Qad dmoui talou."
> [Stop, stop, my stepmother!
> I'm on the little henna leaves
> And I've already wept far too much!]

The wicked woman, taken aback for a moment, wanted to assure herself of this wonder; she opened and closed the door and bent down to check the wedge; each time, at the merest touch, the skin began to sing again:

> "Hday, hday, ya mart bâ... Hday, hday, ya mart bâ ..."

Irritated by the refrain, repeated endlessly, the stepmother tore the skin out and threw it far away.

The desert wind caught it up in a whirl and dropped it in the sultan's gardens.

Now this king—may Allah give him long life—had an only son whom all the people loved; he was a friendly young man without any haughtiness, who was not too proud to enter anyone's home and share in the joys and sorrows of his father's subjects. All the Kasbahs loved and honoured him.

That day, the prince was wandering in the palace gardens when he saw the skin lying on the green grass. He picked it up in surprise and no sooner had he touched it with the tips of his fingers than he heard this song:

> "Hda, hda, ya ould Sältan...!"
> "[Stop, stop, O sultan's son!
> I'm on the little henna leaves
> And I have wept a long time!]

The prince, amazed and delighted, decided to keep this wonder secret; he hid the skin under his burnous and as soon as he was in his chamber he used it to cover a "tara",[5] which he carried everywhere with him from that day on; whenever he was alone in his private apartments or in a remote corner of the garden, he would strike the skin gently to make it sing.

In the Kasbah it became a common sight to see him go past with his tara under his arm, and no one was surprised.

Days passed... nights passed...

For a long time they went on in this way.

One day the father came home. The village children saw him and ran to warn his wife of his arrival, each wanting to be the first so as to get more of the roasted chickpeas and sweets that he was sure to give them.

Forewarned, the wife had prepared her reply and was waiting for her husband. So, when he enquired "Where are my two daughters?", she replied without a blush: "The older one is at the well; the younger one has gone to fetch the 'chtab'".[6]

The father, reassured, asked nothing more.

The little house was soon full of friends and neighbours who had come to welcome the traveller home. Everyone wanted to see him and hear all about his adventures.

The father responded pleasantly to everyone's questions, but his thoughts were elsewhere. He was thinking about his daughters and worrying because they had not come back yet.

Just as he was about to question his wife again, the door opened and the sultan's son came in. He too had come to greet the man, whom he knew well and respected. While they exchanged the conventional greetings, the prince, without thinking, brushed the tara with his fingers. Straight away, the wondrous song was heard:

"Hda, hda, ya ould Sältan...!"
[Stop, stop, O sultan's son!]

Intrigued, and thinking he recognised the echo of a familiar voice, the father asked the prince to lend him the tara. After a brief

---

[5] A sort of flat drum covered on one side with the skin of a goat or sheep; to play it, one holds it in the left hand, puts one's thumb through a hole designed for this purpose and strikes it with the right hand and the other fingers of the left hand.
[6] A hardy plant that grows in clumps in the desert and is used for feeding animals or making the fire.

SUMMARIES AND FURTHER OBSERVATIONS

hesitation, the young man held it out to him. Impatient to hear again the sweet voice that had so moved him, the man rubbed the skin gently with the open palm of his hand and the lament rose up again:

> "Hda, hda, ya biyi!"
> [Stop, stop, dear little father!
> I'm on the little henna leaves
> and I have wept a long time!]

Then the father understood that his daughters were dead. He looked at his wife, saw the fear and panic in her eyes and knew she was guilty. But he said nothing.

That evening at sunset, when the visitors had left, the stepmother was about to go out. The father stopped her and pushed her violently towards the bed.

"You stay here, woman; I have understood everything".

Realising all was lost, she tried to touch his heart. She threw herself at his feet, weeping, begging him to spare her, but the father, totally possessed by the desire for revenge, was unmoved. With unflinching hand, he slit the shrew's throat and cut her body into pieces, which he piled into the pannier of the "shwari",[7] carefully hiding at the bottom her head, hands, feet, and breasts.

The next day, without telling him what was in it, he asked one of his friends to take the shwari to his parents-in-law and not to forget to say to them:

"Ha salam n'eskibum, your son-in-law greets you".

The friend did as he was asked and the parents-in-law, surprised but pleased at their son-in-law's generosity, showered him with thanks.

Then, following the custom, they began to distribute pieces of the still-bleeding meat to their relatives:

> "One piece for the grandmother...
> One piece for the cousin...
> Another for the aunt..."

---

[7] A saddle-bag in the form of two large panniers linked by a strap, which is loaded on the back of a donkey or mule.

Little by little the panniers were emptied and soon they could see the grim remains—head, hands, feet and breasts. Horrified, the parents recognised their daughter.

All the people who had been rejoicing now began to lament and, in the deepest desolation, among the cries and groans of the women, they gathered together the macabre pieces. They washed them piously and, after wrapping them and sewing them into a shroud, they buried them following the rites.

When all this was done, they went to their son-in-law and demanded an explanation.

"*Bach ktalt tmut a malik l'mut*", he replied. "Angel of death, you shall die in the same way you caused others to die".

And he added sternly:

"I am the most to be pitied, I killed your daughter but she had killed mine. If you are not satisfied, there is the cadi".

The parents-in-law, devastated by the perfidy and cruelty of their daughter, said not another word; they departed without delay and went back to their house.

This is the end of my story.

Chapter Eighteen from 1985 edition

Further observations

The configurations of the Skin-ego that I have examined above are neither exhaustive (the list is open-ended) nor fixed (their stability varies according to individuals and circumstances); nor are they always found in a pure state (I have tried to distinguish the topographically simple forms, but these may be embedded in complex and varied ways).

The main configuration that I have not discussed separately or extensively is that of the visual wrapping, together with its variant, or rather its complement, the chromatic wrapping. Not having had the opportunity to analyse any painters, I did not feel qualified to talk about the latter. As for the theory of the visual wrapping, which is touched upon in many of my case studies, it has been well developed by Sami-Ali in *Corps reel, Corps imaginaire* [*Real Body, Imaginary Body*] (1977), in which he discusses the stages of its construction, and in *Le Visuel et le Tactile: Essai sur l'allergie et la psychose* [*The Visual and the Tactile: An Essay on allergy and psychosis*] (1984), in which he analyses how the visual world is established by separating from the tactile wrapping—see also Gérard Bonnet, *Voir-Être vu* [*To See and Be Seen*] (1981), on the unconscious cathexes of the visual).

I have devoted a chapter to the wrapping of sound, but it merits further commentary. For example, the skin of words has a different structure when found in the form of poetry (including prose-poetry or poetic prose) and in fiction, in which what I have termed the "body of the creative work" is dominant (Anzieu, 1981, pp. 118–121). The sound wrapping specific to music has been studied by Michel Imberty, in *Les Écritures du temps* [*Writings of time*] (1981, pp. 114–224).

The role of coenesthetic and vestibular sensations in the constitution of the Skin-ego requires detailed amplification.[1]

Mixed configurations

Within the same person, a part of the Self may function according to one particular configuration of the Skin-ego while another part functions according to a different one. Here is an example of such a mixed configuration.

Case study: Stéphane

Stéphane had been dreaming a lot since he began couch-based analytic sessions; he made great efforts to understand his dreams, for he had developed a good working relationship with me, after a difficult start in face-to-face analysis. Little by little we defined a set of points on which his understanding regularly came up against a brick wall: when he said that our relationship could not last for ever and he expected to end up feeling and expressing hostility towards me, not least because his father's verbal and sometimes physical violence had been such, all through his childhood and youth, that it had robbed him of the freedom to experience aggressive emotions of his own towards the father.

During our sessions a new phenomenon began to appear, more and more often and more and more loudly: Stéphane's stomach rumbled. He was particularly upset and mortified by this because it did not happen to him anywhere else. The particular session I am

---

[1] Herbinet, Busnel et al. (1981), *L'Aube des sens* [*The Dawn of the Senses*], brings together data relating to the infant's development of the five senses and the sense of balance.

reporting was overwhelmed by this rumbling, and Stéphane had no idea what it could mean. As for me, I could not come up with anything; I forced myself to think about it and then I perceived a connection with the previous sessions.

Me: "What's rumbling in you is aggression and you don't know if it's yours or your father's."

Stéphane confirmed this: in the last few days he had been dreaming of knives stabbing him in the stomach.

At that moment, my stomach started to rumble too. I made an effort to stop myself feeling guilty about it or trying to hide it, but instead to understand it as an effect of the transference from Stéphane onto me. I offered him the following interpretation:

Me: "your father deposited his aggression into you because he found it unpleasant and he wanted to get rid of it; in the same way, you have communicated the rumbling to me because you find it unpleasant, so that it will be mine and not yours."

Stéphane: "I'm sorry about that; I'll take it back."

Indeed my stomach had stopped rumbling and his had begun again. My psychical Ego, no longer taken over by his bodily Ego, recovered its ability to think and I noted to myself that it was not enough to interpret what was at work here—the underlying drive (the aggression) and the defence mechanism (projective identification)—but I also needed to find out the specific meaning connected to the part of the body affected by this symptom (the topographical point of view).

Me: "This rumbling was in your belly: a mother and her baby communicate emotions directly through the belly."

This very general, exploratory interpretation gave Stéphane a framework in which at last he could formulate the hybrid configuration of his Skin-ego (half crustacean Skin-ego, half sieve Skin-ego).

Stéphane: "I am like a tortoise. I have a shell on my back and a soft stomach underneath. If I fall on my back, my stomach is full of holes and it gets taken over by other people's aggression and I can't get up again into an active position."

In his analysis, lying down on the couch in front of me, his stomach was indeed exposed in phantasy. Thus it was that the transference gave Stéphane the opportunity to become conscious of his particular Skin-ego configuration.

The psychical wrappings of autism[2]

"The wrapping of agitation" has been described as characteristic of encapsulated secondary autism [ESA] which presents between the ages of six and eighteen months; in this condition, by contrast to primary autism, excitation takes the place of inhibition.

Children with ESA have an armour, a thick skin—comparable to the second muscular skin described by Esther Bick (1968), a crustacean Ego, with a protective shield turned towards the outside but no internal skin. They try to find a bodily and relational wrapping through psychomotor agitation, walking or running about, vocalising compulsively, creating disarray among objects the grownups have tidied away, forcing themselves parasitically on their mother by screaming if she shows signs of going away, whirling around, tearing their clothes to shreds; they refuse to communicate, indifferent to both looks and words. Anxiety appears when this psychomotor defence is restrained by neuroleptic drugs or by tying them to their beds. This anxiety is manifested in self-mutilation: they scalp themselves, fracture their skulls and rip their skin: the skin, as a potential organ of inscription and exchange, is torn away.

The ESA child creates a zone of security by projecting outside itself an impenetrable barrier of agitation. It has learnt the difference between animate and inanimate objects, inside and outside. It has a protective barrier but no enveloping surface or interface. It functions according to the paranoid-schizoid position, but its defence mechanisms remain bodily ones; it has not yet developed the psychical defences of splitting, projection, disavowal, etc. The tactile Skin-ego is refused. The way to enter into contact with this child is by creating a wrapping of sound: singing, playing music, echoing back to it its own cries and vocalisations—however piercing or disruptive they may be.

In regressive secondary autism [RSA] the child has acquired a thin psychical skin—hence the hypersensitivity which it hides behind confusion and disorder.

---

[2]Here I am drawing on the descriptions of Frances Tustin (1972, 1981) and Donald Meltzer et al. (1975), summarised and amplified by Claudine and Pierre Geissmann in *L'Enfant et sa psychose* (1984) [published in English as *A History of Child Psychosis* (1997)].

In childhood schizophrenia, the mother and child are wrapped inside each other in a relationship of mutual inclusion: here at last there is a psychical wrapping, but it is modelled on an intra-uterine phantasy and is not yet formed as the common skin which both separates and unites mother and child.

We come now to the most serious and also earliest pathology (all its presentations occur before six months). In abnormal primary autism [APA] the child's body is soft, floppy, amoeba-like and hypotonic. The result is an amoeboid Ego. Neither the skin nor the Ego performs the function of holding or supporting. The child is quiet, motionless for hours at a time, indifferent, passive, seeming far away; it avoids visual exchanges but watches everything "out of the corner of its eye" without seeming to look. If one tries too hard to attract its attention or if there is a slight change in its surroundings or daily habits, it reacts with rage or terror. It can sit for hours, rocking slowly backwards and forwards. It does not respond to sound signals. It is indifferent to body manipulations or pain. But a slight unexpected noise, or if one simply brushes lightly against it, can provoke reactions of agitation or screaming.

This child has neither a wrapping of touch nor a wrapping of sound. Its visual wrapping is rudimentary. The function of protective shield is served by withdrawal and isolation. It may be that the rhythmical rocking provides an auto-erotic postural wrapping. These children maintain the foetal position; they are immobile and demand surroundings that similarly never change; their body seems to burrow into their mother's lap. Their whole body (and psyche) is folded in upon itself, as if to make itself into a skin and prolong the intra-uterine wrapping. The person caring for them is subsumed into this universe: transparent, manipulated like an inanimate object, plunging into dizzying depths. If they go away the child falls apart.

The child's despair is profound. It manifests itself in rages, self-mutilation, attacking its head, eyes, and skin—all the parts of the body that a Skin-ego might lean on anaclitically.

Having no Skin-ego causes problems in all the bodily functions—hygiene, feeding (sometimes the baby does not seek the nipple), and sleeping. The distinction between animate and inanimate objects is not learned. APA children "play", in a stereotypical way but doubtless for auto-erotic pleasure, with their hands, feet and clothes, with string or twigs or pieces of rough material; they suck their tongue or the inside of their cheeks, hold back their stools, blow bubbles with their saliva, handle water, mud or sand, or listen endlessly to the same record. They do not have transitional objects or learn the difference between inside and outside. They touch their own and other people's genitals.

For them, in sum, the point is to

- artificially prolong the intra-uterine wrapping, and thus to deny birth;
- reject all wrappings offered by the mother or the environment (tactile, visual, auditory, and kinaesthetic);
- not perform the functions of the skin or the sense organs and not acquire the representation of an interface;
- keep the body undifferentiated from objects and fragmented into separate elements, each with its own auto-erotic value;
- make a protective shield for themselves out of isolation, keeping their body immobile, refusing any change in their world and inhibiting their functions.

Is autism always pathological, or could one say that in the first few weeks of life "normal" autistic phenomena occur (see Tustin and Meltzer) which would correspond to an "autistic position" (Daniel Marcelli, 1983) preceding the paranoid-schizoid position? Having no clinical experience in this field myself, I shall not take a view; but in relation to this question, I would cite one of Klein's rare notes concerning the pathology of the psychical wrapping—the description of an autistic phantasy of the mother's body as empty and dark:

> Dick cut himself off from reality and brought his phantasy-life to a standstill by taking refuge in the phantasies of the dark, empty mother's body. He had thus succeeded in withdrawing his attention also from the different objects in the outside wold which represented the contents of the mother's body—the father's penis, faeces, children. (Klein, 1930 [1975], p. 227)

This description seems to me to anticipate Meltzer's notion of the Claustrum. Frances Tustin has pointed out that the normal autistic wrapping includes spots—which correspond no doubt to sensitive points like pimples on the skin or sense organs—while a pathological autistic wrapping is "dismantled" (to borrow Meltzer's expression) and has "black holes", which correspond to the anxiety of being emptied of one's internal vital substance and the terror of being sucked in by the void, since without a Skin-ego the primary function of holding is not fulfilled. Both the autistic child's fascination with circular or whirling movements found in the outside world and its own stereotypical spinning movements reflect the danger of being engulfed by these black holes and are a desperate attempt to stop that happening (Houzel, 1985b).

Marcelli characterises the "autistic position" as follows: thinking by contiguity rather than symbolically, having part-objects situated in a two-dimensional plane, with object-relations that are autistic (in pathological cases) or narcissistic (in normal cases) and having an Ego that leans anaclitically on the skin and the proximal senses (touch, smell, and taste). The two defence mechanisms are

- adhesive identification: Marcelli describes a new form of this: "the child taking an adult's hand in order to use it as an extension of its own upper limb", i.e., including the other person in a limitless Ego; "the child taking an adult's hand or pressing its body close against their body [...] equates to using the sense of touch in a contiguous relationship without boundaries"; the same process is found in the senses of smell and taste (the proximal senses); indeed the distal senses are also used in a way that cancels out the gap between Ego and non-Ego: the autistic child "hears" the music of a phrase and reproduces it in an exaggerated, chanting form; or "catches" the object with its gaze;
- dismantling: autistic children prevent intersensoriality from being set up, with the skin as a continuum combining the different sense organs: "they dismantle their Ego into separate perceptual capacities" (Meltzer) and reduce the "common sense" object into a "multiplicity of uni-sensory events in which animate and inanimate become indistinguishable".

An autistic child refuses visual and verbal communication because it refuses to accept boundaries or the separation from the mother's body: if this is denied, it panics or flies into a violent rage. A normal child, by contrast, will use "pointing" (Vygotsky): it reaches out its hand to grasp the object it wants; if the object is too far away, the hand stays in the air, and for those around the child this gesture acquires a semiotic value; and for the child itself, the gesture is used for communicating (*cf.* Diatkine's "anticipatory illusion").

The Skin-ego is a wrapping that emits and receives signals in interaction with the world around: it "vibrates" in resonance with it; it is animated, alive inside, bright and luminous. An autistic child has the idea of this wrapping—no doubt it is genetically pre-programmed—but because it has no concrete experience of it, the idea remains empty, dark, inanimate, and mute. Autistic wrappings thus provide a proof in negative form of the structure and functions of the Skin-ego.

From skin to thought

In this volume I have described how the sense qualities are arranged within an internal space, that of the Self, which is bounded by an interface with the external objects that constitute the Ego (and then by other interfaces—between the psychical and bodily Egos, between the Ego and the Superego, between the various internal objects, etc.). In turn, the topographical differentiation of psychical space causes sense qualities to change into the elements of phantasies, symbols, and thoughts. I have been able to offer only a glimpse into how these changes are instigated: to study them in detail would require another book. However, many authors have proposed theories about the stages of these changes—Winnicott, Hanna Segal (1957), with "symbolic equation", Bion with his "grid" whose eight levels extend to formalised abstract thought, etc. As for me, I intend to show one day how each of the nine functions of the Skin-ego provides one of the frameworks or processes of thought.

Finally

Another person's speech, if it is appropriate, lively and true, allows the hearer to reconstitute their containing psychical wrapping, and it does this when the words they hear weave a symbolic skin that is a phonological, semantic equivalent to the original echotactilisms exchanged between a baby and its mother or other family members. This is how friendship, psychoanalytic treatment or reading literature can work. Writing too can be a way of speaking to oneself and for oneself alone: from adolescence it can fulfil the same function of restoration following a strong emotion, tension in one's relationships or an inner crisis. This is true not only for many writers—even though the motive of repairing a temporarily weak Skin-ego often remains hidden under more banal aims: writing for pleasure, to save oneself from death, to compete with women's fertility, etc.—but it is even more true of the majority who just choose to write without aesthetic aims or any intention of publication. Micheline Enriquez (1984) uses the term "representative writing" to describe an activity by which the patient secures their presence in the world and for themselves (i.e., maintains their Ego in a position I have called the interface) by noting down word for word on paper the time-space setting in which they live, their immediate perceptions, the concrete actions they have just performed. This was the case with Fanchon (whose case study is reported on pp. 233–236). Here is Fanchon's own comment on this episode, which was an important stage in her recovery: "It was as if this writing allowed me to get back a skin" (Enriquez, 1984, p. 213). It is equally true of Doris Lessing who, in *The Golden Notebook* (1962), describes how she uses the blue notebook in her struggle against depression:

> [...] if I am at a pitch where shape, form, expression are nothing, then I am nothing [... my] intelligence is dissolving and I am very frightened.
>
> It was then that I decided to use the blue notebook, this one, as nothing but a record of facts. Every evening I sat on the music-stool and wrote down my day, and it was as if I, Anna, were nailing Anna to the page. Every day I shaped Anna, said: Today I got up at seven, cooked breakfast for Janet, sent her to school, etc., etc., and felt as if I had saved that day from chaos. (Lessing, 1962 [2008], pp. 350–351)

This self-observation by a woman writer demonstrates the common source between two different kinds of writing: that of intellectuals (essayists, critics, etc.) and that of writers of fiction. In my *Pour un portrait psychanalytique de l'intellectuel* [*Towards a psychoanalytic portrait of the intellectual*] (Anzieu, 1984), I describe a configuration of the Skin-ego, typical of intellectuals, in which the skin is the surface of the brain projected onto contact with things, following a reciprocal process in which things (seen, heard, touched, smelt or tasted) are directly transposed into ideas which, in their turn, filter the perception of things.

Spoken words—and, even more, written words—have the power of a skin. My patients have taught me this, and familiarity with many great works of literature have confirmed it. At first it was a personal intuition and it took some time for me to transform it into an idea. When I wrote this book it was also to defend my Skin-ego by writing. With this act of acknowledgment, I may consider the present volume complete.

TABLE OF CASE STUDIES

Case studies whose pseudonyms are not followed by the name of an author are drawn from my personal practice. For all others, the name of the person to whom I owe or from whom I have borrowed the case study is given in brackets.

Author's note

About half the present volume is composed of unpublished texts and the other half of previously published articles which have been reworked, re-divided or recombined. I am indebted to the journal editors who have given me permission to republish my articles in whole or in part.

In Part I, Discovery, Chapters Two ("Four sets of data") and Three ("The notion of the Skin-ego") used and extended elements of the following texts:

- My original article: Anzieu, D. (1974), Le Moi-peau. *Nouv. Rev. Psychanal., 9*: 195–208.
- Anzieu, D. (1968). De la mythologie particulière à chaque type de masochisme. *Bulletin de l'Association Psychanalytique de France*, June 1968, 4: 84–91.
- Anzieu, D. (1974). La peau: du plaisir à la pensée. In: D. Anzieu, R. Zazzo, et al., *L'Attachement*. Neuchâtel: Delachaux et Niestlé.

Part II, Structure, functions, overcoming, includes a more or less complete reproduction of the following texts:

- Anzieu, D. (1981). Quelques précurseurs du Moi-peau chez Freud. *Rev. Franç. Psychanal., XLV, 5*: 1163–1185, reproduced in my Chapter Six.
- Anzieu, D. (1984). Actualidad de Federn. In: P. Federn: *La psicologia del yo y las psicosis*. Buenos Aires: Amorrortu, reproduced and extended in my Chapter Six.
- Anzieu, D. (1984). Fonctions du Moi-peau. *L'Information psychiatrique, 8*: 869–875, reproduced amd completed in my Chapter Seven.

- Anzieu, D. (1985). Altérations des fonctions du Moi-peau dans le masochisme pervers. *Revue de médecine psycho-somatique, 2*, reproduced in my Chapter Seven.
- The case study of Pandora (Chapter Eight) is taken—with extensions—from Anzieu, D. (1982). L'échange respiratoire comme processus psychique primaire. À propos d'une psychothérapie d'un symptôme asthmatique. *Psychothérapies., 1*: 3–8.
- Anzieu, D. (1978). Machine à décroire: sur un trouble de la croyance dans les états limites. *Nouv. Rev. Psychanal., 18*: 151–167: this article was entirely rethought and rewritten as my Chapter Nine.

Chapter Ten comprises three articles:

- Anzieu, D. (1984). Le corps de la pulsion. In: the Acts of the conference *La Pulsion, Pour quoi faire?* Association Psychanalytique de France.
- Anzieu, D. (1984). Le double interdit du toucher. *Nouv. Rev. Psychanal., 29*: 173–187.
- Anzieu, D. (1984). Au fond du Soi, le toucher. *Rev. Franç. Psychanal., 6*: 1385–1398.

In Part III, Principal configurations, Chapter Eleven picks up material from Anzieu, D. (1976). L'enveloppe sonore du Soi. *Nouv. Rev. Psychanal., 13*: 161–179, and Chapter Eighteen reproduces passages from Anzieu, D. (1990). *L'épiderme nomade et la peau psychique*. Paris: Apsygée.

REFERENCES

Abraham, N., & Török, M. (1978 [1987, 2001]). *L'Écorce et le noyau*. Paris: Flammarion.

Angelergues, R. (1975). Réflexions critiques sur la notion de schéma corporel. In: *Psychologie de la connaissance de soi*. Acts of Paris Symposium of September 1973. Paris: PUF.

Anzieu, A. (1974). Emboîtements. *Nouv. Rev. Psychanal.*, 9: 57–71.

Anzieu, A. (1978). De la chair au verbe. In: D. Anzieu, et al., *Psychanalyse et langage*, 2nd edn. Paris: Dunod.

Anzieu, A. (1987). L'enveloppe hystérique. In: D. Anzieu, et al., *Les Enveloppes psychiques*. Paris: Dunod, pp. 114–137.

Anzieu, A. (1989). *La Femme sans qualité. Esquisse psychanalytique de la féminité*. Paris: Dunod.

Anzieu, D. (1970). Freud et la mythologie. *Nouv. Rev. Psychanal.*, 1: 114–145.

Anzieu, D. (1975a). *L'Auto-analyse de Freud*. 2 volumes. New edn. Paris: PUF.

Anzieu, D. (1975b). Le Transfert paradoxal. *Nouv. Rev. Psychanal.*, 12: 49–72.

Anzieu, D. (1979). La Démarche de l'analyse transitionnelle en psychanalyse individuelle. In: Kaës R. et al., *Crise, rupture et dépassement*. Paris: Dunod.

Anzieu, D. (1980a). Du corps et du code mystiques et de leurs paradoxes. *Nouv. Rev. Psychanal.*, 22: 159–177.

297

Anzieu, D. (1980b). Les Antinomies du narcissisme dans la création littéraire. In: Guillaumin, J., *Corps Création, Entre lettres et Psychanalyse*, 2nd par, Chapter One. Lyon: Presses Universitaires de Lyon.

Anzieu, D. (1981a). *Le Corps de l'œuvre*. Paris: Gallimard.

Anzieu, D. (1981b). *Le Groupe et l'inconscient. L'imaginaire groupal*. New edn. Paris: Dunod.

Anzieu, D. (1982a). Le Psychodrame en groupe large. In: Kaës R. et al. *Le travail psychanalytique dans les groupes*, volume 2: *Les Voies de l'élaboration*. Paris: Dunod.

Anzieu, D. (1982b). Sur la confusion primaire de l'animé et de l'inanimé. Un cas de triple méprise. *Nouv. Rev. Psychanal.*, 25: 215–222.

Anzieu, D. (1983a). Le Soi disjoint, une voix liante/l'écriture narrative de Samuel Beckett. *Nouv. Rev. Psychanal.*, 28: 71–85.

Anzieu, D. (1983b). À la recherche d'une nouvelle définition clinique et théorique du contre-transfert. In: Sztulman, H. et al., *Le Psychanalyste et son patient*. Toulouse: Privat.

Anzieu, D. (1984). La Peau de l'autre, marque du destin. *Nouv. Rev. Psychanal.*, 30: 55–68.

Anzieu, D. (1985). Du fonctionnement psychique particulier à l'intellectuel. *Topique*, 34: 75–88.

Anzieu, D. (1987). Les signifiants formels et le moi-peau. In: D. Anzieu & D. Houzel, *Les enveloppes psychiques*. Paris: Dunod, pp. 1–22.

Anzieu, D. (1990). *L'épiderme nomade et la peau psychique*. Paris: Apsygée.

Anzieu, D. (1993a). La fonction contenante de la peau, du moi et de la pensée: conteneur, contenant, contenir. In: *Les contenants de pensée*. D. Anzieu (ed.), Paris: Dunod, pp. 15–40.

Anzieu, D. (1993b). *Samuel Beckett et le psychanalyste*. Lausanne: L'Aire.

Anzieu, D. (1994a). *Le Penser*. Paris: Dunod.

Anzieu, D. (1994b). L'esprit inconscient. *Nouv. Rev. Psychanal.*, 48: 149–162.

Anzieu, D. & Monjauze, M. (1993). *Francis Bacon ou le portrait de l'homme désespéré*. Lausanne: L'Aire/Archambaud.

Atlan, H. (1979). *Entre le cristal et la fumée. Essai sur l'organisation du vivant*. Paris: Seuil.

Aulagnier, P. (*see also* Castoriadis-Aulagnier) (1979). *Les Destins du plaisir*. Paris: PUF.

Aulagnier, P. (*see also* Castoriadis-Aulagnier) (1984). *L'Apprenti-historien et le maître sorcier*. Paris: PUF.

Balint, M. (1968). *The Basic Fault*. Tavistock: London.

Balint, M. & Balint, A. (1952). *Primary Love and Psycho-Analytic Technique*. London: Hogarth.

Beauchesne, H. (1980). *L'Épileptique*. Paris: Dunod.

Beller, I. (1973). *La Sémiophonie*. Paris: Maloine.

Berenstein, I. & Puget, J. (1984). Considérations sur la psychothérapie du couple: de l'engagement amoureux au reproche. In: A Eiguer et al. *La Psychothérapie du couple*. Paris: Dunod.

Bergeret, J. (1974). *La Personnalité normale et pathologique*. Paris: Dunod.

Bergeret, J. (1975). *La Dépression et les états limites*. Paris: Payot.

Bergeret, J. (1984). *La Violence fondamentale*. Paris: Dunod.

Bettelheim, B. (1954). *Symbolic Wounds*. Glencoe, Ill.: The Free Press.

Bettelheim, B. (1967). *The Empty Fortress*. The Free Press: New York.

Bick, E. (1968). The experience of the skin in early object-relations'. *Int. J. Psycho-Anal., 49*: 484–86.

Bion, W. R. (1962). *Learning from Experience*. London: Heinemann.

Bion, W. R. (1963). *Elements of Psycho-Analysis*. London: Heinemann.

Bion, W. R. (1967). *Second Thoughts*. London: Heinemann.

Bioy Casares, A. (1992 [1940, 1964]). *The Invention of Morel*. Ruth L. C. Simms (trans.). New York: New York Review of Books.

Birch, H. G. & Lee, J. (1955). Cortical inhibition in expressive aphasia. *Archives of Neurology and Psychiatry. 74*: 514–517.

Biven, B. M. (1982 [2005]). The role of skin in normal and abnormal development with a note on the poet Sylvia Plath. In: *True Pretences*. Leicester: Troubadour, pp. 70–108.

Bleger, J. (1967). Psycho-Analysis of the Psycho-Analytic Frame. *International Journal of Psychoanalysis, 48 (4)*: 511–519.

Bonnet, G. (1981). *Voir-Être vu*. 2 volumes. Paris: PUF.

Bonnet, G. (1985). De l'interdit du toucher à l'interdit de voir. *Psychanal. Univ., 10 (37)*: 111–119.

Botella, C. & Botella, S. (1990). La problématique de la régression formelle de la pensée et de l'hallucinatoire. Monographs of the *Revue Française de Psychanalyse*. In: *La Psychanalyse: questions pour demain*. Paris: PUF, pp. 63–90.

Boulery, L., Martin, A. & Puaud, A. (1981). Des enfants sourds-aveugles… et des grottes. *L'Évolution psychiatrique, 46 (4)*: 873–892.

Bourgignon, O. (1984). *Mort des enfants et structures familiales*. Paris: PUF.

Bowlby, J. (1958). The nature of the child's tie to his mother. *Internat. J. Psycho-Anal., 39*: 350–373.

Bowlby, J. (1961). L'éthologie et l'évolution des relations objectales. *Rev. Franç. Psychanal., 24 (4–5–6)*: 623–631.

Bowlby, J. (1969). *Attachment and Loss, volume 1: Attachment*. London: Hogarth and IPA.

Bowlby, J. (1973). *Attachment and Loss, volume 2: Separation*. London: Hogarth and IPA.

Bowlby, J. (1980). *Attachment and Loss, volume 3: Loss, Sadness and Depression*. London: Hogarth and IPA.

Brazelton, T. B. (1981). Le Bébé: partenaire dans l'interaction. Aviva Luke (trans.). In: *La Dynamique du nourrisson*. Paris: Éditions ESF, pp. 11–27.

Brazelton, T. & Cramer, B. T. (1990). *The Earliest Relationship: Parents, Infants and the Drama of Early Attachment*. London: Karnac.

Cachard, C. (1981). Enveloppes de corps, membranes de rêve. *L'Évol. Psychiatr.*, 4: 847–856.

Castoriadis-Aulagnier, P. (1975). *La Violence et l'interprétation*. Paris: PUF.

Chauvin, R. et al. (1970). *Modèles animaux du comportement humain*. Paris: CNRS.

Chiva, M. (1984). *Le Doux et l'amer*. Paris: PUF.

Ciccone, A. & Lhopital M. (1991). *Naissance à la vie psychique*. Paris: Dunod.

Corraze, J. (1976). *De l'hystérie aux pathomimies*. Paris: Dunod.

Debru, C. (1990). *Neurophilosophie du rêve*. Paris: Hermann.

Dejours, C. (1988). *Le Corps entre biologie et psychanalyse*. Paris: Payot.

Denis, P. (1992). Emprise et théorie des pulsions. *Revue française de psychanalyse, 41*: 1297–1421.

Dorey, R. (1992). Le désir d'emprise. *Revue française de psychanalyse, 41*: 1423–1432.

Doron, J. (1987). Les modifications de l'enveloppe psychique dans le travail créateur. In: D. Anzieu, et al., *Les enveloppes psychiques*. Paris: Dunod, pp. 181–198.

Duyckaerts, F. (1972). L'Objet d'attachement: médiateur entre l'enfant et le milieu. In: *Milieu et développement*, Acts of Lille symposium of 1970. Paris: PUF.

Enriquez, M. (1984). *Aux carrefours de la haine*. Paris: L'Épi.

Federn, P. (1952 [2012]). *Ego Psychology and the Psychoses*. Repr. New Delhi: Sarup.

Fisher, S. & Cleveland, S. E. (1958). *Body Images and personality*. Princeton & New York: Van Nostrand.

Frazer, J. G. (1929). *The Golden Bough*. London: Macmillan.

Freud, S. (1887–1902 [1954]). *The Birth of Psychoanalysis: Letters to Wilhelm Fliess*. Marie Bonaparte, et al. (eds.) London: Imago.

Freud, S. (1891b). *On Aphasia: A Critical Study*. S.E., 1. London: Hogarth. Sourced from a 1953 translation by E. Stengel. New York: International Universities Press.

Freud, S. (1900a). *The Interpretation of Dreams [Die Traumdeutung]*. S.E., 4. London: Hogarth, 1953; Vintage 2001.

Freud, S. (1905d). *Three Essays on the Theory of Sexuality [Drei Abhandlungen zur Sexualtheorie]*. S.E., 7, 1901–1905. London: Hogarth, 1953; Vintage 2001, pp. 125–245.

Freud, S. (1909d). Notes upon a case of obsessional neurosis. *S.E., 10.* London: Hogarth.

Freud, S. (1914c). On narcissism: an introduction. [Zur Einführung des Narzissmus]. *S.E., 14,* 1914–1916. London: Hogarth, 1957; Vintage 2001, pp. 69–102.

Freud, S. (1915e). The unconscious. [Das Unbewusste]. *S.E., 14,* 1914–1916. London: Hogarth, 1957; Vintage 2001, pp. 161–215.

Freud, S. (1919h). The uncanny. [Das Unheimliche]. *S.E., 17,* 1917–1919. London: Hogarth, 1955; Vintage 2001, pp. 217–256.

Freud, S. (1920g). *Beyond the Pleasure Principle. [Jenseits des Lustprinzips]. S.E., 18,* 1920–1922. London: Hogarth, 1955; Vintage 2001, pp. 3–64.

Freud, S. (1923). Das Ich und das Es. In: A. Freud, et al. (eds.), *Gesammelte Werke, chronologisch geordnet.* Band XIII. London: Imago 1940; Frankfurt: Fischer 1999, pp. 235–289.

Freud, S. (1923b). *The Ego and the Id.* [Das Ich und das Es]. *S.E., 19,* vol XIX, 1923–1925. London: Hogarth, 1961; Vintage 2001, pp. 3–66.

Freud, S. (1925a [1924]). Note upon the "mystic writing pad". [Notiz über den "Wunderblock"]. *S.E., 19,* 1923–1925. London: Hogarth, 1961; Vintage 2001, pp. 225–232.

Freud, S. (1933). *Neue Folge der Vorlesungen zur Einführung in die Psychoanalyse.* In: A. Freud et al. (eds.), *Gesammelte Werke, chronologisch geordnet.* Band XV. London: Imago 1940; Frankfurt: Fischer 1999.

Freud, S. (1933a). *New Introductory Lectures on Psycho-Analysis. [Neue Folge der Vorlesungen zur Einführung in die Psychoanalyse]. S.E., 22,* 1932–1936. London: Hogarth, 1964; Vintage 2001.

Freud, S. (1941). Ergebnisse, Ideen, Probleme: London, Juni 1938. In: A. Freud et al. (eds.), *Gesammelte Werke, chronologisch geordnet.* Band XVII Schriften aus dem Nachlass 1892–1938. London: Imago 1941; Frankfurt: Fischer 1999.

Freud, S. (1941f [1938]). Findings, ideas, problems. [Ergebnisse, Ideen, Probleme: London, Juni 1938]. *S.E., 23,* 1937–1939. London: Hogarth 1964; Vintage 2001, pp. 299–300.

Freud, S. (1950a [1895]). Project for a scientific psychology [Entwurf einer Psychologie]. *S.E., 1* 1886–1899. London: Hogarth, 1966; Vintage 2001. 281–397.

Freud, S. & Breuer, J. (1895b). *Studies on Hysteria [Studien über Hysterie]. S.E., 2,* 1893–1895. London: Hogarth, 1955; Vintage 2001.

Gantheret, F. (1984). *Incertitudes d'Éros.* Paris: Gallimard.

Garma, A. (1970). *Le Rêve: traumatisme et hallucination.* Paris: PUF.

Geissmann, P. & Geissmann, C. (1984). *L'Enfant et sa psychose.* Paris: Dunod.

Gendrot, J. A. & Racamier, P. C. (1951). Fonction respiratoire et oralité. *L'Évol. Psychiatr., 16 (3)*: 457–478.

Gibello, B. (1984). *L'enfant à l'intelligence troublée*. Paris: Le Centurion.

Gori, R. (1975). Les Murailles sonores. *L'Évol. Psychiatr.*, 4: 779–803.

Gori, R. (1972). Wolfson ou la parole comme objet. *Mouvement Psychiatr.*, 3: 19–27.

Gori, R. (1976). Essai sur le savoir préalable dans les groupes de formation. In: R. Kaës, et al., *Désir de former et formation du savoir*. Paris: Dunod.

Gori, R. & Thaon, M. (1976). Plaidoyer pour une critique littéraire psychanalytique. *Connexions*, 15: 69–86.

Grand, S. (1982). The body and its boundaries: a psychoanalytic study of cognitive process disturbances in schizophrenia. *Internat. Rev. Psycho-Anal.*, 9: 327–342.

Graves, R. (1960). *The Greek Myths*, volume I. Harmondsworth: Penguin.

Green, A. (1984). *Narcissisme de vie, narcissisme de mort*. Paris: Minuit.

Green, A. (1990). La Folie privée: *psychanalyse des cas limites*. Paris: Gallimard.

Green, A. (1993). *Le travail du négatif*. Paris: Minuit.

Grotstein, J. S. (1981 [1986]). *Splitting and Projective Identification*. Northvale, N.J. & London: Jason Aronson.

Grunberger, B. (1971). *Le Narcissisme*. Paris: Payot.

Guillaumin, J. (1979). *Le Rêve et le Moi*. Paris: PUF.

Guillaumin, J. (1980). La Peau du centaure, ou le retournement projectif de l'intérieur du corps dans la création littéraire. In: Guillaumin, J., *Corps Création, Entre Lettres et Psychanalyse*, 2nd part, Chapter Seven. Lyon: Presses Universitaires de Lyon.

Harlow, H. F. (1958). The nature of love. *Americ-Psychol.*, 13: 673–685.

Herbinet, E., Busnel, M. -C. et al. (1981). *L'Aube des sens*, Les Cahiers du Nouveau-né 5. Paris: Stock.

Hermann, I. (1930 [1973]). *L'Instinct filial*. Paris: Denoël.

Herren, H. (1971). La Voix dans le développement psychosomatique de l'enfant. *J.franç. oto-rhino-laryngol.*, 20 (2): 429–435.

Houzel, D. (1985a). L'Évolution du concept d'espace psychique dans l'œuvre de Mélanie Klein et de ses successeurs. In: *Mélanie Klein aujourd'hui*. Lyon: Editions Césura.

Houzel, D. (1985b). Le Monde tourbillonnaire de l'autiste. *Lieux de l'enfance*, 3: 169–183.

Houzel, D. (1987). Le concept d'enveloppe psychique. In: D. Anzieu, et al., *Les Enveloppes psychiques*. Paris: Dunod, pp. 23–54.

Houzel, D. (1990). Pensée et stabilité structurelle. In: *Revue internationale de psychopathologie.*, 3: 97–122.

Imberty, M. (1981). *Les écritures du temps. Sémantique psychologique de la musique*, volume 2. Paris: Dunod.

Kaës, R. (1976). *L'Appareil psychique groupal*. Paris: Dunod.

Kaës, R. (1979a). Introduction à l'analyse transitionnelle. In: R. Kaës, et al., *Crise, rupture et dépassement*. Paris: Dunod.

Kaës, R. (1979b). Trois repères théoriques pour le travail psychanalytique groupal: l'étayage multiple, l'appareil psychique groupal, la transitionnalité. *Perspectives Psychiatr.*, *71*: 145–157.

Kaës, R. (1982). La catégorie de l'intermédiaire chez Freud: un concept pour la psychanalyse? *(unpublished)*.

Kaës, R. (1983). Identification multiple, personne conglomérat, Moi groupal. Aaspects de la pensée freudienne sur les groupes internes. *Bull. Psycholog.*, *37* (*363*): 113–120.

Kaës, R. (1984). Étayage et structuration du psychisme. *Connexions*, *44*: 11–46.

Kaës, R. (1993). *Transmission de la vie psychique entre générations*. Paris: Dunod.

Kaës, R. (1994). *La Parole et le lien*. Paris: Dunod.

Kafka, F. (1919). In the penal colony [In der Strafkolonie]. *Sämtliche Erzählungen* Frankfurt: Fischer, pp. 100–123.

Kaspi, R. (1979). L'histoire de la cure psychanalytique de Mme Oggi. In: R. Kaës, et al. (eds.), *Crise, rupture et dépassement: analyse transitionnelle en psychanalyse individuelle et groupale*. Paris: Dunod.

Kaufman, I. C. (1961). Quelques implications théoriques tirées de l'étude du fonctionnement des animaux et pouvant faciliter la conception de l'instinct, de l'énergie et de la pulsion. *Revue française de psychanalyse, 24* (*4–6*): 633–649.

Kernberg, O. (1975). *Borderline conditions and pathological narcissism*. New York Jason Aronson.

Khan, M. (1974). The Grudge of the hysteric. In: *Hidden Selves*. New York: International Universities Press, pp. 51–58.

Khan, M. (1983). *Hidden Selves*. New York: International Universities Press.

Klein, M. (1930 [1975]). The Importance of Symbol-Formation in the Development of the Ego. In: *Love, Guilt and Reparation and other works 1921–1945*. London: Hogarth, pp. 219–232.

Kohut, H. (1971). *The Analysis of the Self*. New York: International Universities Press.

Lacombe, P. (1959). Du rôle de la peau dans l'attachement mère-enfant. *Revue française de psychanalyse, 23* (*1*): 82–102.

Laplanche, J. (1970). *Vie et mort en psychanalyse*. Paris: Flammarion.

Laplanche, J. & Pontalis, J. B. (1967). *Vocabulaire de la psychanalyse*. Paris: PUF.

Lecourt, E. (1987). L'enveloppe musicale. In: D. Anzieu, et al., *Les Enveloppes psychiques*. Paris: Dunod, pp. 199–222.

Lecourt, E. (1992). *Freud et le sonore*. Paris: L'Harmattan.

Lessing, D. (1962 [2008]). *The Golden Notebook*. New York: Harper Perennial Modern Classics.

Lewin, B. D. (1946). Sleep, the mouth, and the dream screen. *The Psychoanalytic Quarterly, 15*: 419–434.

Loisy, D. de (1981). Enveloppes pathologiques, enveloppements thérapeutiques (le packing, thérapie somato-psychique). *L'Évol. Psychiatr., 46 (4)*: 857–872.

Lorenz, K. Z. (1949). *King Solomon's Ring*. M. K. Wilson (trans.). London: Methuen.

Luquet, P. (1962). Les identifications précoces dans la structuration et la restructuration du Moi. *Rev. Franç. Psychana., 26*: 197–301.

M'Uzan, M. de (1972). Un cas de masochisme pervers. In: *La Sexualité perverse*. Paris: Payot.

M'Uzan, M. de (1977). Un cas de masochisme pervers. In: *De l'art à la mort*. Paris: Gallimard.

Marcelli, D. (1983). La position autistique. Hypothèses psychopathologiques et ontogénétiques. *Psychiatr. Enfant., 24 (1)*: 5–55.

McDougall, J. (1978). *Plaidoyer pour une certaine anormalité*. Paris: Gallimard.

Meltzer, D. et al. (1975). *Explorations in Autism*. Strath Tay: Clunie.

Missenard, A. (1979). Narcissisme et rupture. In: R. Kaës, et al., *Crise, rupture et dépassement*. Paris: Dunod.

Montagu, Ashley (1986 [1971]). *Touching: The human significance of the skin*. New York: Harper & Row.

Nancy, J. -L. (2006). *Corpus*. Paris: Métailié.

Nassif, J. (1977). *Freud, L'Inconscient*. Paris: Galilée.

Oleron, P. (1976). L'Acquisition du langage. *Traité de Psychologie de l'enfant, volume 6*. Paris: PUF.

Pasche, F. (1971). Le Bouclier de Persée. *Revue française de psychanalyse, 35 (5–6)*: 859–870.

Piñol-Douriez, M. (1974). Les fondements de la sémiotique spatiale chez l'enfant. *Nouv. Rev. Psychanal., 9*: 171–194.

Piñol-Douriez, M. (1984). *Bébé agi, bébé actif*. Paris: PUF.

Pomey-Rey, D. (1979). Pour mourir guérie. *Cutis 3*. (2 Feb): 151–157.

Pomey-Rey, D. (1989). *Bien dans sa peau. Bien dans sa tête*. Paris: Centurion.

Pontalis, J. B. (1977). *Entre le rêve et la douleur*. Paris: Gallimard.

Ribble, M. (1944). Infantile experiences in relation to personality development. In: J. McVicker Hunt. *Personality and the behavior disorders*. New York: Ronald Press, volume 2.

Rosolato, G. (1969). *Essais sur le symbolique*. Paris: Gallimard.

Rosolato, G. (1978). *La Relation d'inconnu*. Paris: Gallimard.

Rosolato, G. (1984). Le signifiant de démarcation et la communication non verbale. In: *Art et fantasme*. Paris: Champ Vallon, pp. 165–183.

Roussillon, R. (1991). *Paradoxes et situations limites de la psychanalyse*. Paris: PUF. Ruffiot, A. (1981). Le groupe-famille en analyse. L'appareil psychique familial. In: A. Ruffiot, et al., *La Thérapie familiale psychanalytique*. Paris: Dunod.

Sami-Ali, M. (1969). Étude de l'image du corps dans l'urticaire. *Revue française de psychanalyse, 33 (2)*: 201–242.

Sami-Ali, M. (1974). *L'Espace imaginaire*. Paris: Gallimard.

Sami-Ali, M. (1977). *Corps réel, corps imaginaire*. Paris: Dunod.

Sami-Ali, M. (1984). *Le Visuel et le tactile. Essai sur l'allergie et la psychose*. Paris: Dunod.

Sami-Ali, M. (1990). *Le corps, l'espace et le temps*. Paris: Dunod.

Schilder, P. (1950). *The Image and Appearance of the Human Body*. New York: International Universities Press.

Searles, H. (1959). The Effort to Drive the Other Person Crazy. *British Journal of Medical Psychology, 32*: 1–18.

Searles, H. (1979). *Countertransference and Related Subjects*. New York: International Universities Press.

Segal, H. (1957). Notes on symbol formation. *International Journal of Psychoanalysis, 38*: 391–405.

Soulé, M. (1978). L'Enfant qui venait du froid: mécanismes défensifs et processus pathogènes chez la mère de l'enfant autiste. In: *Le Devenir de la psychose de l'enfant*. Paris: PUF, pp. 179–212.

Spitz, R. (1965). *The First Year of Life*. New York: International Universities Press.

Sterne, D. (1993). L'Enveloppe pré-narrative. 4th Monaco Conference 1992. In: *Journal de la psychoanalyse de l'enfant, 14*: 13–65.

Tausk, V. (1919). On the origin of the "influencing machine" in schizophrenia.

Thévoz, M. (1984). *Le Corps peint*. Geneva: SKIRA.

Thom, R. (1972). *Stabilité structurelle et morphogénèse. Essai d'une théorie générale des modèles*. New York: Benjamin.

Tinbergen, N. (1951]). *The Study of Instinct*. New York: OUP.

Tisseron, S. *La Honte, psychanalyse d'un lien social*. Paris: Dunod.

Tristani, J. L. (1978). *Le Stade du respir*. Paris: Minuit.

Turquet, P. M. (1974). Menaces à l'identité personnelle dans le groupe large. *Bull. Psychol.* Special number *Groupes: Psychologie sociale et psychanalyse*: 135–158.

Tustin, F. (1972). *Autism and Childhood Psychosis*. London: Hogarth.

Tustin, F. (1981). *Autistic States in Children*. London: Routledge & Kegan Paul.

Valéry, P. (1932). *L'Idée fixe,* in *Œuvres complètes* volume 2. J. Hytier (ed.). Paris: Pléiade.

Vincent, F. (1972). Réflexions sur le tegument des Primates. *Ann. Fac. Sciences Cameroun, 10:* 143–146.

Widlöcher, D. (1984). Quel usage faisons-nous du concept de pulsion?. In: *La Pulsion, pour quoi faire?* Paris: Association Psychanalytique de France.

Wiener, P. (1983). *Structure et processus de la psychose.* Paris: PUF.

Winnicott, D. W. (1951 [2002]). Transitional objects and transitional phenomena. In: *Through Paediatrics to Psychoanaysis.* London: Karnac, pp. 229–242.

Winnicott, D. W. (1958 [1965, 1990]). The capacity to be alone. In: *The Maturational Processes and the Facilitating Environment.* London: Karnac, pp. 29–36.

Winnicott, D. W. (1962a). Ego integration in child development. In: *The Maturational Processes and the Facilitating Environment.* London: Karnac, pp. 56–63.

Winnicott, D. W. (1962b). Providing for the child in health and crisis. In: *The Maturational Processes and the Facilitating Environment.* London: Karnac, pp. 64–72.

Winnicott, D. W. (1962c [1960]). The theory of the parent–infant relationship. In: *The Maturational Processes and the Facilitating Environment.* London: Karnac, pp. 37–55.

Winnicott, D. W. (1966 [1989]). Psycho-somatic illness in its positive and negative aspects. *International Journal of Psychoanalysis, 47 (4):* 510–516, repr. in *Psycho-Analytic Explorations.*

Winnicott, D. W. (1971). Mirror role of mother and family in child development. In: *Playing and Reality.* London: Tavistock Publications.

Zazzo, R. (1972). L'Attachement. Une nouvelle théorie sur les origines de l'affectivité. In: *L'Orientation scolaire et professionnelle,* pp. 101–128.

Zazzo, R., et al. (1974). *L'Attachement.* Neuchâtel: Delachaux et Niestlé.

INDEX